# RELIGION AND THE SOCIAL ORDER

*Volume 3* • 1993  (Part B)

## THE HANDBOOK ON CULTS AND SECTS IN AMERICA

# RELIGION AND
# THE SOCIAL ORDER

## THE HANDBOOK ON CULTS AND SECTS IN AMERICA

*Editors:*  DAVID G. BROMLEY
*Department of Sociology
and Anthropology
Virginia Commonwealth University*

JEFFREY K. HADDEN
*Department of Sociology
University of Virginia*

OFFICIAL PUBLICATION OF THE
ASSOCIATION FOR THE SOCIOLOGY OF RELIGION

---

VOLUME 3 • 1993 (Part B)

 **JAI PRESS INC.**

*Greenwich, Connecticut*                    *London, England*

*Copyright © 1993 JAI PRESS INC.*
*55 Old Post Road, No. 2*
*Greenwich, Connecticut 06836*

*JAI PRESS LTD.*
*The Courtyard*
*28 High Street*
*Hampton Hill, Middlesex TW12 1PD*
*England*

*ISBN: 1-55938-715-7 (Part B)*
*ISBN: 1-55938-477-8 (Set)*

*Manufactured in the United States of America*

# CONTENTS

**PART IV.   THE ROAD TO MATURITY.
FROM EPISTEMOLOGY TO A COMPREHENSIVE RESEARCH AGENDA**

# CONTENTS

## PART A

## PART I.  EMERGENCE AND DEVELOPMENT OF CULTS AND SECTS

### Section A.  Maturing Inquiries

### Section B.  Emerging Issues

# LIST OF CONTRIBUTORS

*William Sims Bainbridge*

Department of Sociology
and Anthropology
Towson State University

*Robert Balch*

Department of Sociology
University of Montana

*Eileen Barker*

Department of Sociology
London School of Economics

*James A. Beckford*

Department of Sociology
University of Warwick

*Frederick B. Bird*

Department of Religion
Concordia University

*David G. Bromley*

Department of Sociology
and Anthropology
Virginia Commonwealth University

*William V. D'Antonio*

Washington, DC

*Lynn Davidman*

Department of Sociology
University of Pittsburgh

*Helen Rose Ebaugh*

Department of Sociology
University of Houston

*Roger Finke*

Department of Sociology
and Anthropology
Purdue University

*Arthur L. Greil*

College of Arts and Sciences
Alfred University

Jeffrey K. Hadden                    Department of Sociology
                                     University of Virginia

Phillip E. Hammond                   Department of Religious Studies
                                     University of California, Santa Barbara

Laurence R. Iannaccone               Department of Economics
                                     Santa Clara University

Janet Jacobs                         Women's Studies Program
                                     University of Colorado

Theodore E. Long                     Provost and Vice President
                                       for Academic Affairs
                                     Merrimack College

David W. Machacek                    Department of Religious Studies
                                     University of California, Santa Barbara

Richard Machalek                     Department of Sociology
                                     University of Wyoming

Armand L. Mauss                      Department of Sociology
                                     Washington State University

Meredith B. McGuire                  Department of Sociology
                                       and Anthropology
                                     Trinity University

J. Gordon Melton                     Institute for Study of
                                       American Religion
                                     University of California, Santa Barbara

James T. Richardson                  Department of Sociology
                                     University of Nevada, Reno

Thomas Robbins                       Rochester, MN

Wade Clark Roof                      Department of Religious Studies
                                     University of California, Santa Barbara

John A. Saliba                       Religious Studies Department
                                     University of Detroit Mercy

*Anson Shupe*

Department of Sociology
and Anthropology
Indiana/Purdue University

*David A. Snow*

Department of Sociology
University of Arizona

*Rodney Stark*

Lafayette, IN

*Karen Walsh*

Department of Religious Studies
University of California, Santa Barbara

*Bryan Wilson*

All Souls College
Oxford University

*Stuart A. Wright*

Department of Sociology
Lamar University

# PREFACE

In October 1989 a group of scholars met during the annual meetings of the Society for the Scientific Study of Religion in Salt Lake City to discuss a number of issues relating to new religious movements (NRMs). *The Handbook on Cults and Sects in America* is one product that began with those discussions.

Four topics were high on the agenda of that initial meeting. First, there was concern about how to communicate more effectively the growing body of knowledge about cults and sects to the general public. Second, there was concern about the role of expert witness testimony in litigation on the issue of alleged "brainwashing" by cults and sects. A third topic discussed was the potential usefulness of an inventory and assessment of the literature that has emerged over the past two decades. Finally, there was discussion of the desirability of developing a research agenda for the balance of the twentieth century.

The question of how social scientists might more effectively communicate their knowledge about religious movements to the general public was of interest to all of the scholars studying NRMs. There was a general feeling that secular religion newswriters have become more aware of social scientists and are now calling upon them with greater frequency in their preparation of news and feature stories. Indeed, religion writers have become regular attenders at the annual meetings of SSSR, and three persons present at the Salt Lake City gathering had been featured speakers at the annual meetings of the Religious Newswriters Association in recent years. There was a general consensus that the problem of sensationalized coverage of "cult controversies" does not rest with professional religion writers. The problem, rather, is that new editors often do not assign religion writers to cover the potentially sensational developments. One person observed, for example, that while over 400 members of the press corps were in attendance at Jerry Falwell's first press conference after taking control of Jim Bakker's Heritage USA and PTL Network, only one was an established member of the Religious Newswriters Association. There was no immediate consensus that those assembled, or the professional societies to which they belonged, had resources to carry out a plan of action that could significantly impact mass media coverage of new religious movements over the short term. But there was a strong consensus that social scientists should continue to work with the media so that knowledge generated by SSSR and ASR scholars is fairly and accurately represented in media reports.

Second, during the 1980s there was significant growth in litigation grounded in the allegation that "destructive cults" gain and hold young recruits by "brainwashing" them. Several of those present at the Salt Lake City meeting had served as consultants or expert witnesses in various legal cases, but without exception there was great reservation about becoming too deeply involved in the political and judicial conflicts over the cult/brainwashing issues. At the same time, it was felt that the collective knowledge of social science scholars was not being accurately communicated in forensic proceedings. The group engaged in spirited discussion about possible action that might be collectively taken. On the one hand, there was a sense that professional responsibilities to the judicial system (e.g., as defined in the Frye standard) should be honored; on the other hand, there was deep concern about the inherent conflicts between consultant and scholarly roles. The outcome of this conversation was the preparation of a resolution that was subsequently introduced and, with some modifications, adopted by several professional societies that are engaged in the social scientific study of religion. The resolution stated simply that the knowledge base of the social sciences is inadequate to permit informed, responsible scholars to claim sufficiently definitive evidence to support the conclusion that the techniques of persuasion used by new religious movements constitute coercive influence of the character alleged by those who promote concepts like "brainwashing," "mind control," "thought reform," and "coercive persuasion."

Over the past two decades, vigorous research activity has produced a veritable explosion of knowledge about cults and sects. A third discussion topic focused on assessing the general state of knowledge about new religious movements. What has been accomplished? What are the obvious, and not so obvious, gaps in the extant knowledge base? These concerns led naturally to a fourth topic, namely, the desirability of developing a research agenda that might encourage scholars to engage in research that would contribute to the systematic development of the knowledge base. While there have been some notable assessments of fragments of this literature, none of these efforts is either comprehensive or forward-looking in the sense of identifying knowledge gaps and research tasks to be undertaken. Perhaps the time was ripe, the group concluded, for a systematic assessment and attempt at integrating this knowledge, as well as the development of a research agenda to stimulate and focus research.

This task might have been pursued by an individual or a collaborative effort of a few scholars, but there was a general consensus that the undertaking was sufficiently large and compelling to warrant a collective effort by those scholars who have been centrally involved in the production of this research literature. With the encouragement of other participants in the Salt Lake City discussions, we (David Bromley and Jeffrey Hadden) assumed the role of coordinators of a project that would seek to pursue these generally stated objectives. Over the next several months we sought to engage as many active NRM researchers as possible in discussions to sharpen and develop a plan for accomplishing mutually identified objectives. The discussions and correspondence that ensued identified six specific benefits that might accrue to the production of a publication that would assess the state of knowledge about new religious movements:

1. sharpening scholars' awareness of the theoretical and methodological strengths and weaknesses of NRM research;
2. pinpointing critical gaps in knowledge and outlining the kinds of research required to fill these gaps and thereby;
3. helping to sustain the interests and motivation of those who have been active researchers to continue to conduct research on NRMs;
4. providing an inventory of worthwhile projects and thereby;
5. encouraging students and professional scholars with a wide range of backgrounds, interests, training, and skills to pursue research on NRMs; and
6. communicating the tenuous and incomplete nature of knowledge about NRMs and thereby helping to neutralize unsubstantiated claims both from NRMs themselves and their adversaries.

The worthiness of the undertaking having been affirmed, there remained the need to design a strategy for producing a product that would be, on the one hand, as comprehensive as possible while, on the other hand, completing the task in an expeditious and timely manner. This involved identification of topics and authors, establishing time schedules and assessing publication options.

As the list of topics for inclusion grew, cursory examination of extant literatures revealed that many of the proposed topics were too narrowly defined and/or research literatures were insufficiently developed to warrant inclusion. Some of the more narrowly defined issues were incorporated under broader topics. In this final product, there remain a few topics that ideally should have been included. The most obvious to readers will likely be that broad, amorphous phenomenon of contemporary culture that is referred to as New Age. While the New Age movement has produced an enormous literature advocating a wide panorama of spiritualities, there is as yet very little social science literature on the New Age per se. Readers will, however, find numerous references in this handbook to groups and processes that are part of the New Age movement.

Persons familiar with the new religious movement literature will immediately recognize that virtually all of the most active research scholars on NRMs are contributors to this handbook. This is testimony to their assessment of the need for such a resource. As productive research scholars, every contributor sacrificed time away from other projects in order to meet the production schedule. Contributors to this volume, as well as scholars not here represented, have been supportive of the project in numerous ways—offering critiques of early drafts and sharing unpublished materials.

In order to hasten the production of manuscripts and offer a forum for criticism and feedback, Janet Jacobs, Program Chair of the 1990 SSSR meetings, set aside four program sessions for public workshops. The sessions were conceived as a mechanism to encourage contributors to produce early drafts of their papers that would then be critiqued by other contributors to this handbook. These objectives were achieved and, in addition, the sessions were well attended and produced valuable feedback from scholars who were not contributors to this handbook.

Two factors guided the pursuit of a publisher. The first was to locate a publisher who could move from completed manuscript to a published volume in a timely fashion. The second publishing objective was to maximize availability of the handbook to students and scholars. When both the Society for the Scientific Study of Religion and the Association for the Sociology of Religion agreed to lend their imprimaturs to the project, JAI Press quickly agreed to accept the handbook as part of the series on Religion and the Social Order. Members of both societies will be able to purchase the volume at a significant discount over market price. The editors and contributors will donate all royalties to a special fund of the Association for the Sociology of Religion that will support small research grants.

As the project comes to fruition, the editors wish to acknowledge a large number of persons who have contributed to this project. First and foremost, we express our sincere thanks to all of the contributors to this handbook. To those who completed their manuscripts on or ahead of schedule, our sincerest appreciation for their promptness. To those who had to be nudged as the final deadline drew near, our gratitude for turning to the task.

To the Councils of the Society for the Scientific Study of Religion and the Association for the Sociology of Religion who authorized sponsorship of the project, our appreciation for the trust they placed in us to shepherd the project to completion. We wish also to commend the councils for this action. The handbook is the first formal joint adventure of these two professional organizations. We trust it is but a beginning of many ventures that will promote scientific scholarship on the subject of religion. Thanks also are due to Donald Capps and Theodore E. Long, who were presidents of SSSR and ASR.

J. John Palen and Murray Milner were, respectively, our department chairs at Virginia Commonwealth University and the University of Virginia during the development of this project. They contributed to various editorial costs of the project during a time in which Virginia institutions of higher education suffered severe fiscal cutbacks. Their support was greatly appreciated. Christina Mahoney and John Bozeman provided able and loyal student assistance in a variety of computer and editing tasks.

Numerous professional colleagues contributed both directly and indirectly to this project. At the risk of failing to mention persons to whom we clearly are in debt, we would be remiss in failing to mention the following for a variety of contributions, including encouragement, constructive criticism, and sage counsel: Dick Anthony, Lorraine D'Antonio, James D. Davidson, Barbara J. Denison, Mark Galanter, Benton Johnson, Dean Kelley, Edward C. Lehman, Jr., James R. Lewis, John Lofland, Perry London, H. Newton Maloney, Donna Oliver, Robert O'Neil, Herbert L. Rosedale, James Rudin, James E. Wood, Jr., and Benjamin Zablocki.

Finally, a special thanks to Dean M. Kelley who encouraged us to pursue this project. From 1960, Kelley served as a program executive for religious liberty at the National Council of Churches. Throughout his distinguished career he has championed the rights of racial and religious minorities, often taking unpopular stands for just causes. A gentle man, Kelley has also been provocateur to social scientists who, until he came along, missed one of the most important developments of the century in American Protestantism. The publication of his book, *Why the Conservative Churches Are Growing* (1972), was received with less than enthusiasm by social scientists and church leaders alike. The former were perhaps bemused by the advent of such an important publication coming from the pen of a "church bureaucrat," while the latter decried the messenger of bad news. Kelley's treatise addressed not only the question of conservative church growth but also the reasons why liberal churches were losing ground. Today, scholars recognize not only that Kelley was right, he was right about something very important. Our dedication of this volume to Kelley is in recognition and deep appreciation of his dedication both to human liberty and to tough-minded scholarship.

**David G. Bromley**
**Jeffrey K. Hadden**
*Editors*

# EXPLORING THE SIGNIFICANCE
# OF CULTS AND SECTS IN AMERICA:
## PERSPECTIVES, ISSUES, AND AGENDAS

David G. Bromley and Jeffrey K. Hadden

Before there were anthropologists there were explorers and soldiers and missionaries and traders who traveled to the four corners of the earth where they observed and reported back home on the "primitive folk" they had found in their natural habitat. As their diaries, autobiographies, and travelogues attest, it was virtually impossible to encounter native peoples without being made aware of their "strange" beliefs and practices about the supernatural. Missionaries saw an opportunity to bring these "heathens" to the "true faith," and not infrequently, the armies of the explorers were the instrument for coercing indigenous populations into accepting the religion of the missionaries. Later we learned that the indigenous people of the world were not totally subdued but, rather, created amalgams of faith that retained significant elements of their native religions. Something else of importance happened as well. From the ranks of these subdued cultures arose charismatic prophets who brought messages of hope and liberation, and so were born *new religions*. Anthropologist Anthony Wallace (1966, p. 3) estimates humankind has produced something on the order of 100,000 *different* religions.

In the nineteenth century, after much of the world had been conquered by western civilization, there followed gentlemen of leisure in pursuit of new experience and knowledge. Some pursued hunting safaris, others traveled to observe the wondrous flora and fauna of far away places, while still others were fascinated by the native peoples. The latter were the forerunners of the

Religion and the Social Order, Volume 3B, pages 1-48.
Copyright © 1993 by JAI Press Inc.
All rights of reproduction in any form reserved.
ISBN: 1-55938-715-7

modern science of anthropology. They learned of myths and rituals, observed magic, witchcraft, and divination, and pondered the meaning of taboos and totems.

The discipline of anthropology emerged as the task of recording the cultures of "primitive" peoples became progressively more systematic and comprehensive. The ethnography—a thick description of the social organization, institutions, values, beliefs, and behavioral patterns—soon provided a point of entry into scores of cultures heretofore barely imagined by western culture. One need not read many of these early ethnographies before it becomes evident that religion is central to the lives of native peoples around the world. It is simply not possible to understand their cultures without comprehending the central role of their religions.

The world of religion was all the more fascinating to anthropologists because, as it did to their colleagues in the other disciplines of the emerging social sciences, religion appeared as an anomaly. Whereas sociologists and psychologists were happy to let religion wither on the vine of secular culture—some even believed it their duty to help usher its passing—anthropologists were intrigued with the prospects of finding in religion clues that would help them understand the development of culture and humankind from its primitive inception.

In time anthropology would offer the social sciences two paradigms regarding the role of religion in the development of human culture. The first substantially parallels the inherited paradigm of the other social sciences. Secularization is the cognitive dimension of the emerging modern world, driven by science and technology. Secularization theory holds that belief in a supernatural is simply not tenable to rational humankind. In the fullness of time, religion, having lost its raison d'être, will fade away.

The second paradigm of anthropology may more appropriately be described as a *nascent paradigm,* for its principal proponents are clearly fellow travelers of the secularization theorists. This nascent view postulates that under certain conditions religion can be the dynamo for cultural rebirth. Most clearly articulated by Wallace (1966, p. 265), *revitalization movements* are "deliberate, organized, conscious effort[s] by members of a society to construct a more satisfying culture."

Anthropological observations of revitalization are found around the world in locations where dominant invaders have left the host culture in a state of submission and disintegration. Historical examples are abundant among native American Indians, especially the Ghost Dance movement of the Plains tribes, and among Polynesian and Melanesian cultures there were Cargo Cults. Numerous twentieth-century examples are found in Africa, and in the Caribbean one finds the Jamaican Rastafarians. In the post-World War II era there emerged an abundance of "new religions" in Korea and Japan.

Over the long haul, Wallace sees little hope for the survival of religion in the modern world. In his classic treatise on religion he writes: "Belief in supernatural beings and in supernatural forces that affect nature without obeying nature's laws will erode and become only an interesting historical memory" (1966, pp. 264-265). Revitalization movements, thus, are a rear guard activity in the linear trajectory of history toward a rational social order. In this sense, Wallace and his revitalizationist colleagues have not offered a new paradigm at all but, rather, an accounting of how religion manages to linger yet a little longer.

The revitalization thesis is important, however, because it provides the embryo for thinking about religion in new ways that break the grip of a linear historical model. While Wallace sees the birth of religions occurring under the unusual conditions of cultural distress, it is possible to entertain the proposition that new religions emerge for other reasons. Perhaps religions, like cultures, go through cycles of growth, maturation, stagnation, and decline, followed then by revitalization, reshaping, or displacement by new religions. This is, in fact, what Wallace said, but he postulates a very limited application of the model in the modern world.

The very notion that the birth of new religions is a normal process permits one to entertain a wide array of theoretical speculations. For beginners, we can postulate with Wheeler (1971, p. 8) that "a death-of-god" era is also a "god-building" era. The erosion of the plausibility structures upon which particular religions have been grounded does not so much spell the demise of the religion as it signals the coming of new religious ideas in the religious economy (Stark and Bainbridge 1985). Entertaining the thought that secularization may not be a one-way superhighway and that cultures traveling the road are not necessarily destined to find their religious precepts shattered and left scattered along the way, is a rather new idea in the social sciences. But we get ahead of ourselves.

The United States has provided fertile soil for new religions from nearly the beginning; and, to a greater degree than most historians have acknowledged, these new religions *are* the story of the making of America (Moore 1986). New waves of immigrants constantly changed the religious landscape as they brought the faiths of their motherland, thus making the United States ever more pluralistic. Moreover, new religions (e.g., Baptists and Methodists) were spawned, grew, and eventually gained major market shares. During the late nineteenth and early twentieth centuries North America saw an effervescence of new religious activity that has few parallels in recorded world history.

Religious historians have scarcely taken notice of these groups (Stark and Finke 1992) and sociologists have done little better. In the celebrated presidential commission on *Recent Social Trends,* Fry (1933, p. 1009), summarizing changes in American religious organizations, mentions that "[some] non-traditional sects like the Mormons and the Christian Scientists have very greatly increased their membership since 1906." But that is all he has to say about new religions in an essay that is almost 25,000 words in length. The ignoring of new religions seems all the more curious when we consider that the sociologists devoted considerable attention to elaboration and refinement of the Weber-Troeltsch "church-sect" typology. Clearly sociologists were aware of cults and sects, but they hardly ever went out and studied them. The study of unconventional religious groups seemed to remain in the purview of anthropologists (e.g., La Barre 1962).

To every generalization, of course, there are exceptions. One can readily find isolated studies of sectarian and cultic groups, but prior to the late 1960s, there simply was no substantial, cumulative, and systematic body of literature. A self-conscious literature begins to emerge as "new religions" blossomed in the wake of the youth counterculture. The San Francisco Bay Area was the mecca of the counterculture, and it was there that new religions began to flourish as well. Scholars affiliated with the University of California and the Graduate Theological Union became actively engaged in investigating the broad array of unconventional religious practice. In 1970 a Graduate Theological Union seminar led by Charles Y. Glock and Robert Bellah evolved into the *New Religious Consciousness Project.* An edited volume from the project involved fifteen contributors (Glock and Bellah 1976), and many of these contributors published other books and papers that were spawned by the seminar. As other scholars across the country took up the task of studying new religions in their locales, most were soon in contact with at least one, often several, of the Berkeley scholars.

In fairly short order, a small cottage industry became one of the hottest topics within the sociology of religion, attracting some of the subdisciplines' more able young scholars. By the 1980s the study of new religions may have become the largest subdiscipline within the sociology of religion. Saliba's (1990) herculean bibliography, *Social Science and the Cults,* annotates over 2,200 items, almost all of them published after 1970.

There are numerous reasons why scholars were attracted to studying new religions. First of all, the very idea of a spiritual revival attracting youth appeared as a cultural anomaly. Saliba (1990, p. xvii) summarizes well the conventional theoretical wisdom:

> This was the age when religion appeared to be in decline, when secularization, the process through which religion becomes less of a factor in sociopolitical matters and in the public domain in general, was deemed irreversible, and when religious beliefs looks as if there were crumbling under the advance of modern science.

Also during this time frame, Protestant theologians proclaimed the "Death of God" and began to write theologies for the post-religious era. The apparent flurry of new religious movement activity indicated religion was alive. Scholars of religion naturally were interested in discovering why this was happening.

Studying new religions was also attractive because it offered the opportunity to observe the organization, growth, and development of a new faith as it was happening. The uniqueness of this situation may not have been immediately apparent to scholars, but many soon realized that there were few previous incidents in which social scientists were present to study a new religion as it developed. In 1929 Faris urged sociologists to study the "origin and evolution of specific religious sects" (cited in Stark and Bainbridge 1979), but scholars did not pick up the challenge. Stark and Bainbridge (1979, p. 130) repeated the challenge a half century later:

> The origin of many social institutions and much human culture "is lost in mystery." We have no time machine to permit study of the past. But religious sects and cults can be studied from the start and thus can furnish a body of information "concerning the rise of institutions," and the invention of culture.

By the time this second challenge was issued, there was already a burgeoning literature.

Yet another incentive for studying new religious movements was the fact that several groups exhibited more than casual curiosity in being studied. For some groups there was a sense that the sociologists were part of a providential plan that would facilitate the spreading of the word—that is, when the scholars studies were published, people would read them and be attracted to the group. However naive, it was a posture that made it easier for scholars to gain entry to some groups. Others groups seemed to recognize the value of chronicling their development and viewed sociologists as valuable resources toward this end. Whatever the motives of the NRM leaders, a number of scholars were permitted to make scholarly observations and collect various kinds of research data.

It has now been over two decades since the study of new religious movements began in earnest. The cumulative literature is substantial. Selected portions have been reviewed previously (e.g., Snow and Machalek 1984; Greil and Rudy 1984), and Robbins (1988) has written a monograph length essay that seeks to assess the extant literature.

This *Handbook on Cults and Sects in America* seeks to provide a comprehensive assessment of the literature as well as to identify the kind of work that needs to be done to move the study of new religious movements toward a mature subdiscipline. The handbook is organized around three broad topics: (1) organization and development, (2) the sociocultural environment, and (3) the individual. Each of these three parts is in turn subdivided into what we have called "maturing inquiries" and "emerging issues." These designations are in some sense arbitrary, but they do help to underscore the dynamic, unfolding character of the research and the issues that warrant systematic inquiry. A final section of the handbook addresses important epistemological and methodological questions.

Our charge to the contributors asked them to address five questions: (1) what are the most important questions regarding the topic? (2) what is the state of empirical knowledge? (3) what are the knowledge gaps? (4) how can these knowledge gaps be filled? and (5) how does the literature treat interface with the broader corpus of social science literature?

Recognizing that space would not permit scholars to address each of these questions adequately, we allowed the authors to exercise discretion in determining the priority of these questions for their particular topics. On some of the topics identified as "emerging" issues, there is not much research to draw upon and, hence, authors have necessarily focused on the nature of the knowledge gaps and how they might be filled. Authors working in more established areas often have attempted to consolidate and synthesize research findings.

From the beginning of this project, there has been much concern with the integration of knowledge about new religious movement into the core body of sociology of religion literature and, in an even broader sense, into the corpus of social science literature. Beckford (1985) and more recently Wuthnow (1988) have expressed the view that the sociology of religion has become a fragmented and significantly differentiated subdiscipline that is in danger of losing intellectual strength and integrity. The prospect that the study of new religious movements might become a subspecialty within a subdiscipline that some have judged as fragmented and cut off from the mainstream of sociological inquiry gives cause for sober reflection. We took this criticism seriously and asked our contributors to address the issue to the extent that it seemed appropriate for their topic.

We are heartened by the evidence here amassed. There is certainly room for scholars of NRMs to immerse themselves in broader sociological literatures. At the same time, the papers in this volume demonstrate that the scholars of NRMs are on the cutting edge of a number of basic questions that are important to the core discipline. Even more encouraging is the evidence that NRM scholars have taken seriously the criticism of insularity and have become more self-conscious in locating their work in sociological questions of broader import than new religions.

We believe that the evidence presented here points to the conclusion that the study of NRMs has illumined many of the core issues of the sociology of religion and has contributed to the maturation of this subdiscipline. Readers, of course, will have to judge for themselves.

Before moving to a discussion of the contents of this handbook, a few comments should be offered regarding the concepts or nomenclature here employed. The words "cult" and "sect" have carried a variety of meanings through the years. Sect is defined in *Webster's New Collegiate Dictionary* as (a) an organized ecclesiastical body, (b) a dissenting or schismatic religious body, especially one regarded as extreme or heretical, and (c) a group adhering to a distinctive doctrine or to a leader. Encased within these three dictionary definitions are at least six distinct, and not at all compatible, meanings. The dictionary options on the word "cult" produces an even larger number of ideas.

What then are we to make of the subject matter of a handbook on cults and sects? The Queen in Lewis Carroll's *Alice in Wonderland* said, in effect, that "words mean exactly what I say they mean." In everyday discourse and mass media the concepts "cult" and "sect" are, in very substantial measure, used in a pejorative context. *Such conceptualizations are unacceptable for social science inquiry.* One *may* conclude from a social science inquiry that a particular cult or sect is led by a rascal, or engages in practices unacceptable to some individuals or to broadly accepted cultural conventions. But such are hypothetical conclusions that would only be valid if supported by empirical investigation. To begin with a negative premise is to virtually assure that one will draw negative conclusions. Objective social science inquiry must begin and proceed from value-neutral premises.

Sociologists of religion have generally preferred the designation new religious movements (NRMs) to the concepts cults and sects for the very reason that the former does not carry negative connotations that are culturally ascribed to the latter. The NRM concept is not a totally satisfactory resolution for several reasons. First, not all NRMs are new. Many of the Eastern religions that became highly visible in the United States during the late 1960s can trace their roots to Hindu traditions thousands of years old. While they are new in the United States, they are not new religions. Second, the concept NRM camouflages some important conceptual distinctions between cults and sects. Third, social scientists' attempts to create a value-neutral term has produced a backlash of sorts. To their adversaries, all cults and sects are, by definition, devious and destructive. The use of the concept "new religious movement" is seen as a deceptive means of hiding the true intent of inquiry. By implication, anyone who uses this concept is intentionally or unintentionally aligned with the cults and sects.

Research evidence clearly indicates the inappropriateness of broad sweeping stereotypical statements about NRMs. Some groups are hardly very different from well-established religions, others are culturally quite "strange." As scholars, sociologists would caution against either positive or pejorative generalizations. NRMs are simply too diverse to warrant sweeping generalizations. As individuals, sociologists of religion harbor many sentiments about the groups they have studied—some positive, others quite negative. Sociologists of religion, however, are of one mind in their wish to be nonaligned in the struggle between NRMs and their adversaries. Notwithstanding the negative spin the anti-cultists have given to the concept, sociologists of religion are not likely to abandon the use of the term "new religious movements." Readers will find the use of the concept in virtually all the contributors to this handbook.

We have chosen to use the concepts "cults" and "sects" in the title of this volume for two reasons. First, the concepts do have more or less precise meanings as employed by social scientists. There are many occasions when it is appropriate to designate whether one is speaking of a sect or a cult. Second, it has become abundantly clear that after nearly two decades, the concept new religious movements has virtually no recognition either in the mass media or the general public. By calling attention to the concepts as they are used by social scientists, we hope to begin the long process of educating the mass media and public regarding the non-pejorative meaning of these words.

To place these concepts in context, we should begin by identifying cults and sects in relationship to "conventional" religious organizations which social scientists call churches. A sect is a religious group with beliefs and practices that have a clear lineage to established practices and beliefs (i.e., churches). In most instances, sects are created as the result of schism from an established group. Cults, on the other hand, are religious groups that have sufficiently different believes and practices as to be considered novel and, thus, judged to be outside of established religious traditions.

Religious groups with novel beliefs and practices can come about as a result of three different processes, or some combination thereof. First, a group may begin as a sectarian movement and gradually elaborate beliefs and practices that members of traditional religions judge to be outside of acceptable

8 DAVID G. BROMLEY and JEFFREY K. HADDEN

conventions. The Peoples Temple headed by Jim Jones, for example, began as a sectarian drift from an established Protestant denomination and then gradually developed radical beliefs that placed it outside of conventional Christianity. A second type of cult formation can be characterized as innovation or invention. Scientology evolved from ideas first expressed in the science fiction writings of its founder, L. Ron Hubbard. Third, religions that are well established in one culture may be imported to another where they are viewed as totally novel. The International Society for Krishna Consciousness, or Hare Krishna movement, is an example of the latter.

These basic distinctions could be elaborated upon in great detail, but to do so would invite rejoinders from a number of contributors to this volume who have elaborated on conceptual distinctions elsewhere. As this area of inquiry moves toward maturity, scholars may be expected to adopt some conceptual designations in preference to others. Some variations in the use of these concepts will be evident in the papers of this volume, but the distinctions over above should be helpful to readers who are not familiar with this literature.

## ORGANIZATION OF THE HANDBOOK

This *Handbook on Cults and Sects in America* appears in two parts. For the convenience of readers this introductory essay appears in both parts. It seeks both to provide an overview of the contents of individual contributions as well as some integrative perspective. *Part A* explores issues relating to the *organization* and *development* of cults and sects as well as the *sociocultural environments* in which these processes occur. *Part B* focuses on the *individual* and, in addition, addresses several important *epistemological* and *methodological* issues that are critical to the ongoing development of a body of empirical literature on New Religious Movements. Discussion of the articles appearing in Part A follows immediately; discussions of the contents of Part B begins on page 28.

## I. EMERGENCE AND DEVELOPMENT OF CULTS AND SECTS

### A. Maturing Inquiries

*Historical Comparisons*

American sociologists of religion turned to the study of cults and sects; the studies of Bryan Wilson, a Reader in Sociology at the University of Oxford and Fellow of All Souls College, provided one of the few points of intellectual departure. Wilson had conducted research on cults and sectarian groups on three continents. His comparative analysis of the new religions of late nineteenth and early twentieth centuries in America was extremely helpful for gaining perspective on the "strange" religious flora and fauna spawned by the counterculture of the 1960s.

Over two decades later we again find ourselves turning to this senior scholar of cults and sects for insights about the character of the research that has accumulated since the inception of the research sciences. When we asked Wilson ("Historical Lessons in the Study of Sects and Cults") to take a panoramic view on this scholarship, we envisaged not a summary of what has been learned but, rather, an exercise in the sociology of knowledge or science. How did our knowledge come to be and how can we benefit from these insights? Once again, Wilson provides keen insights about the route we have traveled and sage counsel about what may lie ahead.

Before the emergence of the social sciences, Wilson reminds readers, the task of reflecting upon the role and character of sects fell to historians and theologians, and their point of reference was strictly a juxtaposition of these groups to established Christian doctrines and practices. Objective, dispassionate analysis came only slowly. But even as the quest for a science of society emerged, this particular field of inquiry continued to be shaped by the cultural perception of "sects" as errant deviations from established Christian doctrines and practices.

Ernst Troeltsch, whose work has framed the way scholars have thought about churches and sects for over half a century, believed sectarianism to be "radical," "apocalyptic," and "anti-establishment." These presuppositions, Wilson argues, were "carried forward into sociological analysis...without losing the theological implications." This presumptive framework postulates a gradual transformation of the sect toward characteristics that are church-like. An important implication of this is that sects tend to be compared with established groups almost to the exclusion of comparison with other sectarian groups.

As long as scholars focus analysis around this ideal-typical construct, the possibility of independent origins and developmental trajectories of new religions are missed. Wilson argues what contemporary scholars are beginning to understand, namely that while some groups do tend to fit this "church-to-sect" model, many sectarian movements have natural life histories that do not correspond very closely at all. Many are enduring, relatively stable, and change only slowly; others emerge, develop, and change rapidly in response to dynamics that are quite independent of the inherited classic model.

Wilson postulates several commonalities that historical and contemporary new religions tend to have in common: (1) they tend to be lay movements, (2) offering a more proximate salvation, (3) which is congruous to the life circumstances of (4) the distinctive constituency or market segment to which it appeals, (5) with a correspondingly unique legitimacy. Finally, new religions *appear* to be (6) iconoclastic and desacralizing (i.e., they seem simultaneously to debunk established conceptions and icons of the sacred while offering new alternatives that seem to outsiders not to be religious at all).

Wilson also explores how the changing social climate impacts on the character and structure of new religions. "Accelerated social change," he argues, "has been a powerful factor in stimulating new orientations in religion and in promoting the organization of new cults." Many readers will be familiar with Wilson's traditional formulation of secularization as a process that gradually erodes the plausibility of traditional belief systems and renders religion a private matter. Here he offers a much richer and potentially revolutionary conceptualization of the process. Emile Durkheim postulated that societies render sacred those aspects of their cultural and organizational life that are critical for their collective survival. Wilson sees the new religions as legitimating and sacralizing contemporary hedonistic orientations.

However antithetical or heretical the "salvation now" orientations of many new religions may appear to those who equate religion with the traditional ascetic ethic of Protestant Christianity, the practitioners of these new religions may be the harbingers of global movements rather than residual remnants of a phenomenon known as religion that passed from culture early in the Third Millennium of the Common Era.

The doctrines and practices of all religions evolve, sometimes so slowly that change can hardly be detected, but at other times change occurs so rapidly that ties to tradition appear untenable or ethereal. A final lesson from Wilson's paper is that we should not be too hasty in assuming either the character or the trajectory of contemporary new religions.

## Charismatic Leadership

The concept of charisma is endemic to the study of religion and certainly to the study of new religions. Max Weber's complex analysis of the traditional social order identifies charisma as a central instrument for social change. Standing outside established authority, the charismatic leader repudiates the past while offering a new revolutionary vision. People heed the call for change because charismatic leaders are seen as possessing "supernatural," "superhuman" powers unaccessible to ordinary people. Such are the prophets who found new religions.

Notwithstanding the central role of charisma in classic sociological thought about new religions, Bird ("Charisma and Leadership in New Religious Movements") notes that studies of leadership and authority patterns occupy only a scant proportion of the expanding literature on NRMs. Bird's analysis draws upon a very substantial knowledge about leadership patterns in many new religious groups. His contribution to this volume lays the foundation for more systematic comparative study of religious leadership.

Bird argues that scholars of religion had tended to treat leadership patterns as "idiosyncratic phenomenon" when, in fact, predictable patterns persist that are explicable in terms of "the type of organization [rather] than the unique personalities of the leaders." While focusing on new religions, Bird's analysis moves back and forth between the leadership attributes of new religions and other types of religious organizations. Weber notes that over time charisma becomes routinized and thus accrues to the holder of institutionalized offices. Bird identifies important differences in leadership styles between those whose authority is institutionalized and those who rely on what he terms *personal* charisma.

Personal charismatic leaders are characterized by three common attributes. First, they recruit their own followers. Second, they develop highly personalized relationships with their core followers. Third, they are the author of the normative visions and mandates of their group. The core followers of personal charismatic leaders can typically be characterized as possessing: (1) reverence and commitment to the leader rather than the beliefs and practices, (2) intense dedication to work for the goals and vision of the leader, and (3) high levels of energy or feelings of empowerment.

From this mosaic of leader and follower attributes emerge three master problems. First, personal charismatic leaders tend to become *isolated,* even from the very persons they initially recruited and with whom they developed intense affective bonds. Established institutions typically develop structures for communication and feedback regarding policies and organizational goals. Charismatic leaders, as founders and visionaries, tend to trust their own judgments and/or revelatory insights. Not actively seeking criticism and feedback, they tend to become progressively cut off from communication. Those closest to the leaders are reluctant to criticize them, either out of awe or fear of losing their privileged status. Those further down in the organizational structure must either choose to remain silent or leave.

This problem of isolation produces a second serious problem, namely the absence of structures of *accountability.* The absence of accountability invites persistence of excesses and poor judgments. Isolation and the absence of accountability, in turn, produce a *fundamental instability of leadership* both with respect to sustaining legitimacy and in planning for the inevitable crisis of succession. To sustain legitimacy, charismatic leaders engage in a wide array of strategies and tactics including: (1) more or less continual production of new visions and projects, (2) undermining the legitimacy of competitors or opponents, (3) recruiting new members, (4) "working wonders," and (5) engaging in crisis-mongering.

While these problems are typical, they are not universal. Bird observes that Eastern religious, more often than groups emerging in Western cultures, have succeeded in creating organizational structures more nearly resembling traditional "denominational" character. This he attributes in substantial measure to the fact that the founding leaders have seen their roles more as "transmitting, translating, and interpreting" established religious messages rather than creating new messages.

Characteristically, charismatic leaders are not successful in planning for succession, which is a reason that many NRMs do not survive the passing of their founder. Bird presents a provocative commentary on the problem of succession in NRMs. He speaks of a "pentecostal model" wherein "individual groups may disappear, [but] new leaders...attract new groups of followers." The key idea here is that the movement evolves sustainable dogmas and organizational forms. When leaders pass without having arranged for their succession, a free market invites new leaders to compete for extant constituencies.

Bird's analysis provides substantial evidence for the proposition that NRMs have common organizational imperatives that tend to produce the personal charismatic style of leadership. He analyzes why this style seems to be nearly imperative and also provides important insights regarding the liabilities that accrue to personal charisma.

## NRM Development

The typology of church-sect development has been a central ideal in sociology of religion literature nearly from the onset of the discipline. In the simplest terms, dissident factions splinter off from established church traditions and then, over time, gradually evolve so that they take on the church-like characteristics of the group from which they seceded. Over the decades scholars have produced a very substantial literature that has sought to refine the conceptual details of this transformation and to develop empirical measures of the process of change. Several recent critiques have highlighted the virtues and methodological shortcomings of this literature (e.g., Stark and Bainbridge 1979).

Hammond and Machacek ("Cults and Sects in America: Organizational Development") eschew the task of reviewing this rather substantial literature in favor of a carefully selected focus on emerging issues. They begin with what they characterize as a "modest map for guidance through the now vast literature" on organizational development. After a brief inventory of key issues pertaining to *emergence* and *development* of NRMs, they focus attention on important conceptual issues that constitute the cutting edge of thought about organizational development.

One important development is the anchoring of knowledge about new religions in the theory of secularization. Stark and Bainbridge (1985) are credited with explicitly treating secularization as a central concern in theorizing about new religions. The conceptual thought of two theorists, Wilson and Bell, provide helpful illustrations of how NRM development has been linked to secularization.

As noted above, Wilson has long been associated with the view that secularization is an inexorable process that eventually will render religion impotent as a cultural force. "Nowhere in the modern world does traditional faith influence more than residually and incidentally," writes Wilson (1982, p. 179). New religions represent futile attempts to recreate meaning and intimacy in a world characterized by anonymity and impersonality.

Bell (1977) is less concerned with the structural implications than with individual effects. Secularization, Bell argues, produces broad cultural experimentation. When these experiments fail, individuals turn to religion for meaning and understanding. New religions are the evidence of traditional religions' failure to satisfy the quest for meaning.

The church-sect model postulates a one dimensional process of NRM development based on fissures in established structures. In light of over two decades of active research, it is evident that this is an oversimplified description of how new organizational forms emerge. Hammond and Machacek examine three prominent conceptualizations. The first is Ellwood's "diachronic" model. Following a long tradition in anthropology, Ellwood views new religions as epiphenomenal. New religions are not really new but, rather, renewed "outcroppings" of cultural ideas that have long been present.

Wallis echoes Ellwood's notion of a religious substratum with the idea of a "cultic milieu." He sees a continuum ranging from a cultic milieu to centralized cults to sects. The cultic milieu is ever present and characterized by a high degree of individual autonomy. Individuals participate much like consumers or clients. "Centralized cults" are organized around a leader whose principle resource is charisma sans tradition. Seldom does the centralized cult survive beyond the organizing founder. Sects are characterized by a greater degree of organization and authority.

Stark and Bainbridge (1985) offer three models of cult formation: psychopathological, entrepreneurial, and subcultural evolution. These are complementary, not mutually exclusive, ideas about how cults emerge. The psychopathological model postulates an "episode" or "personal crisis" which provides the genesis of new religious ideas. The entrepreneurial model sees creative people inventing and borrowing to create marketable religious ideas. Subcultural evolution stresses the role of group interaction in the production of novel religious ideas.

In the final section of their paper, Hammond and Machacek examine how the considerable theoretical activity about NRMs has produced concepts and ideas that can inform sociological theory that has "no intrinsic reference at all to religion." They see promising possibilities for interface with the "neoclassical" approach and "poststructuralism." Both traditions stress meaning and could benefit from more systematic concern with religious meaning. Finally, Hammond and Machacek see value in viewing religion as a "nurturing institution" and conclude that religion, with the family, will not disappear. Implicit is an invitation to examine the two institutions in tandem.

## B.   Emerging Issues

### Historical Issues

Social science theory has long been dominated by the presupposition that religious belief is *irrational.* In this volume Stark and Finke ("A Rational Approach to the History of American Cults and Sects") challenge the fundamental premise that religious belief is irrational. The paper opens with an identification of several "theories" of religion grounded in the assumption that religious belief and behavior are irrational.

Freud viewed religion as a "psychopathology," an illusion to be removed from culture and a neurosis to be erased from individual consciousness. Marx saw religion as "false consciousness" which would gradually disappear with the growth and development of the socialist state. This, of course, is a direct corollary of secularization theory. A close cousin, expressed in the vernacular, is the "ignorance and poor reasoning" or "backwardness and ignorance" theory.

Here education is seen as a means for overcoming the irrational in the rational world. Still another corollary, again in the vernacular, they call the "fear and trembling theory of revivals." This perspective is anchored in the notion that in periods of hardship and fear people will harken back to religion and its irrational assumptions.

Briefly surveying each of these perspectives, Stark and Finke conclude that the irrationalist position is now in serious difficulty. "Empirical evidence," they maintain, "has failed to cooperate." Furthermore, they argue that the a priori relegation of religion to the domain of the irrational has constituted a serious obstruction to the development of theory. If scholars assume religion to be irrational, it follows that religion will be constantly subjected to the eroding influences of reason in modern secular culture. If religion survives, even periodically thrives, it follows that the reasons must necessarily be the result of irrational behavior. This presuppositional framework structures how scholars think about religion to the point that it utterly precludes the exploration of questions that might be grounded in the presumption of religion as rational behavior. Furthermore, the presumption of irrationality can result in ignoring many kinds of social phenomena because the theory renders them nonproblematic.

Consider, for example, the presumption of periodic Great Awakenings in American religious history. Each awakening is postulated to have occurred during a period of social crisis. The theory that people turn to religion in response to crisis thus provides self-validating evidence that awakenings occurred as theologians and historians have argued. The search for confirming historical evidence is unnecessary because the idea of awakening is compatible with the theory. Emerging evidence, however, is beginning to seriously challenge the thesis of Great Awakenings during the eighteen and nineteenth centuries.

A significant body of contemporary literature has attempted to explain the development of cults and sects during the second half of the twentieth century with the same general notion of cultural crisis or disruption that has been postulated as an explanation for the Great Awakenings. Three broad movements are believed to have occurred: (1) a "Consciousness Reformation," corresponding to the period of the youth counterculture during the 1960s and early 1970s, (2) the "sudden influx" of Eastern religions, and (3) the "explosion" of evangelical Protestantism.

Stark and Finke examine these developments with previously unpublished data and find the case for each alleged movement to be wanting. Rather, they present evidence for "gradual, long-term, linear shifts" rather than "sudden eruptions." We see two important contributions in this work. First, Stark and Finke have presented data that seriously challenge the assumptions of cult and sect formation during the second half of this century as "sudden," "explosive," and so forth. It would appear that both cults and sects have emerged in a much more gradual and orderly fashion. What has been sudden is public discovery of their presence. Both the unfolding of new religions and public response to them are fodder for fresh conceptual thinking. A second contribution is their argument for and demonstration of the payoff of thinking about religion as rational rather than irrational behavior. By challenging conventional wisdom, they are likely to stimulate a lively response.

## NRMs and Social Movements

In the conventional lexicon of social science literature, a *religious movement* is understood to be a subcategory of *social movements*. In reality, the two have become relatively independent subfields of the larger discipline of sociology. Over the past quarter-century both literatures have experienced a renaissance of interest and a parallel elaboration of both theoretical and empirical scholarship. The proliferation of these two literatures, however, has produced little cross-fertilization.

Mauss ("Research in Social Movements and in New Religious Movements: The Prospects for Convergence") is one of only a few scholars who has actively contributed to both literatures. His task here is to identify many of the common conceptual concerns and thereby lay a foundation for mutual leavening. Following the organizational presentation of McAdam, McCarthy, and Zald (1988) in Smelser's *Handbook of Sociology*, Mauss utilizes a four-fold typology that pivots on the cross-cutting dimensions of macrolevel vs. microlevel of analysis, and movement emergence vs. movement development or maintenance.

At the macrolevel of analysis, all movements go through a phase of emergence; those that survive then enter a longer phase of maintenance and development. At the microlevel of analysis, the parallel issues are recruitment followed by the tasks of retention, socialization, and mobilization of participants. Mauss finds that both the social movement (SM) and the sociology of religion (NRM) literatures have addressed each of these conceptual tasks, albeit with different vocabularies, orientations, and emphases. The common points of departure in these literatures provide an opportunity for leavening. Following are some examples that illustrate Mauss's argument for cross-fertilization.

Both literatures have elaborated fairly comprehensive explanations of why movements emerge in particular environments. The social movement literature emphasizes political, economic, and/or underlying demographic conditions as key factors giving rise to movements. The NRM literature tends to focus on symbolic and cultural elements of the environment. Mauss argues that the study of NRMs would benefit by giving attention to demographic, political, and economic factors that facilitate or constrain the development of religious movements. Similarly, SM literatures "like those for women's rights (including abortion) or gay rights would benefit by looking beyond political and economic resources (important as these are) to religious, symbolic and other cultural shifts in the meaning of sex, sexuality and female roles in order to understand when the why such 'secular' movements have emerged."

Both SM and NRM literatures now recognize that the classic "sects" to "churches" model inspired by Weber and Troeltsch is far too simple to account for the varied trajectories that movements take. Both literatures have benefitted by the application of "resource mobilization" theory and market metaphors, although the NRM literature has lagged behind in these applications.

The NRM and SM literatures pose very different models of success. A successful cult or sect maintains a sufficiently high level of tension with the broader culture so that it is differentiated and thus attractive to participants and potential recruits. Reduction of tension suggests a path toward assimilation. A sect that becomes "just like" a church has not succeeded, but has been coopted and lost its raison d'être. Social movement literatures, in contrast, have traditionally defined success in terms of the broader culture accepting and assimilating the agenda of the movements even though the movement's goals remain unrealized. In reality, this may be another kind of cooptation.

These contrasting perspectives call for a reexamination of the meaning of movement success. It seems reasonable to search for some level of *optimal tension* whereby a movement is not coopted or assimilated. A derivative of this perspective is that retention of commitment to a movement may be grounded in placing *high costs* on membership. Low demands are simply not commensurate with high performance expectations.

Social movement literature has conceptualized the acquisition of new movement followers as "participants," whereas the NRM literature is framed in terms of "converts." Mauss finds the NRM literature to be more developed, although the emerging models focus on an interactive *process* of engagement and disengagement. This direction deemphasizes conversion as it has been traditionally understood.

Finally, Mauss notes that neither literature has devoted much attention to understanding differential experiences and retention rates of recruits from different social and demographic categories.

Other contributions to this handbook suggest that Mauss may have understated the degree to which the literatures of social movements and new religious movements have been "carried on largely in mutual disregard." The stimulating analysis he presents indicates that there is much room for cross-fertilization and considerable benefit to be derived from doing so.

## Para-Religions and Quasi-Religions

The growth of interest in new religious movements raises anew the question of locating boundaries between religion and other activities which may, in some ways, closely resemble religion. Social scientists have sometimes made the case for the inclusion of almost everything from selling Amway products to practicing Hatha Yoga as religion. Much time and ink has been spent arguing over whether Marxism is religion, or at least a "functional equivalent." At the other extreme, theologians tend to establish criteria for inclusion or exclusion resting on the distance of the group in question from their own orthodoxy.

In his paper, "Explorations Along the Sacred Frontier: Notes on Para-Religions, Quasi-Religions, and Other Boundary Phenomena," Greil takes on the difficult task of delineating boundaries . Greil discusses two classes of activity that fall outside the boundaries of what he calls "the American folk category of 'religion'." "Quasi-religions" are groups that embrace ideas of the sacred, but are viewed as anomalous vis-à-vis the American folk category. "Para-religions," on the other hand, are ostensibly nonreligious entities, but they have features that are common to religions.

The Unification Church, Scientology, Alcoholics Anonymous, and many Human Potential groups are examples of quasi-religious groups. Para-religions are groups that prima facie appear not to be religious, but nevertheless engaged in activities (functions) that are religious-like in character. For example, much has been written about "sports as religion," (e.g., Novak 1976) and direct sales organizations socialize their personnel with techniques that are "revival-like" and that tend to produce zealous loyalty (Biggart 1989; Bromley forthcoming).

While there is no explicitly identifiable body of literature on para-religious and quasi-religious groups, as such, Greil identifies substantial literatures that help clarify the meaning of these concepts. Two important payoffs are readily evident from the organization of scholarly literature in this manner. First, it helps illumine the fact that most sociological definitions are not very different from "folk" or "actor" definitions. Sociological definitions tend to incorporate the idea of a transcendent deity and organizational forms pivoting on churches and denominations. Sociological definitions stand oblique, but neither conceptually nor ideologically in real juxtaposition to folk definitions.

Greil's analysis circles back to the vexing question of whether scholars have traveled a great distance from the days when theologians delineated the boundaries between religion and nonreligion. He underscores the important insight that even scholarly conceptions and definitions have subtly, perhaps unknowingly, smuggled in political agendas. Delineating boundaries between religious and nonreligious, or the sacred and the secular, is a political process.

A second important insight emerging from Greil's delineation of para-religious and quasi-religious groups is also evident in Wilson's analysis of the changing face of the sacred in the modern world and the Stark and Bainbridge hypothesis of the self-limiting character of secularization. The apparent eclipse of a transcendent deity in quasi-religions may not so much be a demise of religion as a reshaping and revitalization in new forms. Greil observes that "the line between religion and nonreligion is getting fuzzier." Traditional sociological theory would view this as evidence of secularization. It is possible, rather, that the face of the quasi-religions provide us a glimpse of religion in the post-modern era. We would agree with Greil that the examination of para-religious and quasi-religious group "phenomena provide us with a useful vantage point from which to watch and try to comprehend the transformation of American religion."

## II.  THE SOCIOCULTURAL ENVIRONMENT
## OF CULTS AND SECTS

### A.  Maturing Inquiries

*NRM Opposition*

Organized opposition to the new religions of the current era dates back almost to the beginning of the movements themselves. From early on, parents of young people who joined NRMs found one another and developed communication networks. Distraught families provided one another emotional support, shared information about groups, tried to locate their children, and served as liaisons to "deprogrammers."

In time, the counter organizations to NRMs developed increasing sophistication in communication and organizational skills. Working initially from kitchen tables, the anti-cult movement (ACM) forged coalitions with parents in other locations across the country and gradually transformed ad hoc operations into nation-wide professional organizations. Fly-by-night "deprogrammers" gave way to quasi-credentialed "exit counselors." As mental health professionals became involved, they helped transform a highly charged emotional language into an intellectual perspective, thus lending legitimacy to the cause. From an initial position of legal defensiveness—because some NRMs had successfully pressed claims of coercive restraint—the ACMs became aggressive litigators, pursuing multimillion dollar suits against NRMs for various kinds of mental/emotional damage inflicted on former members who had escaped their influence.

Bromley and Shupe have been observers of the ACM for over fifteen years. Shortly after they commenced their investigation of the Unification Church, they decided their research would be enhanced if they also attempted to understand the perspective of the parents. *"Moonies" in America* (Bromley and Shupe 1979) and *The New Vigilantes* (Shupe and Bromley 1980) are companion volumes that represent a simultaneous investigation of movement and countermovement.

Over the years, their collaboration on this subject reflects an evolving perspective, even as the character of NRMs and the ACMs have evolved. In their contribution to this handbook, Bromley and Shupe ("Organized Opposition to New Religious Movements") pursue the broader cultural import of NRMs and ACMs locked in conflict. Several important themes are developed.

First, they argue that the sociological significance of social movements derive from the insight they provide into the larger structure of social relations against which they are in rebellion. Movements that seriously challenge the prevailing social order can be expected to generate countermovements. Countermovements are less likely in contexts where major social institutions have the resources and interest to deal directly with social movements.

Second, when countermovements do emerge, their life course, including structure and development, is best understood in dialectical relationship to the movement they oppose. Movements and countermovements significantly influence and feed upon one another. Thus, argue Bromley and Shupe, movements and countermovements should be studied in tandem.

Bromley and Shupe here develop a broader sociocultural and historical context for explaining the emergence of the NRMs and ACMs than has appeared in their earlier collaborations. The rapid growth of both groups can be traced to historically evolving *contractual-covenantal tensions* in the American social order. The long-term structural pattern in modern cultures is toward the expansion of contractual relationships, which can necessarily only expand at the expense of covenantal relationships.

By the 1960s, the dominant mode of youth socialization was toward the goal of preparation for competitive position in a world based on contractual relationships. Suspended between adolescence and adulthood, youth rebelled against both familial control and looming bureaucratic control.

NRMs enter the scene with world-transforming messages that support this rebellion while further undercutting both parents and the legitimacy of secular institutions. Along with their critique of the existing social order, the NRMs bring the good news of humanity's "new beginning." Youth are offered a new vision of themselves and of a world transformed. The path to be followed requires total loyalty and commitment, to the exclusion of any other competing claims.

This historical backdrop lends perspective on both the ideological and organizational form the ACM assumed at its inception and hence the point from which its subsequent development emanated. Given the crisis that families of NRM converts experienced, they predictably sought a meaningful cultural interpretation of their circumstances and a remedial course of action. The resolutions the ACM formulated, a cult-brainwashing explanation for NRM affiliations and a family-association network to combat NRMs, were consistent with its position vis-à-vis the NRMs and the larger social order. These resolutions developed dialectically in interaction with NRM target groups.

In addition to their discussion of the dialectical relationship between movements and countermovements and an analysis of how the NRM and ACM conflict is anchored in the broader sociocultural context of changing contractual-covenantal relations, the paper also offers valuable insights about ACM ideology and a history of the organizational development of the ACM.

## NRMs and the State

The First Amendment to the Constitution of the United States guarantees both the freedom to establish and to exercise religion. The first sixteen words to the Bill of Rights read simply: "Congress shall make no law respecting an establishment of religion, or prohibiting the free exercise thereof."

For nearly a hundred years this First Right stood unencumbered by judicial opinion. Not a single case involving religion came before the Supreme Court until 1878, when George Reynolds, personal secretary to Brigham Young, appealed his conviction for violating the Morrill Act that prohibited the practice of polygamy in the Territories. The Supreme Court upheld the conviction and constitutionality of the law (*Reynolds* v. *United States* 1878). A decade later, the court upheld the conviction of another Mormon, Samuel Davis (*Davis* v. *Benson* 1890). Davis did not practice polygamy but, rather, was convicted of falsely signing a voter registration oath in the Territory of Idaho which declared he was not a member of an group that teachers or practices "the crime of bigamy or polygamy." In yet another decision (*Church of Jesus Christ of Latter-Day Saints* v. *United States* 1890) the court ruled that a federal statute revoking the charter of the church was constitutional.

Here, then, we have laws written for the explicit purpose of restricting the Mormon Church from practicing its beliefs along with court decisions upholding the constitutionality of these laws. The rationale for these decisions was spelled out by Chief Justice Waite who wrote the *Reynolds* v. *United States* decision. Justice Waite drew a distinction between *belief* and *action* wherein belief is absolute, but action is not.

The United States enjoys broader religious liberties than almost any other country. These first cases before the Supreme Court are significant because they demonstrate the precariousness of religious liberty when the group in question is unpopular. After nearly a century without religious liberty cases, and another half century with only a few cases, the past quarter-century has seen a flood of cases in both state and federal courts. For the past two decades, there have been few sessions of the Supreme Court without a religion case. Over the years, a significant number of religious liberty cases have involved cults and sects.

Some First Amendment scholars have argued that dislike of, or even discomfort with, unconventional religious groups can subtly bias jurors and judges alike. The enduring significance of court decisions involving unpopular religious groups is that they set precedent for all religions.

In 1991 the Supreme Court upheld the denial of unemployment benefits to two members of the Native American Church who were fired for ingesting peyote as part of a religious ceremony (*Smith* v. *Employment Division of Oregon*). Justice Antonin Scalia concluded that the First Amendment does not excuse religious groups from obeying "otherwise valid law[s] that the state is free to regulate." In an unusual move, Justice Sandra Day O'Connor voted with the majority, but wrote that the decision "dramatically departs from well-settled First Amendment jurisprudence...and is incompatible with our nation's fundamental commitment to individual religious liberty." The "fundamental commitment" to religious liberty has been grounded in the concept that there must be a "compelling state interest" before the courts could prohibit religious practice. With only very narrow exceptions, *Smith* negates the compelling interest test. First Amendment scholars have widely viewed the *Smith* decision as a serious erosion of the *free exercise* clause.

The growing number of religious liberty cases before the courts, especially cases involving groups "outside the mainline religious denominations," or cults and sects, presents a set of intriguing questions for social scientists. Robbins and Beckford ("Religious Movements and Church-State Issues") examine three interrelated theoretical questions in their paper: "(1) the construction of moral boundaries, (2) the organization and operation of the state and (3) the shifting position of marginal groups with respect to judicial legitimation." In the final section of the paper, Robbins and Beckford explore church-state relations in Western Europe and compare this diverse scene with the United States.

"Controversies over cults," argue Robbins and Beckford, "have elicited from authorities and citizens an articulation of a society's implicit ideology of social control and its latent premises regarding the proper balancing of the obligations of citizens to the state, to extra-governmental associations, to their families, and to their selves." While Americans take religious liberty seriously, the authoritarian style of some sects is viewed as a contradiction of individual liberty. The balancing of obligations places a higher value on the individual rather than corporate religious structures. The perception that some authoritarian groups "encapsulate" recruits to such a degree that they lose rational mental capacities is viewed as a legitimate reason to act on behalf of the devotee. Observation of collective responses to the activities of NRMs with respect to their membership is a way of identifying culturally perceived moral boundaries. The boundary disputes can be located in such activities as debates over the meaning of "authentic" religion, the legal status of the idea of brainwashing, and efforts to define "deprogramming" as a legitimate therapeutic activity.

The second broad question explored by Robbins and Beckford is the role of the state in shaping NRMs. They discuss the anomalous situation of U.S. concern for protecting religious liberty and the growing role of the government in the oversight of religion. The more immediate factor precipitating growing government oversight is the expanding mentality of "consumer protection" in the culture. "Fraudulent religions" become just one among a growing number of activities the government is expected to regulate on behalf of a consumer public. The broader context of regulation is to be found in the expanding role of government in the modern Western welfare state.

Robbins and Beckford identify two types of discrimination against marginal religious groups: (1) affirmative discrimination (manifest) and (2) indirect or rule-based discrimination (latent). Among regulatory authorities of the state, the IRS is probably the most influential in the emerging shape of NRMs. The pursuit of tax exempt status and/or the avoidance of tax problems with the IRS pushes NRMs toward earlier formal organization while simultaneously molding the shape of these organizations.

As already noted, new religions have become increasingly enthralled in litigation. In many instances, NRMs are in the courts as plaintiffs in pursuit of rights they believe have been abridged, but more often they are defendants against a broad array of charges. Robbins and Beckford identify and briefly discuss eight broad categories of litigation.

The third section of this paper reviews the changing legal legitimacy of NRMs. Following Way and Burt (1983), they argue that important Supreme

Court cases in the 1960s and 1970s, which established the principle that free exercise should not be infringed upon unless there is a compelling state interest, appear to have tipped the law in favor of marginal groups. More recent impressionistic evidence and the 1991 *Smith* decision suggest the scales are again tipping against NRMs.

In the final section, Robbins and Beckford survey the situation of NRMs in Western Europe and draw important comparisons with the United States. "Despite many striking similarities [between the United States and Western Europe]...there are nevertheless some sharp contrasts." In general, European countries are more likely to treat religious organizations under laws pertaining to voluntary associations. This tends to have the impact of blunting state-church conflict. European societies, as part of the great complex of modern Western welfare states, tend to view "cult controversies" as "managerial problems." There are, of course, exceptions and some troubling issues unfolding, such as growing demands among the rapidly growing Moslem population in the United Kingdom that the they be treated as a "Moslem state-within-the-state."

## NRMs and Families

Families figure prominently in mass media treatment of cults and sects. Probably the single most worked theme in movies, television drama series, and mass magazine stories about cults is the emotion-wrenching tale of a family struggling to regain control of a son or daughter who has joined an unconventional religious group. Almost without exception we find the "brainwashing" theory presented uncritically as an explanation of how the young person fell under the influence of a ruthless charismatic leader.

Wright and D'Antonio ("Families and New Religions") observe that the problem of families breaking up is an old cultural theme and a long concern of the social sciences. In 1933, William F. Ogburn wrote a classic essay in which he explained why and how the traditional functions of the family were eroding and that this demise in family stability had been taking place over a long period of time (p. 663). Ogburn wrote of *changing functions*, but much of his analysis pivots on the theme of *eroding functions*. Increasingly the family has become an institution to service the socioemotional needs of its members. "The future stability of the family," Ogburn wrote, "will depend...on the strength of the affectional bonds" (1933, p. 708).

Across the twentieth century social science literature has mirrored many popular themes about troubled families, but social scientists have tended not to jump on the bandwagon to scapegoat cults for the break-up of families. Wright and D'Antonio identify four distinct theories of why youth join new religions that are explicitly linked to family life: (1) identity formation, (2) functional analysis, (3) family deprivation, and (4) pathology.

Each of these theories may be seen as a play on Ogburn's theme that the modern family is increasingly called upon to do heavy-duty work fulfilling socioemotional needs of members. The first three theories explain joining a religious movement as a means to fulfilling developmental needs that are either missing or being impeded by the family. For example, the identity formation theory holds that parents can impede their children's developmental need for independence. Joining a religious movement serves as a kind of halfway house en route to independence. Only the pathological model posits that "cults" are responsible for disrupting the normal familial growth and development process. This perspective is found mainly among persons engaged in therapy and counseling activities. Wright and D'Antonio note this perspective suffers from several methodological deficiencies including generalizing from clinical patients without any control groups.

The conflict between NRMs and families is thoroughly understandable. Parents typically feel fear, anger, incomprehension, and guilt when that child joins a group that does not meet with their approval. Even though the child is typically a legal adult, the distressed parent is likely to impose a psychological definition of child to the situation. Well meaning but distressed parents can engage in desperate acts. They may succeed in "rescuing" their child, but this victory may come at the price of exacerbating the problems that contributed to the youth's joining the group in the first place.

The tension between parents and the movements their children join has so dominated the literature that many other potentially interesting questions about new religions and families have gone virtually unexplored. For example, given the high level of marital dissolution in the United States, it would be interesting to know whether youth coming from broken homes are more or less likely to join NRMs. Very little is known about the social demographics of the families of NRM joiners. Some NRM members overcome or never experience real conflict with parents. Why and how does this happen? The list of interesting and theoretically important questions about families and religious movements is substantial. Most of them remain unexplored.

There is some literature on family, marriage, and sexuality in new religions which is the subject of the second half of the Wright and D'Antonio paper. Three topics are explored: (1) sex and social control, (2) gender and power, and (3) marriage and raising families in new religions. Each topic raises important questions.

Communally organized religions tend to have either highly restrictive *or* very liberal orientations toward sexual behavior. Both extremes legitimate their posture theologically, and in both instances, sex is regulated as a mechanism of social control.

Wright and D'Antonio again find wide variance between groups with respect to sex roles, gender, and power. Whereas new religions can function as a source of empowerment, in other groups they provide a legitimation of status quo roles for persons looking for a rudder in a highly ambiguous secular world.

Finally, studies of several new religions point to the tensions and ambiguities encountered when members move into the child-bearing phase of the life cycle. Having children creates demands and emotional rewards that must be balanced with the group as a surrogate family. This dynamic almost necessarily is destabilizing and results in some loss of control by the leaders. Wright and D'Antonio conclude by noting that several groups are now going through this stage and call upon social scientists not to miss this "exceptional opportunity to record and analyze the reciprocal effects of families and new religion in the coming years."

## B.  Emerging Issues

### Religion and Rationality

Deductive theories are built upon systematic and interrelated sets of propositions inferred (deduced) from a limited set of given axioms (general principles). Such theorizing is relatively rare in the discipline of sociology, and rarer still in the sociology of religion. In 1979 Stark and Bainbridge published a paper titled "Of Churches, Sects, and Cults" which laid the foundation for deductive theory building. In *A Theory of Religion* (1987) Stark and Bainbridge make good on their promise to produce a systematic theory of religion. From a mere seven axioms, this ambitious treatise developed over 100 definitions and nearly 350 propositions.

While some scholars have rejected the theory outright because it is grounded in exchange theory, which contends that humans seek maximization of rewards and avoidance of costs, many have at least found elements of the theory intriguing, if not compelling. Most sociologists of religion would acknowledge that elements of the theorizing of Stark and Bainbridge have profoundly influenced the *orientation* of scholars who study religion.

Even as scholars are still struggling to come to grips with the full import of the deductive approach of Stark and Bainbridge, Stark has joined in a collaborative relationship with economist Iannaccone in which they have developed a rational choice approach to religious behavior. *Rational choice theory* has thus far been most explicitly elaborated in the discipline of economics. Stark and Iannaccone seek to extend the deductive approach while refocusing the general theoretical approach in the language of rational choice.

The Stark and Iannaccone contribution to this volume ("Rational Choice Propositions About Religious Movements") demonstrates the novelty and originality of applying rational choice models to religion. Some of the propositions elaborated herein will be familiar to those who have read *A Theory of Religion,* but the shift of emphasis offers yet another fresh approach to thinking about religious behavior.

Occasionally even seasoned scholars need to be reminded that theories, like definitions are neither right or wrong, but more or less useful. The utility of rational choice approach is easily demonstrated by the wide array of propositions that shed new light on long-standing problems. For example, it has long been recognized that established churches have large proportions of their membership who are inactive and contribute little to the either the economic or social maintenance of the institution. In the language of economics, these people are "free riders" (i.e., individuals who do not "carry their weight"). New religions are by definition small and could scarcely survive if a large proportion of their members were free riders. New religions screen out free riders by extracting high costs for membership. Those choosing membership do so because they perceive the rewards of belonging to be greater than the stigma and sacrifice (high costs) required of members.

In 1972 Kelley wrote a book that posed a classic dilemma: why are conservative churches growing? The book is equally about why liberal churches are declining. In the end, critics reluctantly admitted that Kelley's thesis that strict churches grow while undisciplined churches decline was correct. Propositions derived from the rational choice model provide fresh insights, at a higher level of abstraction, that explain *why* Kelley was correct.

A second illustration of fresh insight is found in the Stark and Iannaccone discussion of religious monopoly. Sacralization of cultures is greatest in environments where one religion has a monopoly. The deregulation of the religious economy is by definition *de*sacralization. By deductive reasoning they demonstrate why desacralization is not the same as secularization. Demonopolization will lead to secularization because the previous monopoly loses its power to impose its sacred symbols, but demonopolization will also stimulate the movement of more firms (new religions) into the market place.

This decoupling of sacralization and secularization adds explanatory weight to the earlier theorizing of Stark and Bainbridge that posits secularization to be self-limiting. But more importantly, it opens up a wide array of new questions and focuses attention on genuinely important research agendas. Perceptive readers will see that these are only two or many arenas where Stark and Iannaccone have broken new ground.

The application of rational choice theory to religion is certain to be elaborated and revised in future work by Stark and Iannaccone, and others are certain to join the effort both as critics and elaborators of the perspective. This seminal paper will remain a useful point of entry into this innovative theoretical perspective.

## NRMs and Politics

The youth counterculture of the late 1960s exhibited both alienation and a yearning for political reform; there were simultaneously messengers encouraging youth to "drop out and turn on" and prophets exhorting radical political measures to build a better world.

The new religious movements of the late 1960s had some of their greatest successes in persuading youth to get high on religion rather than drugs. What were the political implications of this development? One of the hit songs of the Broadway musical *Hair* proclaimed the "dawning of the Age of Aquarius," an explicit political message. Were the new religions the conduit for political expression, or a "safety valve" as youth turned their energies to otherworldly activities?

Not surprisingly, understanding the political implications of the new religious movements was a central concern of scholars examining the counterculture. Long ("New Religions and the Political Order") reviews this early scholarly literature and finds three dominant foci of interest: (1) the shift from radical politics to new religions, (2) the sociopolitical significance of these groups, and (3) delineation of the political ideologies and agendas of NRMs that perceived themselves to be "world-transforming movements." In a word, scholars were interested in knowing whether these new religions would legitimate and energize unconventional political agendas or contribute to a cooling out of political engagement?

In spite of this initial interest in the relationship between religion and politics, after the formative years of the late 1960s and early 1970s Long finds the literature to be sparse both in quantity and quality. He posits two explanations for this dearth of literature. It may be, Long notes, that after an initial surge of interest scholars have neglected an important area of inquiry. On the other hand, the sparseness of the literature may result from the fact that there really is not much to know, that is, NRMs just may not be all that involved in the political order.

Long's central argument is that the absence of a robust literature on new religions and politics, and why this is so, could be assessed more adequately if inquiry were guided by a better theoretical understanding of the relationship between the two phenomena. His paper provides a valuable contribution toward a clearer conceptualization of the relationship between religion and politics. Long begins by noting that all religious groups can be ordered along two axes: (1) primary *orientation* toward the world [this-worldly or other-worldly] and (2) *attitude* toward the world [world-affirming or world-rejecting]. This simple four-fold typology provides important clues as to how a group might be expected to respond to the political order.

Pivoting on a typology that identifies all religious groups as having an *orientation* that is this-worldly or other-worldly and an *attitude* that is affirming or rejecting of the world, Long identifies four dimensions which characterize how religions enter the political order: (1) interests, (2) ideology, (3) action, and (4) consequences. Delineation of these dimensions from the perspective of the typology provides important insights as to how and why some NRMs become deeply involved in politics while other groups are not very political at all. Furthermore, Long helps clarify the different ways in which groups may be political. This paper, in conjunction with Long's earlier writings (1986, 1988), constitutes an important prolegomenon to a theory of religion and politics. In the concluding section of the paper, Long provides rich illustrations of how this theoretical orientation can illumine understanding of the relationship between religion and politics. For example, one important insight is that NRMs, lacking great resources to directly impact political action, often confine their political relevance to "cultural" or "symbolic" crusades rather than directly impacting organizational or structural character of government resulting from political contests.

## NRMs and Science

As already noted, Stark and Bainbridge (1985, 1987) have offered an important alternative to the classical model of secularization. Neither modern science nor the state, they argue, is capable of providing enduring satisfactory answers to the most fundamental questions concerning the meaning of life and death. Thus, secularization is a self-limiting process and inevitably leads to revival and religious innovation. Cults and sects, the subject of this volume, emerge on the fringe of culture. Some of these new religions are eventually successful and so eventually become victims of the secularization process. Science, which spawns an acceleration of technological change, will also accelerate the debunking/secularization process *as well as* innovation in the emergence of new religious ideas.

Is it possible for new religions to escape the corroding impact of secularization, or might secularization eventually destroy even the potential for faith to be rekindled? From a scientific perspective, the answer might seem to rest in the possibility of religions developing strands that are more resistent to secularization. This might be achieved if religions were to develop plausibility structures (underlying tenets) that are less easily debunked. If science produces the fodder that feeds secularization, it is possible that science might also contribute to the production of strands of religion most resistant to the debunking effects of secularization.

In his paper for this volume, Bainbridge ("New Religions, Science, and Secularization") explores the potential of science itself to spawn new religions. His quest takes him down paths that will be unfamiliar to many readers. First, he examines the cutting edges of theoretical and philosophical thought in the natural sciences. Bainbridge argues that whereas "traditional science contradicts religion both in its determinism and its rejection of causes that cannot be seen and measured...[emerging schools of science regard]...natural processes as a combination of chance and necessity....Stochasticism, the view that chance rules all...has little influence as a school of thought...[but]...its principles can be found in practically all of the natural sciences."

This emerging perspective presents a powerful challenge both to traditional religion and to culture. If modern science brings us to the brink of a paradigmatic view of life as "accidental," "random drift," bordering on "chaos," then the human and cultural need to be able to grasp onto something believable is even greater. Bainbridge postulates that the same scientific processes that have brought us to the brink of the abyss may also be capable of spawning new religions precisely because they provide a *rational* basis for belief.

Science fiction provides one set of clues to scientifically generated religions, but even the finest sci-fi ventures into religion are crudely constructed fantasies. Somewhat less crude are cults grounded in "pseudoscientific" principles. The last two centuries have produced many examples including many out of the New Thought tradition of the late nineteenth and early twentieth centuries that include the word science in their name (e.g., Christian Science and Religious Science).

Bainbridge examines three contemporary groups that have attempted to build faith on principles of science: Transcendental Meditation, Scientology, and the Committee for the Future. He illustrates how each is built upon claims that are vulnerable to contradiction by the very methods and logic of science. But, alas, this need not be the inevitable outcome of religion building in the modern scientific world. To illustrate his point, Bainbridge takes his reader on the religious odyssey of Anson MacDonald, founder of The Experimentalist Church on the first day of the year 2001. To the best of our knowledge, this is the first time a sociologist has outlined the contours of a scientifically grounded religion since August Comte, the acknowledged founder of sociology, created the Church of Humanity. Whether or not careful scrutiny of an elaborated statement of Bainbridge's creation would reveal flaws capable of debunking by science, he offers an extraordinary mind-expanding challenge. Then, in a conclusion that is even more remarkable, and certain to be controversial, Bainbridge makes an argument for sociologists of religion to join in the quest to create new religions. Whether or not one agrees, Bainbridge certainly provides a stimulating and provocative case.

## III.  CULTS, SECTS, AND THE INDIVIDUAL

### A.   Maturing Inquiries

*Conversion*

The idea of conversion conjures up the image of Saul of Tarsus on the road to Damascus. This celebrated Roman soldier had a radical encounter with the holy which transformed his life as well as the life of a new religious movement founded by Jesus of Nazareth.

Through the ages there have been many stories of sudden, radical, life-transforming conversions. To the modern secular mind, however, the very idea of a life-transforming spiritual experience is problematic. Why would rational, normal persons place themselves in a situation where they would experience a radical belief and identity transformation? Early social science literatures offered two explanations. Conversion to sectarian groups was viewed as an indicator of psychological deprivation. A literature on cult conversion transferred the responsibility for conversion from the individual to the agents of conversion. Introducing concepts like "brainwashing" and "coercive persuasion" to identify powerful psychotechnologies available to cult leaders, the proponents of this orientation saw individuals as utterly helpless victims of subversive influence.

The phenomenon of conversion has produced a larger research and theory literature than any other topic pertaining to new religions. Whether this can be attributed to the fact that the early explanations of conversion were viewed as too simplistic, or merely the desire of scholars to explain this novel and esoteric commitment, literature on conversion proliferated from the beginning of the contemporary wave of interest in NRMs.

A literature of such scope and breadth has understandably spawned several literature reviews, including a very able effort by Snow and Machalek (1984). Machalek and Snow ("Conversion to New Religious Movements") seek here "to identify key interpretive themes, analytical approaches, and research findings." Their paper is organized around three questions: What is the *nature* of conversion? What are the *causes* of conversion? And, what are the *consequences* of conversion? To each question they raise keen insights, help focus the issues, and bring to bear significant literatures that have shaped knowledge about conversion.

Following conventional understanding, Machalek and Snow define conversion as "a radical transformation of consciousness, including self and identity." They note that the idea of conversion needs to be located in a broader conceptual web of processes that connote religious change. "Adhesion," "alternation," "consolidation," and "regeneration" are distinct types of religious change that have very important consequences for people, but do not normally imply radical identify transformation. They also distinguish between conversion and *commitment,* on the one hand, and *membership* on the other. Persons may profess conversion, but they may not necessarily exhibit behaviors that leaders would consider behavioral sine qua non of a legitimate member.

One of the most serious problems of studying conversion is the inability to observe the process while it is happening. As a result, little is known empirically about the dynamics of conversion. As a result, much literature is grounded in the assumption that membership is a reasonable surrogate indicator of conversion. Machalek and Snow urge more participant observation and ethnographic studies to fill this knowledge gap.

The literature on the causes of conversion is rich in detail, but uneven in scope and theoretical focus. Machalek and Snow differentiate between *individual* attributes that are postulated to be related to conversion and *contextual* influences. Individual attributes are organized under three subcategories: (1) physical, (2) psychological, and (3) social status. Contextual influences are divided between (1) contextual and (2) sociocultural. Important exemplars of each literature type are examined.

The early literatures are very deterministic, even though there are a wide range of monocausal determinants. This literature is followed by a heavy emphasis on individuals as "active agents" in their conversions, reflecting the influence of the symbolic interactionist and phenomenological traditions. While this latter approach is an important corrective to deterministic models, Machalek and Snow see a movement toward models that combine multiple factors—both individual and contextual. To achieve this requires much more focused attention on "the role of temporal, organizational, and macrosocial factors."

The literature on the consequences of conversion is much less systematically developed than the literature on causes. "The very nature of the conversion process," they argue, "appears to mitigate against reliable assessments of its consequences." One literature on consequences is grounded in the presupposition of "brainwashing" and, by definition, must view consequences in thoroughly negative, pathological terms. "[M]ost researchers challenge the brainwashing model on the grounds that the conditions required for coercive persuasion to be successful simply are not met in the recruitment context available to the vast majority of new religious movements."

A limited, but significant, literature points to positive consequences from converting and joining an NRM, but Machalek and Snow underscore the methodological problems of measurement. The problems of measurement are also pursued in detail by Saliba (this volume). It is virtually impossible to conduct studies that could meet conventional scientific criteria of pre-conversion and post-conversion measures.

Machalek and Snow conclude that conversion research has focused disproportionately on individual attributes and microsocial factors and call for more attention to the development of macrosociological orientations.

*Brainwashing*

It has often been repeated that the wings of the hummingbird are so tiny and their aerodynamic structure so ill-proportioned that the creature could not possibly fly. But there it is. What bird watcher has not delighted in the acrobatics of this tiny creature as it darts methodically from flower to flower, unaware both of the fact that it is being observed and that what it is doing is quite impossible?

Many social scientists view the concept of "brainwashing" as no less improbable. The idea that there are people with the capability of exerting such overwhelming influence that the person influenced becomes a "human robot" and, further, that this influence can be achieved without the atrocity even being detected by the average observer, seems so absurd that it is hard to imagine that anyone could believe such a tale. But there it is. No other idea even begins to come close to rivaling the concept of brainwashing as a master concept dominating public sentiment about the subject of cults.

No one has ever conducted a survey of the membership of the Association for the Sociology of Religion and the Society for the Scientific Study of Religion to determine their evaluation of the idea of brainwashing. If someone were to do so, they would almost certainly find that the overwhelming proportion of the membership of these professional associations would reject the idea as a viable scientific concept.

The ASR and SSSR memberships are a distinct cognitive minority. For example, in one recent public opinion survey more than three-quarters (78 percent) of the respondents professed to believe that brainwashing is real. Another survey found 69 percent of Oregonians believing that the followers of Bhagwan Rajneesh were brainwashed. Other studies have shown that 30 to 45 percent of respondents believe that people just would not join cults unless they were brainwashed.

The general public is not alone in a belief in brainwashing. Some former members of new religious groups claim they have been brainwashed. There exists a new occupational group known as "deprogrammers," also known as "exit counselors," who offer services allegedly undoing the effects of the brainwashers. Courts have allowed experts to testify that former cult and sect members were brainwashed. Movies and television dramas portray the personal tragedies of brainwashed victims and their families. Social scientists' steadfast rejection of the brainwashing concept has been construed by some partisans as evidence of their having been collectively hoodwinked. How do scholars begin to sort out the cant and get to the real issues?

Richardson ("A Social Psychological Critique of 'Brainwashing' Claims About Recruitment to New Religions") was among the first sociologists to pursue studies of the new religions in the late 1960s, and he has continued to research the subject for the past two decades. Richardson is also an attorney. He has both conducted research on mock juries and frequented the courtroom as an expert witness. His contribution here focuses on the *social psychological literature* about brainwashing. Richardson does provide some limited insights regarding why people believe in brainwashing—essentially it provides a variety of groups with a powerful social weapon to use against unconventional religions, but this is not the focus of his paper. Rather, his goal is to explore a significant body of scholarly literature in social psychology that both illumines and points to solid theoretical and empirical conclusions about the concept of brainwashing.

The concept emerged during the Korean War of the early 1950s. A small number of American soldiers, held prisoners by the communists, defected. An English journalist coined the concept and proclaimed that the communists had developed techniques so powerful that they could literally turn people into a slave class that could be trusted never to revolt. After the Korean conflict, a psychologist, Edgar Schein (1961), and a psychiatrist, Robert Jay Lifton (1961), conducted studies for the U.S. government of small samples of the defectors, now returned home of their own volition. Both scholars acknowledged that the communists had exerted significant, albeit rather temporary influence, over American soldiers under conditions of *physical* coercion. Both explicitly rejected the utility of the brainwashing as a scientific concept.

The idea of brainwashing, of course, did not disappear. The Cold War mentality of the 1950s and 1960s found the concept ideal to describe the sinister influence of the communists. *The Manchurian Candidate,* an eerie film about a brainwashed American soldier, was a box office smash in 1962 and did much to solidify the indelible imprint of the word. As with many words that come into popular usage, the idea of brainwashing underwent devaluation so that it came to be used loosely to characterize unwelcome influence, especially by unsavory people or groups.

With the cult phenomenon of the late 1960s and 1970s, the concept was restored to its full original horrific implications. Richardson traces how disregard, and even misrepresentation, of the classic studies of Schein and Lifton facilitate reinvention of the myth of brainwashing. Advocates of the "second generation" theory of brainwashing see it as much more powerful because the new brainwashing is grounded in psychological manipulation rather than physical coercion. Richardson explores also a variety of other kinds of evidence that should give rise to skepticism regarding the viability of the concept.

After critiquing the underpinnings of the brainwashing concept, Richardson systematically explores social psychological literature that is relevant for understanding the dynamics of becoming a member of a NRM. Three general factors alleged to be central to the "second generation" brainwashing are explored in depth: (1) isolation, (2) group pressure, and (3) physical coercion.

*Isolation* is used by some, but by no means all NRMs to discourage contact between potential recruits and their families and friends. Research supports the conclusion that a large proportion of potential recruits are already isolated from significant others when they enter interaction in which they are potentially receptive to recruitment. There is little evidence to suggest that coercion is used against people who attempt to leave. Furthermore, many groups—including parents, social clubs, and the military—use isolation to discourage contact with persons or groups that might reduce their ability to influence or control youth.

*Group pressure* takes on a myriad of forms, but the literature in social psychology does not support the conclusion that actors are passive agents incapable of resisting influence that is incompatible with their interests or predispositions.

*Coercion* may be characterized as either physical or psychological. There is no evidence to support the contention of physical coercion. Further, if such techniques were imposed, social psychological theory would hypothesize rebellion. Psychological coercion, as Robert Cialdini so ably demonstrates in his book, *Influence* (1984), is an integral part of the human experience. People in all kinds of social situations seek to influence other people. But influence usually does not persist for long periods of time unless the subject of influence wishes to be so influenced. Richardson's paper concludes with a discussion of three alternative social psychological models to the idea of brainwashing. All three are grounded in the presupposition that recruitment/conversion to a new religious group is much like the processes whereby people become involved in any group or diadic relationship. Engagement involves reciprocal and consensual influences.

If the idea of "brainwashing" did not exist, the subject of cult and sects would be much less acrimonious, perhaps even uninteresting. However, it is not an idea that is likely to recede from public consciousness. It is too deeply ingrained and, as we shall explore elsewhere in the volume (Bromley and Shupe), there are well organized interest groups in America and Europe that are dedicated to keeping the myth of brainwashing alive. Some anti-cultists, sensing the vulnerability of brainwashing as a viable legal concept, prefer concepts like "mind control," "thought reform," and "Systematic Manipulation of Social and Psychological Influence." But as one of the leading exponents of the perspective has acknowledged in a recent legal deposition, the terms all refer to the same phenomenon. Richardson's article does not review the important issues in the evolving legal status of the concept, nor is this explored in depth in this handbook. These matters are discussed in an excellent essay by Anthony (1990; see also Ungerleider and Wellisch 1989).

## Mental Health

Saliba ("The New Religions and Mental Health") is author of two massive annotated bibliographies on the scholarly literature about cults and sects. The first volume surveyed publications of psychiatry (1987) and the second explored the literatures of the social sciences (1990). Combined, the two volumes provide exquisite annotations of the theory and research of over 4,000 books and articles. It is hard to imagine that any scholar in the world could be better qualified to examine the difficult and controversial questions surrounding new religions and mental health.

Saliba begins by noting that the latest edition of the *Diagnostic and Statistical Manual of Mental Disorders* (*DSM-III*), a widely used reference manual published by the American Psychiatric Association, still endorses "the position that cultic beliefs and lifestyles contribute to mental illness and are an obstacle to the development of a health personality." This quasi-official position of the APA stands in sharp contradiction to much research and to resolutions endorsed by several social science groups that find scientific evidence inadequate to reach such a conclusion.

Saliba's paper for this volume examines three broad literatures to shed light on the controversies relating to: (1) converts to Eastern religious movements, (2) members of Pentecostal and fundamentalist sects, and (3) persons practicing various types of meditation. Most of the literature falls into two broad categories: studies of members and studies of persons who were pressured to leave their groups. Three-quarters of the studies of members "tended to show that the psychological profiles of individuals tested fall well within 'normal' bounds." On the other hand, a very high incidence of "serious mental and emotional dysfunctions" is found among those subjects who left NRMs involuntarily.

Researchers of subjects who left involuntarily typically attribute the observed mental health problems to participation in the religious group. Saliba notes that such an inference in not methodologically sound. Further, there is some evidence to support the conclusion that the source of emotional disturbances for some ex-members pivots on the traumatic circumstances surrounding their departure. Methodologically, it is equally important to note that most of these research reports have no reliable evidence on the mental health of these subjects *before* the subjects entered the group. A relatively small number of studies do provide mental health diagnoses prior to entering the NRM. Typically, they report high levels of psychological distress prior to entering with significant improvements in mental health as a result of participation in the group. Psychiatrist Marc Galanter has referred to this dramatic change as the "relief effect." But most of these studies, too, are not without methodological shortcomings.

Substantially missing from the literature are studies of persons who left NRMs of their own volition. In terms of sheer numbers, there are far more ex-members of cults than members. Further, the overwhelming majority of ex-members do leave voluntarily. Thus, little is known about the single largest category of persons who have been affiliated with NRMs. Such investigations are critical before it is possible to approach a comprehensive assessment of the impact of cult membership on mental health.

As might be inferred, a substantial proportion of Saliba's paper is devoted to methodological issues. *In spite of the vast amount of literature, a large proportion of it is deficient insofar as one is interested in an overall assessment of cult and sect life on the mental health of participants.* Saliba appears to come down hardest on the research about ex-members who left involuntarily and the sweeping generalizations of DSM-III. But he also makes clear that it would be inappropriate to conclude that the research literature supports the contentions of many NRMs that membership has an efficacious effect on the mental health of members. In the end, Saliba concludes that "[c]ontemporary research does not offer an unequivocal answer to the intriguing question of whether the cults are adverse or beneficial to individual mental health."

Scholars who are interested in moving toward a resolution of the controversies surrounding the questions of NRMs and mental health will find Saliba's paper invaluable in identifying the kind of research that is required. His contribution to this volume does not go into detail about the research literature on "brainwashing." For a comprehensive review of this literature, readers are encouraged to consult the introductory essay to Saliba's volume *Psychiatry and the Cults* (1987).

## B.   Emerging Issues

### Exiting

The subject of conversion, as noted above, has occupied more scholarly attention than any other topic relating to the subject of religious movements. While sociological scholars noted early that a high proportion of joiners of NRMs do not remain affiliated for a very long period of time, systematic investigations of the process of leaving have been rare until about a decade ago. To capture in a nutshell what the growing number of investigations are finding, leaving new religions is in many ways a mirror image of joining. Some scholars use the concept "deconversion," but research does not support the popular radical "road to Damascus" conversion model. Rather, both joining and leaving religious movements tend to be gradual processes.

Ebaugh was one of the early scholars to investigate the process of leaving a "totalistic" religious organization (1977). Her study of Roman Catholic nuns who gave up their vows and left their religious orders is a landmark investigation of the dynamics and dilemmas people face when leaving a religious order. In this volume Ebaugh collaborates with Wright, who has conducted the most extensive research on voluntary leavetakers from NRMs, to provide a valuable review of the emerging literature on leaving new religions.

Wright and Ebaugh ("Leaving New Religions") identify three broad issues in the emerging literature on leaving NRMs: (1) conceptual, (2) methodological, and (3) theoretical. Conceptually, defection from a religious group is not a unidimensional phenomenon. One may feel disaffection that results in emotional withdrawal and detachment. One may feel disillusioned, with the result that disbelief undermines the authority of the leader and the group. But neither the deterioration of affective bonds nor erosion of belief will necessarily lead to withdrawal from the group. Theoretically, there are many reasons individuals might elect to remain in a group. The existing research literature has only begun to conceptualize the dynamic interaction of affective, cognitive, and organizational dimensions of leaving religious groups. The authors suggest that leaving a religious group is analogous to divorce, and elsewhere Wright (1991) has explored the conceptual parallels.

One of the most complex problems in understanding the dynamics of leaving religious groups is that the accounts exiting members formulate often appear to be at variance with other evidence. Wright and Ebaugh identify several methodological hazards in interpreting these accounts. The most important problem pivots on the precariousness of retrospective reporting. The real dilemma is that there are seldom opportunities to gain other kinds of accounts. Theoretically, and from much ethnomethodological research, scholars know that biographies are socially constructed to fit a specific occasion and set of life circumstances. The interpretations former adherents construct of their lives in NRMs reveal as much about the circumstances in which they are recalling the experience as they do about their actual experiences. Retrospective accounts are particularly suspect when individuals have been "deprogrammed."

Role theory and social process models have figured prominently in the research literature on conversion or joining NRMs. These perspectives have now been elaborated in considerable detail to explain why members leave NRMs. Wright and Ebaugh provide a fairly comprehensive delineation of both perspectives. They also provide a very helpful examination of social movement theory. People leave social movement organizations because of: (1) movement transformation, (2) movement decline, or (3) movement failure. Mauss' contribution to this volume encourages greater interpenetration of the literatures of religious movements and social movements. Wright and Ebaugh offer here further evidence of the conceptual value of this counsel.

In the final section of their paper, Wright and Ebaugh note that expulsion and extraction are also reasons why people leave NRMs. The number expelled is not large, but examination of the circumstances that lead organizations to force members to leave provides interesting insights about organizational growth and development.

## Health and Healing

Rene Descartes' seventeenth-century bifurcation of man into mind and body set in motion the fundamental principles upon which modern biomedicine is built. Illness results from the invasion of agents that disrupt normal anatomical functions. The goal of modern biomedicine is to develop procedures—principally alchemy and surgical intrusion—to counteract the invading agents. So pervasive is this mode of thinking that the average person believes all other methods of health care are merely varieties of quackery.

Part of what makes Pentecostals and New Age advocates seem bizarre, for example, is that both practice "faith healing." Televangelists who counsel audiences to place their hands on a cathode ray tube and be healed, and lecture circuit riders (the likes of Shirley McLaine and Marianne Williamson) are thought to be fellow travelers in the perpetuation of a giant hoax upon persons too ignorant or gullible to resist their siren calls (Randi 1987).

This contemporary secular perception notwithstanding, the subterranean practice of alternative health and healing is so pervasive that it hardly qualifies as a novel or deviant activity. Several recent surveys reveal that very substantial numbers of Americans believe in and practice a wide variety of unconventional health and healing strategies.

Unconventional or alternative health and healing methods are much like Evangelicals who were discovered by the mass media in 1976 when Jimmy Carter ran for president. Evangelicals were not a new phenomenon, nor had they been growing at an extraordinary pace. They had been present in very large numbers for a very long time. So also have alternative healing methods been present in American culture in large numbers for a long time. A large proportion of these alternative methods are spiritually grounded. Virtually all of the significant new religions of the late nineteenth and early twentieth centuries preached doctrines that linked health and healing to faith. Consider the following.

- *Pentecostalism* practices the "laying on of hands" to heal the sick.
- *Mormons, Seventh-Day Adventists,* and *Jehovah's Witnesses* all link disciplined care of the body (including prohibitions against certain foods, alcohol, tobacco, and stimulants) to theological imperatives.
- One of the central theological tenants of the *Christian Science* tradition is the belief that the mind can transcend physical maladies which are really only imagined.
- Several New Thought traditions (e.g., *Unity* and *Religious Science*) practice doctrines that promote the power of the mind (spirit) over the body.

Virtually all of the surviving new religions of this period taught and took seriously a powerful link between faith and health. But the late nineteenth and early twentieth centuries were not particularly unique. A case can be made for an integral connection between faith and health in most religious traditions throughout history (Numbers and Amundsen 1986). The puzzling question is not that contemporary new religions stress a faith-health connection but, rather, how does it happen that we have forgotten history?

Harvard cardiologist Herbert Benson, author of *The Relaxation Response* (1975) came to the annual meetings of the Society for the Scientific Study of

Religion in 1984 to encourage social scientists to study the relationship between what he called the "faith factor" and health. At the time, Meredith McGuire was practically the only scholar in the society who was already engaged in serious research on the subject. McGuire's *Ritual Healing in Suburban America* (1988) has contributed much to the "rediscovery" that faith and health care go together, not just among esoteric groups and peoples but also in the mainstream of American culture. In her ethnographic research, McGuire encountered scores of healing groups, not in inner city store-front missions or Southern rural churches but in middle- and upper middle-class neighborhoods in suburban New Jersey.

McGuire's contribution to this volume ("Health and Healing in New Religious Movements") provides an analytical foundation for much research that needs yet to be done before we understand more clearly the implications of alternative healing. Four basic questions are identified and then extant research on each is examined: (1) what are the definitions of health, illness, and healing of different religious groups? (2) what are their specific practices? (3) what is the place (centrality) of health and healing in various religious traditions? and (4) what are societal responses to the wide array of unconventional health/healing practices?

Health and illness, McGuire argues, are socially constructed cultural ideas. While modern biomedicine links health to the absence of intrusive agents that interrupt normal functioning of body organs, there are theoretically many alternatives to this dominant paradigm. For example, one alternative conception of health and healing views wellness as a state of harmony between mind/spirit and the body. Persons with Parkinson's disease cannot be relieved of the progressive deterioration of the nervous system, but they may be "healed" of the anger and anxiety that knowledge of this disease brought on and so may be made "well" in the sense that they are "at peace" with their condition.

Biomedicine places great credence in the capability of professionals to dispense proper technique, while alternative healing methods see the physician as having a much lesser role, or even no role at all. At least two broad categories of alternative conceptions of healing are discernable from extant research. One type sees healing as having *transcendent* origins while the other sees the power to heal as coming from *within*.

Useful though this typology may be for ordering and comparing groups, it does not get to the heart of the *meaning* of health and healing. McGuire argues, on the one hand, for systematic delineation of the wide array of groups with the goal of developing useful typologies; on the other hand, she pleads for "thick ethnographic description" that will probe the phenomenological meaning of health and illness of people who practice alternative medicines.

Commentary on existing research literature is carefully framed in a very cautious concern for important methodological issues. In doing so, McGuire raises all manner of fascinating questions. For example, how can social scientists know that the wide array of alternative healing communities today represent an increase over the alternative communities of a generation or two generations ago? For that matter, how do scholars know that persons attracted to alternative healing groups practice more alternative healing techniques than the general population?

A huge research literature in medical sociology deals with patient noncompliance with physician's advice and prescriptions. McGuire suggests this literature may be improperly framed. Rather than investigating why people do not follow doctor's orders, it might be more useful to explore factors affecting the selective acceptance of physician counsel. To what extent is noncompliance a result of preference for the efficacy of alternative methods?

McGuire addresses several questions of broader cultural importance, including the significance of the professional dominance of medicine. Related to this is the tendency of culture to "medicalize" deviance, that is, to label socially undesirable behaviors as illness and thereby invoke the full professional and legal authority of the health care professions as social control agents. These power relationships stand in dynamic tension with the challenges posed by alternative religions. There is, in many of the health conscious new religions, a conception of health as salvation. This has very important implications for the questions Wilson poses regarding the direction and character of new religions.

*Life Course*

A recurring fallacy of scholars and mass media communicators during the 1950s and 1960s was the conclusion that lower rates of religious belief and participation among younger people constituted evidence of secularization. The fallacy, of course, was the failure to consider that religious engagement changes during the course of the life cycle. Younger people are more likely to express doubts about religious belief and to attend church less frequently.

Inspired by the developmental stages of Erik Erikson, psychologists have elaborated various typologies of life cycle that include stages of spiritual-religious development. Sociological literature has emphasized *changing roles* as individuals age rather than *stages* of psychological maturation. Sociological literature has offered another important observation: generations have unique cultural experiences that cut across "normal" life-cycle effects. For example, the common experience of war, depression, or radical value transformations may have lasting effects on an entire population, albeit differently experienced by different age cohorts. Any given age cohort is thus a carrier of both age-role-specific development and unique experiences.

The implication of this observation is that scholars should not necessarily expect to find a constant relationship between religion and age. Sociologists of religion have generally been slow to study the relationship between age and faith or to incorporate the growing theory and research literature on *life cycle* and *generational* effects. Roof, one of the few scholars to systematically study religion and the *life course,* collaborates here with Walsh ("Life Cycle, Generation, and Participation in Religious Groups") to explore the implications of this literature for understanding cults and sects.

"Despite the huge proliferation of literature on cults and sects since the 1960s," write Roof and Walsh, "virtually no attention has been given to thinking about life cycles and generational cohorts." The focus of their inquiry is on the age cohort that matured during the 1960s, the so-called "baby boomers." They examine the implications of interaction between generation and life cycle for: (1) religious disaffiliation, (2) cult recruitment, and (3) contemporary religious and spiritual trends.

Life cycle theory postulates that as youth leave home and the direct influence of their parents, they are likely to disaffiliate from religious institutions. The "boomer" generation, comprising almost a third of the population, is the largest single cohort ever to pass through American culture. As predicted, large numbers did drop out of religion, but the rate of disaffiliation was strongly influenced by their exposure to the counterculture of the 1960s. Among those deeply exposed to the counterculture, 84 percent dropped out of religion, compared to 56 percent who were only nominally exposed.

The large number of dropouts has the simultaneous effect of creating an unusually large pool of potential recruits for new religions. Who was recruited into the ranks of new religions during the late 1960s and 1970s? Persons with the same demographics as the church dropouts: "young, college-educated, mobile, middle-class." This group, writes Roof and Walsh, "were the most vulnerable to the cultural strains in America at the time, and hence more alienated and more likely than working class youth to turn to cults as an alternative to organized religion." Following Wuthnow's analysis of San Francisco Bay Area youth in the early 1970s, they conclude that while life cycle partially explained involvement in NRMs, "generational effects were of greater impact."

But what of all the boomer youth, most of whom did not join NRMs, who are now middle aged? Are they following the expectations of life cycle theory and returning to religion? Forty percent who dropped out are exploring religion, but not necessarily in conventional ways. Roof and Walsh report that a large proportion returning are "seekers" in contrast to "belongers." They are more likely to "explore" religious ideas than to "commit" to an institution: "[I]mage is more central than word, journeying more important than a fixed faith or following."

Much of the data presented in this paper comes from a study conducted by Roof for the Lilly Foundation and is forthcoming in a book titled: *To Dwell in Possibility: America's Baby Boomers and Their Quest for a Spiritual Style.* The boomer generation data provides compelling evidence of the importance of examining both life cycle and age cohort for insights about the development of NRMs. Roof and Walsh conclude with a set of questions to stimulate further research.

## Feminism

The period of intense interest in new religious movements parallels the development of the feminist movement and the growth of interest in feminist grounded knowledge. Davidman and Jacobs ("Feminist Perspectives on New

Religious Movements") examine the growth of a body of feminist literature on the development of research and theory about new religious movements. Secondarily, their work explores racial and other marginalized groups.

Three significant areas of research about NRMs are examined for evidence of explicit analysis and theory about gender. The three topics explored are: (1) origins of NRMs, (2) family, and (3) conversion and commitment. Davidman and Jacobs conclude that the impact to date has not been particularly profound. "[G]ender has not become a basic category of analysis," nor has "[t]he impact of feminism [been] integrated into the theoretical work on the contemporary sociology of religion." Still, they see the prospects for introducing feminist perspectives and thereby enriching and broadening sociological knowledge about new religions as considerable.

Of the three issues explored, gender is most frequently and explicitly explored in the literature on the family. This attention results from two attributes of many NRMs. First, some groups self-consciously function as surrogate families and attribute theological meaning to their socially constructed family life. Second, some NRMs are patriarchal and have detailed, theologically grounded prescriptions for sex role behaviors. A frequently offered explanation for the attractiveness of patriarchal groups for women is that they offer unambiguous and stable sex roles in a world of great ambiguity. This research literature also produces some unanticipated findings. For example, a number of researchers find evidence among manifestly patriarchal Evangelical Christian groups of the incorporation of feminist goals.

The literatures on origins of NRMs and conversion are quite thin in the elaboration of gender-specific data and in the incorporation of gender-grounded theoretical ideas. On both topics Davidman and Jacobs review major research findings and offer suggestions as to how the incorporation of feminist perspectives would enrich theory and research. For example, Davidman and Jacobs note new religions and therapeutic groups offer meaning and integration to individuals adrift in a highly differentiated culture. But do men and women feel that anomic disruption of a highly differentiated culture to the same degree and in the same ways? The literature does not tell us, but the question raises important possibilities for research.

Davidman and Jacobs note also that the "self-in-relation" school of feminist thought finds women experience deeper "interconnectedness" than do men. This suggests that women may be less likely to experience the stress of a highly differentiated world than men. It suggests also that they may be less willing to break social ties and join an NRM, particularly a group that requires radical discontinuity with past affiliations. This may account for the higher ratio of males in NRMs and also explain why women are more likely to participate in occult groups.

In the final section of their paper, Davidman and Jacobs offer feminist insights on two gender-grounded topics: (1) sexuality and sexual exploitation and (2) women-centered religious communities. Both topics have received some research attention, but both categories offer important prospects for deeper understandings both of new religions and of the role of women in these groups.

## IV. THE ROAD TO MATURITY: FROM EPISTEMOLOGY TO A COMPREHENSIVE RESEARCH AGENDA

### Epistemology

Epistemology is the disciplined inquiry into the nature of knowledge. It addresses the fundamental question of how we know what we know. Sociology of knowledge explores much of the same domain with the theories and methods of inquiry that have developed in the discipline of sociology.

In the simplest of societies, people knew little about the world beyond their immediate first-hand experience. In the modern world, personal experience constitutes only a small fraction of what people know or, more precisely, what they know about. Literacy and mass communications expose almost everyone to enormous amounts of information about which they have little or no first-hand experience. The vast majority of what we know is mediated through other people, the printed word, or electronic communication.

This is clearly the case with public knowledge about new religions. The vast majority of the public in North America and Europe has virtually no first-hand knowledge of any cult or sect. Of those who have any direct knowledge, most simply have witnessed or personally been approached by NRM fundraisers or proselytizers. Such encounters may well leave a lasting impression, but they hardly qualify as firsthand knowledge about the groups.

Few, if any, scholars can even begin to rival Barker's wealth of firsthand knowledge of many new religious groups around the world. Even before there was a firm commitment to produce this volume, we asked Barker to address the epistemological question of knowledge about new religions. Her contribution to this volume ("Will the Real Cult Please Stand Up? A Comparative Analysis of Social Constructions of New Religious Movements") is a penetrating analysis of our cultural sources of knowledge about cults and sects.

Beginning with the sociological proposition that knowledge is socially constructed, Barker distinguishes between *primary* and *secondary* constructions. Primary constructions initially are the product of the founder(s) of an NRM, but this reality constantly changes and incorporates new information and ideas as the group and its leadership evolve. Secondary constructions come from a variety a sources, including the group itself and also persons and groups that may have no firsthand knowledge of the NRM.

Barker describes her task here as a *tertiary* construction, by which she means an analysis of secondary constructions. Four secondary constructions are examined: (1) those of the NRMs themselves, (2) the anti-cultists, (3) the media, and (4) sociologists of religion.

The perceptions or presuppositions that inform an individual's understanding of any group or social phenomenon are not random ideas but rather are more or less systematically related to subcultural assumptions, values, interests, and so forth. One would thus expect the social constructions of a parent who feels distraught as a result of their child's joining of an NRM to be qualitatively different from that of the child. And different still are the constructs of a sociologist whose interest in the group is to *understand* the complex details of its social organization.

Barker's analysis begins with the secondary constructions of the NRM itself. As groups grow and become more complex it becomes inevitable that the group will engage not only in the primary task of creating its own world but also in the creation of a reality for the outside world. This will likely involve amplification of attributes which the group feels will be positively received by those outside the group and, very likely, the camouflaging of beliefs and practices perceived to be controversial to the outside world.

Barker offers a fascinating discussion of the reasons why cults and sects, even though they often feel uncomfortable with sociologists, may promote the secondary constructions of the sociologists. First, they are savvy enough to know that the general consumer of knowledge does not trust their own constructs. Second, they recognize the sociologist is less likely to present misinformation than anti-cultists or the media. This creates a dilemma for sociologists who, on the one hand, need to retain rapport with NRMs if they are to have any reasonable access through which to conduct research and, on the other hand, need to avoid being portrayed as apologists or closet members of a group.

In sharp contrast to the social constructions of the NRMs themselves, the world created by the *anti-cultists* will be a mirror image—amplifying the negative and downplaying anything positive. This observation invites the comment that "Bundles of ideas can be communicated through the use of a single concept." The label "cult" is itself such a word. Barker acknowledges that the concept "anti-cultist" can carry similarly negative connotations.

Anti-cults, like the cults, are anything but homogeneous, but all who have been so labeled have in common "a negative evaluation of NRMs." What they propose to do with their negative evaluations runs the gamut from exposing and warning to employment of methodologies intended to destroy NRMs. If the goal of this movement is "to persuade people that 'something ought to be done' about NRMs," writes Barker, "it is only logical that the ACM [anti-cult movement] would be disposed to construct pictures of the movements in which only, or at least mainly, negatively evaluated aspects are included." Further, the logic of their action agenda excludes any positive information, ambiguous or nonevaluative information such as might be expected from sociologists. Indeed, the sociologist's construction, if publicly accepted, is a threat to their own social construction. As a result, there exists considerable tension between the two groups.

As for *media* constructions, Barker acknowledges at the beginning and the conclusion of her discussion that the media has produced some "excellent and accurate information," but she also credits them with "most irresponsible and fantastic constructions." She is, however, sympathetic of the conditions under which the media must operate.

Mass media, first and foremost, must produce a product that sells. Second, reporters operate under constant constraints of time and space. As with many other categories of news, the very definition of newsworthiness pivots on a sensational or emotional spin. "The grieving mother" is more interesting than a professor's lecture on the theories of why young people join a cult.

An additional factor that plays heavily into the structural constraints under which news is produced, is an active, symbiotic relationship between reporters and the anti-cultists. The Cult Awareness Network, for example, courts mass media and produces a media kit that identifies issues along with names of their experts.

"All secondary constructions," Barker concludes, "must select some aspects and leave other aspects...The NRMs can be expected to select those aspects they believe...will put them in the best light, the ACM will select those that put the NRM in a bad light and the media will select what they believe, according to a range of criteria, will make a good story."

In the midst of this triumvirate with competing interests and needs, Barker finds the sociologist's role limited:

> [Sociology]...cannot pronounce on the truth or falsity of a theological or ideological position...; it cannot decide between opposing moral claims...; it cannot make Platonic statements about what is the true content of a definition.... A sociological criterion for judging a sociological account is the degree to which it furthers our understanding of a social phenomenon, not the degree to which it furthers the advancement or the curtailment of the phenomenon or how good a story it makes.

In an extra-sociological role, Barker founded INFORM (Information Network Focus on Religious Movements), an information dissemination group in Great Britain, that seeks to build constructive communication between families and their children who have become affiliated with NRMs. Her success in building bridges is unparalleled by any other organization in Europe or the United States. INFORM has a research and information gathering component so that clearly the sociological role is evident in this endeavor. One may be tempted to conclude that Barker's modesty understates the role of sociology in promoting understanding and good will among the parties in this conflict. But Barker would certainly counsel that this is not intrinsically the sociological role.

## A Research Agenda

The contributors to this volume have repeatedly advised readers of gaps in the existing research literature, of opportunities for more research, and of the need for research of a higher quality. Some of the research on NRMs, it has been argued, is of mediocre to poor quality because researchers have brought ideological presuppositions to their inquiries that virtually preclude objective inquiry. Much of the methodologically objectionable research has been carried out by persons who believe new religions to be a pernicious force in culture. They assume that "right thinking" people would not get involved in a sect or cult. Therefore, they bring a strong predisposition to define cult and sect members as victims. But to keep the record straight, it needs to be acknowledged that social scientists contributing to this volume have been accused of being "soft," even sympathetic to cults.

The stability of research findings necessarily hinges on the quality of the data. When scholars of new religious movements come together to discuss research issues, most readily admit that some research on NRMs fails to meet optimal standards of methodological soundness. Many of the reasons why this is so that have little or nothing to do with investigator bias.

Studying movements, religious or social, is an inherently precarious task. Movements tend not to keep detailed organizational records and, moreover, tend to be secretive about information they do gather. Leaders tend to be suspicious of being observed or too busy with the movement to cooperate with scholars, and members may be reluctant to cooperate with researchers unless leaders have approved. In a word, the obstacles to inquiries about NRMs are substantial while the resources available to pursue studies of religious movements are usually quite thin. As a result, researchers are often faced with compromising ideal research designs if they expect to obtain any research data at all.

Take, for example, the problem of sampling for a study of former cult or sect members. Persons who leave NRMs voluntarily constitute the large majority of former cult and sect members. Most simply disappear back into society. The groups to which they belonged soon lose track of them, and there are no other readily available resources to track them down. On the other hand, persons who have left a group involuntarily (i.e., as a result of being deprogrammed or receiving "exit counseling") frequently end up in anti-cult associations. Given what is known about the role of deprogrammers or exit counselors in framing the experience of the former members they counsel, there is every reason to be suspicious about a study that relies on subjects who left involuntarily. The limited data available suggest the two groups are quite different. So how does one proceed with a study? Not surprisingly, most of the studies of former members have used the networks of anti-cult groups to identify subjects.

Richardson, Balch, and Melton have each written independently about the problems of developing and maintaining high standards of research. Their collaboration here ("Problems of Research and Data in the Study of New Religions") provides a catalogue of methodological problems that need to be addressed if the quality of research is to be elevated. The second half of their presentation provides a blueprint of research that needs to be pursued. Far more issues are pursued than can be summarized here, and so a few points of particular importance will be highlighted.

First, there are hundreds of new religions in North America and Europe, but the large majority of all the accumulated knowledge comes from the study of only a few groups. It is important to encourage investigations of groups that have heretofore not been investigated.

Second, while there is a substantial accumulation of knowledge about a few groups, the examples of comparative research are very thin. Richardson, Balch, and Melton plead for the establishment of an archive like the Human Relations Areas Files, which house raw research data on hundreds of pre-literate groups studied by anthropologists. Such an archive on cults and sects would both raise consciousness about the desirability of comparative research and facilitate the process.

Third, there is much room for improvement of research designs. Typically, investigations are "one shot" encounters with a movement rather than longitudinal inquires capable of discerning change. The concept of "compounded accounts" refers to the tendency of investigators to add their own subjective interpretations to the stories told them by their subjects. Triangulation, the simultaneous employment of multiple research methods, is an important strategy for neutralizing subject and researcher bias. Similarly, it is important to recognize the importance of gathering data from a wide range of persons associated with the NRM experience, "from members *and* ex-members, from apologists *and* detractors, from leaders *and* followers,...from parents *and* from sons and daughters who are members." Control groups, while not easily achieved, should not be ignored as a research objective wherever possible. Similarly, greater attention should be paid to replication of research and, when possible, the use of standardized research instruments.

Two particular types of research design flaws are singled out for attention. "Therapy as research" suffers from sample bias and "the worst type of 'compounded account' problem[s]." Because therapy typically involves resocialization of the former group member, the accounts that emerge "are *jointly constructed* by therapist and subject and cannot be treated as independent measurements of individuals or groups." One also needs to be cautious of the "happy member" research syndrome. Because most NRMs tend to have fairly high attrition rates, studies of those happily affiliated is certain to miss important dimensions of group life. The researcher who fails to find any evidence of discord has likely been the victim of a heavy dose of "impression management."

Fourth, the authors join other contributors to this volume in calling for much greater attention to structural and organizational analysis. Research on individual-group relationships is important, but it is only one dimension of the sociological mission.

The final section of the paper is devoted to the identification of neglected substantive research areas. For each area identified, the authors raise a number of questions that may be viewed as a blueprint for research activity.

## CONCLUSIONS

Taken as a set, the contributions to this volume offer a number of fresh perspectives, raise issues significant to both the study of religion and the larger sociological enterprise, and propose research agendas to advance the understanding of NRMs while integrating that knowledge into broader sociological theory.

The section on the emergence and development of cults and sects in the largest sense calls for putting the current cohort of new religions in a broader perspective. If there is a single theme, it is identifying points of continuity and uniqueness: How do NRMs differ from and resemble earlier NRM cohorts? To what extent do cohorts of NRMs constitute sharp historic breaks or long-term continuities? How much resemblance is there between NRMs and other types of social movements? How unique are the leadership patterns of NRMs? What is the basis for determining when social movements cease to be religious and begin to be something else? Are separate theories required to explain NRMs appearance and development, and how can competing theories be reconciled?

The section on the sociocultural environment considers the organizational and institutional matrix within which NRMs operate. The overarching theme of this section is interpreting the relationship between NRMs and a variety of organizations and institutions: To what extent can NRMs and the countermovements arrayed against them be understood as the product of the same social forces and as linked in a dialectical development process? How are NRMs influenced by power expansions/contractions of the state, and what are the long-term patterns and implications for successive NRM cohorts? Do NRMs further or retard the process of secularization? Must science and religion be inherently compatible, or can new religious groups blend science and theology so that these distinctive ways of knowing are rendered compatible?

The section dealing with cults, sects, and the individual works at a social-psychological level, examining individual-group relationships. The central theme is the dynamic interfacing of NRM and adherent: What is the process that is called conversion, and how does it differ from other types of personal-level change that occurs when individuals affiliate with groups? How hegemonic is the personal transformation that accompanies affiliation with NRMs? Is the process sufficiently unilateral that it qualitatively differs from other forms of influence, or can it be understood as simply an extension of normal, routine influence processes? What is the relationship between entering and exiting processes, and how are affiliation and disaffiliation processes shaped by an environment in which serial relationships have become normative? How do age, generation and gender impact the patterning of NRM affiliations and disaffiliations? What is the impact of NRM membership on mental and emotional functioning, and how can the specific effects of NRMs be separated from the myriad of social forces that have impacted on adherents through their lives? What is the significance of healing rituals and health practices in NRMs, and what are the consequences of the availability of mainline and alternative modes of healing for individuals in religious groups?

The final section considers epistemological and research agenda issues. These contributions take a step back from the diverse array of research issues considered in this volume to consider two questions: What are the roles of social scientists and others in constructing what comes to be regarded as knowledge about NRMs, and can a comprehensive research agenda be fashioned so that social scientists work consensually on problems designed to yield an integrated corpus of knowledge about NRMs?

These, then, are some of the perspectives, issues, and agendas delineated in the *Handbook of Cults and Sects in America*. Individually, the papers pursue these matters in depth. Together they establish a base and chart a course for furthering the sociological understanding of new religious movements.

# REFERENCES

Anthony, D. 1990. "Religious Movements and Brainwashing Litigation: Evaluating Key Testimony." Pp. 295-344 in *In Gods We Trust*, edited by T. Robbins and D. Anthony. 2nd ed. New Brunswick, NJ: Transaction Publishers.

Beckford, J.A. 1985. "The Insulation and the Isolation of the Sociology of Religion." *Sociological Analysis* 46: 367-364.

Bell, D. 1977. "The Return of the Sacred?" *British Journal of Sociology* 28:419-444.

Benson, H. 1975. *The Relaxation Response*. New York: William Morrow and Co.

Biggart, N.W. 1989. *Charismatic Capitalism*. Chicago: University of Chicago Press.

Bromley, D.G. forthcoming. "Quasi-Religious Corporations: The Reintegration of Capitalism and Religion." In *Religion and the Resurgence of Capitalism*, edited by R. Roberts. London: Routledge.

Bromley, D.G., and A.D. Shupe. 1979. *"Moonies" in America*. Beverly Hills, CA: Sage.

Cialdini, R.C. 1984. *Influence*. New York: Quill.

Ebaugh, H.R.F. 1977. *Out of the Cloister*. Austin: University of Texas Press.

Ellwood, R. 1978. "Emergent Religion in America: An Historical Perspective." Pp. 267-284 in *Understanding the New Religions*, edited by J. Needleman and G. Baker. New York: Seabury.

Fry, C.L. 1933. "Changes in Religious Organizations." Pp. 1009-1060 in *Recent Social Trends in the United States*. Report of the President's Research Committee on Social Trends. New York: McGraw-Hill.

Galanter, M. 1978. "The 'Relief Effect': A Sociobiological Model for Neurotic Distress and Large-Group Therapy." *American Journal of Psychiatry* 135:588-591.

Glock, C.Y., and R. Bellah, eds. 1976. *The New Religious Consciousness*. Berkeley: University of California Press.

Greil, A.L., and D.R. Rudy. 1984. "What Have We Learned From Process Models of Conversion?" *Sociological Focus* 17: 306-323.

Kelley, D.M. 1972. *Why Conservative Churches Are Growing*. New York: Harper and Row.

La Barre, W. 1962. *They Shall Take Up Serpents*. New York: Schocken Books.

Lifton, R.J. 1961. *Thought Reform*. London: Victor Gollancz Ltd.

Long, T.E. 1986. "Prophecy, Charisma, and Politics: Reinterpreting the Weberian Thesis." Pp. 3-17 in *Prophetic Religions and Politics*, edited by J.K. Hadden and A.D. Shupe. New York: Paragon House.

———. 1988. "A Theory of Prophetic Religion and Politics." Pp. 3-16 in *The Politics of Religion and Social Change*, edited by A.D. Shupe and J.K. Hadden. New York: Paragon House.

McAdam, D. et.al. 1988. "Social Movements." Pp. 695-737 in *Handbook of Sociology*, edited by N.J. Smelser. Beverly Hills, CA: Sage.

McGuire, M.B. 1988. *Ritual Healing in Suburban America*. New Brunswick, NJ: Rutgers University Press.

Moore, R.L. 1986. *Religious Outsiders and the Making of Americans*. New York: Oxford University Press.

Novak, M. 1976. *The Joy of Sports*. New York: Basic Books.

Numbers, R.L., and D.W. Admundsen, eds. 1986. *Caring and Curing: Health and Medicine in the Western Religious Traditions*. New York: Macmillan.

Ogburn, W.F. 1933. *Recent Social Trends in the United States*. Report of the President's Research Committee on Social Trends. New York: McGraw-Hill.

Randi, J. 1987. *The Faith Healers*. New York: Prometheus Books.

Robbins, T. 1988. *Cults, Converts and Charisma: The Sociology of New Religious Movements.* Beverly Hills, CA: Sage.

Roof, W.C. Forthcoming. *To Dwell in Possibility: America's Baby Boomers and Their Quest for Spiritual Style.* San Francisco: Harper Collins.

Saliba, J.A. 1987. *Psychiatry and the Cults: An Annotated Bibliography.* New York: Garland Publishing.

————. 1990. *Social Science and the Cults: An Annotated Bibliography.* New York: Garland Publishing.

Schein, E.H. 1961. *Coercive Persuasion.* New York: W.W. Norton.

Shupe, A.D., and D.G. Bromley. 1980. *The New Vigilantes.* Beverly Hills, CA: Sage.

Snow, D.A., and R. Machalek. 1984. "The Sociology of Conversion." *Annual Review of Sociology* 10: 167-190.

Stark, R., and W.S. Bainbridge. 1979. "Of Churches, Sects, and Cults: Preliminary Concepts for a Theory of Religious Movements." *Journal for the Scientific Study of Religion* 18: 117-131.

————. 1985. The Future of Religion. Berkeley: University of California Press.

————. 1987. *A Theory of Religion.* New York: Peter Lang.

Stark, R., and R. Finke. 1992. *The Churching of America, 1776-1990.* New Brunswick, NJ: Rutgers University Press.

Ungerleider, J.T., and D.K. Wellisch. 1989. "Deprogramming (Involuntary Departure), Coercion, and Cults." Pp. 239-253 in *Cults and New Religious Movements,* edited by M. Galanter. Washington, DC: American Psychiatric Association.

Wallace, A.F.C. 1966. *Religion: An Anthropological View.* New York: Random House.

Way, F., and B.J. Burt. 1983. "Religious Marginality and the Free Exercise Clause." *American Political Science Review* 77: 654-665.

Wheeler, H. 1971. "The Phenomenon of God." *The Center Magazine* 4: 7-12.

Wilson, B. 1982. *Religion in Sociological Perspective.* Oxford: Oxford University Press.

Wright, S.A. 1991. "Reconceptualizing Cult Coercion and Withdrawal: A Comparative Analysis of Divorce and Apostasy." *Social Forces* 70:125-145.

Wuthnow, R.J. 1988. "Sociology of Religion." Pp. 473-509 in *Handbook of Sociology,* edited by N.J. Smelser. Beverly Hills, CA: Sage.

# PART III

## CULTS, SECTS, AND THE INDIVIDUAL

Section A

MATURING INQUIRIES

_____

# CONVERSION TO NEW RELIGIOUS MOVEMENTS

Richard Machalek and David A. Snow

## ABSTRACT

This paper consists of a review and assessment of the theoretical and empirical literature on conversion to new religious movements. Conversion is conceptualized broadly as a radical transformation of consciousness, including self and identity. We review and evaluate recent social scientific studies of conversion to new religious movements and provide recommendations for subsequent scholarship and research. First, we examine the nature of conversion, as it has been conceptualized and investigated by social scientists. Second, we determine that most researchers have attributed conversion to two basic sets of causes: individual attributes (physical, psychological, and social status) and contextual influences (temporal context and sociocultural context). Finally, we review and evaluate studies of the social and psychological consequences of conversion. We conclude by recommending that social scientists conduct more research on the macrosocial, organizational, and temporal contexts within which conversions occur in order to bring more balance to the existing emphasis on psychological and microsocial aspects of conversion.

Perhaps because they are novel and exotic, new religious movements have puzzled social scientists and lay people alike: How and why do people become converted to cults, and what are the social and psychological consequences of conversion? Inspired by their puzzlement, social scientists have made recruitment and conversion to new religious movements one of the most

**Religion and the Social Order, Volume 3B, pages 53-74.**

extensively studied aspects of the new religions (Beckford and Richardson 1983; Rambo 1982; Robbins 1988; Snow and Machalek 1984). Robbins (1988, p. 63) observes that the assumption underlying this research is that "spiritual apotheosis is an unnatural and problematic phenomenon which entails esoteric processes." Few social scientists have questioned whether the "spiritual apotheosis" that they call "conversion" is empirically real and, therefore, amenable to scientific analysis. Instead, the topic of religious conversion has become a minor growth industry among these researchers studying new religious movements.

The putative reality of life-transforming spiritual experiences derives, in part, from the influence of religious culture itself. Religious traditions, great and small, have long celebrated the epiphanies of spiritual virtuosos such as Siddhartha, Augustine, and Paul of Tarsus. Because believers interpret such experiences as evidence of human encounters with the sacred, it is hardly surprising that conversion experiences have commonly come to be regarded, even by social scientists, as extraordinary phenomena that require special explanation. It is perhaps for this reason that social scientists have not hesitated to generate *special* theories of conversion per se rather than attempting first to render conversion tractable to other explanatory approaches such as role theory, socialization theory, and learning theory. Consequently, the proliferation of new religious movements has been paralleled by a burgeoning of theories about and research on religious conversion. Thus, it may be that the ostensible uniqueness of conversion as a behavioral phenomenon owes more to social scientists' largely uncritical acceptance of a *religiously* defined reality than to conclusions drawn from scientific observation. Social scientists, however, are now beginning to explore the extent to which more general sociological and psychological theories of human behavior may be useful in explaining the conversion process.

If we conceptualize conversion broadly as a *radical transformation of consciousness, including self and identity,* then it becomes possible to review and assess a wide range of studies, both empirical and theoretical, in terms of the following basic questions: (1) What is the nature of conversion? (2) What are the causes of conversion? and (3), What are the consequences of conversion? In this paper, we report what social scientists have learned by trying to answer these questions, and we offer suggestions for new types of inquiry that could further enrich our understanding of conversion to new religious movements.[1]

## WHAT IS THE NATURE OF CONVERSION?

What is a conversion, and how do we know that it has occurred? These questions bear on the very nature of conversion as it is conceptualized by social scientists. Some scholars take conversion to mean a process by means of which people simply become affiliated with a religious group, organization, or movement (Albrecht and Bahr 1983; Fee et al. 1981; Harrison 1974; Heirich 1977; Hoge 1981; Hood 1981; Newport 1979; Roof and Hadaway 1979; Stark and Bainbridge 1985). In this view, conversion consists of gaining membership in a religious collectivity. For many researchers, however, mere affiliation does not capture adequately the transformation typifying the conversion process. Instead, they insist that conversion necessarily implies some sort of radical personal change. This is consistent with ancient Biblical meanings attached to the word conversion and associated terms such as the Hebrew word *shub* and the Greek words *epistrephein, strephein,* and *metanoia.* All such terms express the notion of a radical change in self and identity.

The idea of conversion as radical personal change has inspired scholars to attempt to distinguish conversion from other types of personal religious change. Some would separate conversion from other types of personal changes that they see as less thoroughgoing in their nature and consequences. Nock (1933), for example, distinguishes between conversion and *adhesion,* which he sees as a process of acquiring a supplementary, but not alternative, religious orientation. More recently, others have identified *alternation* as a form of religious identity change that preserves continuity with one's previous identity to a greater extent than does conversion (Barker and Currie 1985; Pilarzyk 1978; Travisano 1970). Another form of religious change, called *consolidation,* results in a synthesis between old and new elements of one's religiosity (Gordon 1974), while *regeneration* signifies a process whereby one's previously "dormant" or nominal religious identity becomes biographically vital and salient (Clark 1929; Nock 1933; Lang and Lang 1960). Finally, researchers such as Staples and Mauss (1987) and Barker and Currie (1985) caution against confounding conversion with *commitment.* If conversion consists of a radical change in self and identity, commitment refers to the post-conversion durability of that change. In this view, conversion, in and of itself, does not assure commitment (Barker and Currie 1985, pp. 305-306; Staples and Mauss 1987). Thus, conversion and commitment are analytically and empirically distinct. Because the personal transformation wrought by a conversion may be more or less stable, it is useful to reserve the term "commitment" to capture the dimension of the durability of those changes comprising a conversion.

A review of the literature reveals that conversion subsumes a rather heterogeneous array of phenomena, and several social scientists have attempted to classify these varieties of conversion by proposing various conversion typologies. For example, Parucci (1968) identifies sixteen different types of conversion, Lofland and Skonovd (1981) distinguish conversion types in terms of five basic "motifs," and Kilbourne and Richardson (1988) specify four general types of conversion with eleven subtypes. This perceived diversity may derive, in part, from the broad array of diverse new religious movements that have been investigated by researchers working in this area. Perhaps scholarship in this area is at a relatively early, "natural history" stage wherein researchers find themselves overwhelmed by the apparent diversity of the phenomena they face. Kilbourne and Richardson (1988), however, seem to have made an important advance in codifying this empirical diversity by proposing an elegant scheme for classifying types of conversion based on the dimensions of agency and level of analysis. If all conversions share a finite and specifiable number of common properties, we can hope that an analytical scheme, such as that developed by Kilbourne and Richardson, will allow us eventually to identify the underlying deep structure shared by the diverse expressions of conversion experiences that now deluge the literature (Richardson 1989).

At present, it can be argued that all conceptualizations of conversion share at least one common theme: the notion that conversion constitutes a radical personal change (Snow and Machalek 1984). More specifically, this change is commonly construed as a transformation of consciousness, especially of self and identity. Clearly, this conception of conversion implies a momentous personal change that is unlikely to be produced by simple affiliation with an organization. Viewing conversion as a transformation of consciousness implies that one has undergone something akin to a paradigm shift (Jones 1978), or a change in one's "sense of ultimate grounding" or "root reality" (Heirich 1977, pp. 673-675) or one's "universe of discourse" (Mead 1962, pp. 88-90; Snow and Machalek 1983, p. 265). Snow and Machalek (1983, 1984) argue that membership, in and of itself, should not be taken as an indicator of conversion. Instead, they propose that empirical indicators of conversion can be found in the language used by converts, specifically, in their rhetorical patterns. Based on a study of Nicheren Shoshu Buddhism (Snow 1976), Snow and Machalek (1983, pp. 173-174; 1984) contend that four rhetorical themes characterize converts to this new religious movement: biographical reconstruction, the adoption of a master attribution scheme, a suspension of analogical reasoning, and the embracement of the convert role. If, as Marx (Tucker 1978, p. 158) argued, language *is* practical consciousness, then a transformation of consciousness should be empirically evident in language behaviors. Recently, Staples and Mauss (1987) found evidence of such rhetorical patterns among a group of evangelical Christians. They contend, however, that only one of these rhetorical indicators (biographical reconstruction) signifies conversion, and the remaining three signify commitment rather than conversion.

Although group membership has very little utility as an indicator of the social-psychological changes said to constitute conversion (Snow and Machalek 1984, p. 171), researchers continue to use such forms of affiliation as indicators of conversion, especially when using very large samples. This circumstance may be inescapable, because it may be prohibitively expensive and logistically difficult, if not impossible, to generate data about conversion language behaviors when one is working with large-scale national samples (e.g., Stark and Bainbridge 1985). In such circumstances, nothing better than membership data may be available. While such data are quite informative about patterns of religious group affiliation, they may do little to advance understanding of the nature, causes, and consequences of religious conversion when it is defined as a *transformation of consciousness*. Consequently, a social scientific understanding of conversion may require the use of alternative methodologies less well-suited to generating large data bases. Thus, the study of conversion may, for the time being, remain the domain of participant-observers, ethnographers, content-analysts, and other such qualitative methodologists. The obvious cost of this constraint is the limited generalizability of such studies. On the other hand, it is not at all clear that the greater generalizability afforded by the large sample size "membership" studies actually illuminates our understanding of religious conversion. Rich opportunities exist for truly innovative researchers who could help solve the problem of generating large data bases on conversion as a transformation of consciousness.

## WHAT ARE THE CAUSES OF CONVERSION?

To the believer, the cause of a conversion experience is self-evident, because it is perceived as the result of an encounter with the sacred. Social scientists, on the other hand, seek a causal explanation that need not entail the influence of a transcendent reality. Instead, social scientific studies of conversion attribute causation either to traits possessed by the individual, to the various contexts within which individuals are embedded, or to the relationship between the two. This simple distinction between *individual attributes* and *contextual influences* allows us to summarize and to evaluate critically an extremely broad range of studies that purport to identify the causes of conversion. Furthermore, this distinction also enables us to identify explanatory trends and changes in those trends as social scientists intensify their efforts to isolate the causes of conversion to new religious movements. Individual attributes that have been credited with producing conversions can be divided into three analytic categories: physical traits, psychological traits, and social status attributes. Contextual influences to which potential converts are subject fall into two broad categories: temporal context and sociocultural context. Temporal context is subdivided into biographical context and historical context, and sociocultural context is subdivided into microsocial, mesosocial, and macrosocial context.

In reviewing the past few decades of research on conversion to new religious movements, a noticeable shift in explanatory approach can be discerned. In the early days of conversion research, great emphasis was placed on the role of contextual influences as primary causes of conversion, and this focus is most dramatically apparent in the highly deterministic "brainwashing" or "coercive persuasion" models of conversion (Sargant 1957; Lifton 1961; Schein 1961; Somit 1968; Enroth 1977; Ofshe 1980; Ofshe and Singer 1986). More recently, a new approach that attributes causal significance to a complex of individual propensities, called "active agency" (Kilbourne and Richardson 1988), has gained prominence among researchers. In fact, Richardson (1985) has argued that nothing less than a paradigm shift has occurred over the past two or three decades among those studying conversion. This new paradigm advances the view of the convert as an active, self-determining agent, "author," and "negotiator" of his or her conversion experience. Such people are said to be possessed of a "seekership" or "quest" orientation that motivates them to search for spiritual enlightenment and renewal (Straus 1976, 1979; Batson and Ventis 1982). Attributing conversion to an individual's seekership or a quest orientation entails a more subtle and complex explanatory approach than invoking individual unicausal traits such as brain dysfunction, "addictive" personality, psychological distress, or attenuated ego and superego development (e.g., Sargant 1957; Simmonds 1977; Galanter 1978, 1980, 1985; Levine 1980). Instead, the idea of an active seeker is informed strongly by the symbolic interactionist and phenomenological traditions of social theory, both of which place great emphasis on human agency as a significant force shaping social behavior. While the recent emphasis on the individual as an active agent in the conversion process represents a corrective to the previous tendency to treat individuals as passive recipients of forces acting upon them, it does not deny the contribution of certain individual and contextual factors in generating conversions. The influence of these factors is readily acknowledged in the work of researchers such as Long and Hadden (1983), Lofland and Skonovd (1981, 1983), and Snow et al. (1980). Having noted the trend toward viewing individuals as significant causal agents of their own conversion experiences, we turn to a discussion of conversion studies that examine the influence of individual traits, contextual influences, or a combination of both.

As the popularity of simplistic, monocausal theories of religious conversion (such as the brainwashing model) has begun to decline, more researchers have come to assume that conversions result from the combined and interactive influences of multiple factors, both individual and contextual. Nevertheless, the literature reveals a tradition wherein most researchers have tended to place *primary* explanatory emphasis on one or a few factors at the neglect of others in order to explain conversion. Accordingly, we shall examine, in sequence, the types of individual attributes and the sorts of contextual influences that have been emphasized in research on the causes of religious conversion.

## Individual Attributes

### Physical Attributes

Attempts to explain religious conversion in terms of individual physical attributes, physiological or morphological, are relatively rare. Unlike some social scientists, such as Wilson and Herrnstein (1985), for example, who credit the predisposition to commit crime to biologically based traits such as impulsivity, poor conditionability, depressed arousal level, and so on, conversion researchers generally have avoided efforts to trace the causes of conversion to the physical characteristics of individuals. Yet, certain explanations of conversion imply that the health or physical condition of an individual may help predispose conversion. For example, those who subscribe to the brainwashing model of conversion contend that subjecting an individual to a harsh environmental context will induce stress and fatigue and thereby predispose the person to brainwashing (e.g., Sargant 1957; Somit 1968). Specifically, this interpretation suggests that an adverse environmental context imposes physical and psychological stress on individuals which, in turn, can result in a conversion.

A second explanation of conversion implicates organismic factors as well. Glock and Stark (1965) and Stark and Bainbridge (1985) describe new religious movements as having the capacity to provide "compensators" for those experiencing deprivation.[2] Among the types of deprivation that potential converts can suffer is "organismic" (biological) deprivation. While these researchers do not place great emphasis on biological deprivation as a primary cause of conversion, their theoretical perspective admits the possible causal influence of organismic factors. Thus, individuals who suffer some form of organic deprivation are eligible for compensation in the form of religious rewards.

More recently, Galanter (1989) and Wenegrat (1989) have suggested that the human propensity to join religious groups has an organic foundation in the human genome. Drawing upon sociobiological theory, they argue that humans have evolved powerful psychological needs for group affiliation. Furthermore, Galanter claims that humans will experience neurotic distress in the absence of such affiliation. Consequently, humans experiencing strong affiliative needs will be motivated to join groups that provide "relief" from the distress generated by their alienation, and cults are among the groups available to provide such relief (Galanter 1989, pp. 85-97). It should be emphasized that this sociobiological approach is not designed to explain why some people rather than others join new religious movements. Instead, it represents an attempt to interpret conversion as one expression of a common human need, crafted by natural selection, for group affiliation. In this view, the transformation of consciousness that we call conversion is but a by-product of group affiliation and the sociological mechanisms that maintain group cohesion. Researchers such as Galanter and Wenegrat see the propensity to join cults simply as one manifestation of an evolved human predisposition to organize themselves into "in-groups" whose members exhibit "flexible mutualism" (cooperation) (Wenegrat 1989).

Finally, Crippen and Machalek (1989) have taken this evolutionary reasoning one step farther and have suggested that the human capacity for religious life may have an evolutionary foundation in the peculiar mechanisms by means of which humans recognize kin. Crippen and Machalek do not posit a genetic predisposition for religion per se. Instead, the argument holds that the behavioral capacity and propensity for symbolically mediated "kin recognition" among humans may comprise the behavioral infrastructure upon which cultural evolution eventually constructed religious institutions.

With the exception of the brainwashing model, none of the proponents of the aforementioned approaches seeks to reduce conversion or human religiosity to unique physical traits possessed by converts. Instead, each approach, in different ways, simply implicates the organic dimension of human life in religious conversion, including conversion to new religious movements, *without* embracing a version of biological determinism such as that suffered by criminology in its early history (e.g., phrenology, Sheldon's theory of body types).

## Psychological Attributes

If scholars of new religious movements are reluctant to invoke physical attributes as candidate causes for conversions, they show little such hesitancy in assigning causal significance to individual psychological attributes. The list of such psychological factors is long indeed. They range from relatively simple, situationally induced states such as "neurotic distress" (Galanter 1989), to complex "seekership" orientations that are the product of socialization and biography (Straus 1976, 1979), to distinct personality types such as "addictive personalties" (Simmonds 1977).

As the brainwashing model has faced increasing challenges over the past two or three decades, new types of psychological factors have emerged as contenders for explanatory preeminence. The most noticeable shift in explanatory motif is away from psychopathological attributions (e.g., Salzman 1953) to those entailing a view of conversion as an expression of processes that are seen as psychologically normal, including among others (1) free, rational choice (Gartell and Shannon 1985; Dawson 1990), (2) the pursuit of a meditative state of consciousness (Volinn 1985), (3) a mature quest for spiritual development (Batson and Ventis 1982), or (4) a discriminating consumer's pursuit of the most satisfying available spiritual commodity (Straus 1976, 1979; Balch and Taylor 1977; Richardson 1978). Finally, some seek to explain conversion as a response to psychological needs that are induced by experiences common to all humans, such as various types of deprivation (Glock and Stark 1965; Stark and Bainbridge 1985) and felt tension (Lofland and Stark 1965). As researchers come to rely increasingly on more general social science theories—such as socialization theory, learning theory, role theory, social network theory, exchange theory, power-dependency theory, and so on—in order to explain religious conversion, we can expect researchers to invoke more common, "everyday" psychological factors in their explanations of conversion.

It should be emphasized that while psychological factors can be interpreted properly as proximate causes, they themselves are often the product of more distal contextual influences. For example, if psychological distress is seen as the proximate cause of a conversion, the distress itself is often understood to derive from factors located in the sociocultural and material environments within which individuals must live. This kind of psychological explanation must be kept distinct from those interpretations that see conversion as the product of constitutional traits inherent in the nature of the convert.

*Social Status Attributes*

In addition to physical and psychological characteristics, individuals also possess social status attributes that are sometimes seen as causes of conversion. For example, it is commonly observed that cult converts come from middle- to upper middle-class backgrounds, are highly educated and are young (Judah 1974; Snow 1976; Galanter and Buckley 1978; Nordquist 1978; Bromley and Shupe 1979; Ungerleider and Wellisch 1979; Barker, 1980, 1983; Rochford 1982; Beckford 1983; Shinn 1983). Recent research by Stark and Bainbridge (1985, pp. 394-424) reveals that social status attributes of cult joiners include previous status as a religious "none" or religious socialization as a Protestant or Jew.

Similarly, these researchers report that cult joiners are disproportionately better educated than their counterparts and that females are disproportionately overrepresented (Stark and Bainbridge 1985, pp. 406-407, 413-417).

Taken together, these traits could be assembled into a "social status profile" of those most predisposed to conversion by virtue of their social attributes: young, middle- to upper middle-class, more highly educated, nonreligious or Jewish or Protestant and female. Nevertheless, it is interesting to note that the most recent literature on religious conversion is largely devoid of attempts to generate such diagnostic profiles of either psychological or social attributes of converts. Perhaps because research has shown converts to new religious movements to be heterogeneous in terms of both psychological and social traits, scholars have resisted temptation to proffer psychological or social profiles of converts. This signifies the achievement of a certain level of sophistication by conversion researchers. Instead of trying to provide an inventory of specific social traits that predispose one to conversion, Snow et al. (1980), Snow and Machalek (1984), and Rochford (1985) have proposed the concept of "structural availability" for describing how social traits influence the conversion process. The idea of structural availability means that either possessing certain social characteristics (e.g., power, wealth, prestige) or not being constrained by role obligations (e.g., duties and responsibilities accompanying occupational, family, civic statuses) increases one's availability for potential affiliation with and conversion to a new religious movement.[3] Research on the Hare Krishna movement, for instance, has revealed that the vast majority of its members had neither the role obligations nor social ties that could be construed as countervailing commitments for most people (Rochford 1985, pp. 76-79). More generally, the notion of structural availability helps explain why people of college age are often found in new religious movements; they are young, single, and free from occupational and family obligations. In other words, they lack the "countervailing ties" that bind most people to more conventional lines of action, and they possess the discretionary or unscheduled time to explore and participate in the activities of new religious movements.

Clearly, structural availability, in and of itself, does not ordain conversion to a new religious movement, nor is the idea intended to convey any such notion of determinism, contrary to the misinterpretation of some (Wallis and Bruce 1982). Instead, the idea of structural availability is useful for specifying the social characteristics of populations in which rates of religious conversion are more likely to be higher. It offers no guidance whatsoever about the type of new religion, if any, to which the structurally available are likely to be converted.

## Contextual Influences

In addition to individual attributes, people inhabit various contexts that influence the probability that they will convert to a new religious movement. In broadest terms, two such contexts can be specified: temporal (biographical and historical) context and sociocultural (microsocial, mesosocial, and macrosocial) context. By far, most social scientific research on conversion has examined the causal influence of microsocial factors on people's chances for conversion. The causal contributions made by the other types of contextual influences are often more difficult to ascertain, but they also merit discussion.

*Temporal Context*

People live not only within a sociocultural context, but within a temporal context as well. The temporal context consists of both an individual (biographical) and a collective (historical) dimension. Sociologists have long recognized the importance of time as a "context" that helps shape people's behavior. Mills (1959), for example, virtually defined sociology as the discipline that studies the intersection between biography, history, and social structure.

The influence of biographical context on the propensity for conversion can be illustrated in several ways. Lofland and Stark (1965), for example, discuss the importance of biographical "turning points" (such as graduation, divorce, moving or relocation, etc.) as periods during which people are especially available for conversion. Alternatively, a life-cycle or developmental approach could be employed for specifying those critical periods of life during which the probabilities of conversion increase. Starbuck (1915) and James (1902), for example, were among the earliest observers to document the adolescent inclination toward religious enthusiasm and conversion. More recently, Rudin (1984) contends that the elderly are particularly amenable to cultic conversion. A life-cycle approach also suggests the hypothesis that those undergoing a "mid-life crisis" are more highly predisposed to cultic involvement and conversion. In short, it is plausible to explore the literature on human development and the life cycle for suggestions that the biographical "trajectory" contains various critical periods during which the probabilities of religious conversion increase significantly. Of course, such biographical trajectories are largely shaped by cultural factors, and certain biographical stages, such as adolescence, may be culture-specific, thus affecting cross-cultural differences in patterns of religious conversion. In fact, the cultural invention of adolescence as a life-stage may have increased the rate of religious conversion in those societies where it is found, because adolescence is commonly typified by identity work and cognitive struggle with those beliefs that are acquired through cultural inheritance.

The temporal context also exerts its influence on conversion collectively, in the form of historical circumstance. Certain historical periods may possess properties that generate higher rates of conversion. For example, Wuthnow (1976) labels one such historical period, the 1960s in the United States, as a "consciousness reformation," a time generally conducive to cultural experimentation and innovation. Long before Wuthnow, Sorokin (1937-1941) attempted to characterize cultural epochs as more or less "sensate," "ideational" or "idealistic" with ideational periods typified by an orientation to transcendent realities.

Today, with a very few exceptions (such as Robert Bellah, William Sims Bainbridge, Rodney Stark, and Robert Wuthnow), most social scientists do not attempt to generalize about the types of historical contexts that might be conducive to conversion. More often, such periods are circumscribed and described retrospectively, as "Great Awakenings." Conversion researchers might profit by exploring this underresearched aspect of conversion to new religious movements. If certain types of historical periods do, in fact, represent fertile temporal contexts for conversion, then they deserve effort at formal specification. The investigation of both biographical and historical contexts as facilitators or inhibitors of conversion clearly is a neglected and potentially rich area of inquiry.

## Sociocultural Context

When it was first introduced almost three decades ago, the Lofland-Stark model of conversion heralded a new emphasis on the way in which sociocultural contextual influences the conversion process. By far, most of the subsequent research has addressed microsocial rather than mesosocial or macrosocial or influences on conversion. The *microsocial* context is comprised of the patterns of interpersonal interaction and relationships of which individuals are a part. Most conversion researchers have studied these influences in the forms of social networks (e.g., Stark and Bainbridge 1985; Rochford 1982, 1985; Snow and Phillips 1980; Snow et al. 1980), role behaviors (e.g., Bromley and Shupe 1979, 1986; Kilbourne and Richardson 1985; Snow and Machalek 1983; Balch 1985; Straus 1976, 1979; Balch and Taylor 1977; Richardson and Stewart 1977), and socialization processes (e.g., Wilson 1984; Long and Hadden 1983). Among these various types of microsocial influences, social networks have been found to be particularly significant in relation to conversion. As Stark and Bainbridge (1985, p. 424) conclude in a recent study of cults and sects, "[t]he central factor leading to membership in a novel religion is the development of social bonds with persons who already are members, a process likely to be as wholesome as it is natural." Finally, it should be mentioned that many of the brainwashing theorists also focus on the microsocial context by addressing how manipulative, deceptive, and coercive dimensions of interpersonal interactions and relationships can be said to produce involuntary conversions (e.g., Appel 1983; Clark et al. 1981; Ofshe 1980; Conway and Siegelman 1978; Enroth 1977; Delgado 1977).

One aspect of this research on the microsocial context has been to examine the particular quality of interpersonal interaction and relationships, namely, highly affective bonds linking prospective converts and converts to new religious movements. Beginning with Lofland and Stark's (1965) emphasis on the formation of "affective bonds" between potential converts and new religious group members, numerous researchers have sought to complement the prior emphasis on the cognitive dimension of conversion with a corresponding focus on affective attachment (Jacobs 1984, 1987; Greil and Rudy 1983; Lofland and Skonovd 1981; Barker 1980; Snow and Phillips 1980; Heirich 1977; Harrison 1974). The concern with understanding how affective bonds mediate the acquisition of a new religious ideology has added balance to the older research tradition that tried to explain conversion as primarily a cognitive change.

While research pertaining to microsocial influences on conversion abounds, there are is remarkably little systematic investigation of the way in which *mesosocial* contexts (formal and informal organizational structures and processes) impinge on conversion. Insofar as conversion can be attributed to more than individual seekership, it is typically influenced by the organizational contexts in which it occurs. This is clearly recognized by proponents of the "brainwashing" or "coercive persuasion" explanation of conversion, with its emphasis on systematic and strategic control and manipulation in sharply bounded and highly regimented group settings (Sargant 1957; Delgado 1977; Conway and Siegelman 1978; Clark et al. 1981). Because relatively few conversions occur in such settings, however, the actual manner in which organizational contexts influence conversion remains poorly understood.

There are, however, a number of works focusing more generally on social movement organizations that provide suggestive leads with respect to this type of organizational influence (Zald and Ash 1966; Coser 1967; Gerlach and Hine 1970; Lofland and Jamison 1984; Lofland and Richardson 1984; Snow 1987). Taken together, these studies suggest two propositions: (1) that as movement organizations become more "exclusive" in terms of membership requirements and more "greedy" in terms of membership demands, not only is conversion more likely to be a necessary condition for association, but it is also likely to be facilitated by such organizational tendencies; and (2) some organizational forms, particularly those that link their members to the organization both vertically and horizontally in a segmented yet reticulated fashion (see Gerlach and Hine 1970; Snow 1987) are likely to be more conducive to conversion. These are very general propositions, of course, but they do provide a point of departure for developing more specific hypotheses regarding the relationship between organizational form and conversion.

Given that the study of *macrolevel* social phenomena is both an old and a well-developed tradition in sociology, it is somewhat perplexing to find this approach so poorly represented in the study of religious conversion (Machalek and Snow 1985). Of course, exceptions are to be found. For example, Wuthnow (1976) has discussed the way in which general patterns of institutional cultural change within societies promote changes in religiosity, Bellah (1975) has discussed how crises in national institutions stimulate religious change, and Lenski and Lenski (1982) have linked major structural changes, such as the Agrarian Revolution, to patterns of religious effervescence. A related line of research focuses on macrosocial forces that give rise to religious revivals (e.g., Wimberly et al. 1980).

The recent work of Stark and Bainbridge (1985) is also relevant here. They devote considerable time and effort to specify the types of sociocultural environments in which sectarian and cultic movements are likely to emerge and flourish. For example, they develop a compelling case that secularization, a complex of macrosocial processes, is a significant factor in generating new religious movements. In so doing, they make the case for considering macrostructures, macroprocesses, and demographic characteristics of populations as important factors in the rise of new religious movements.

Similarly, they posit the existence of macrolevel religious "economies," regulated by basic processes of supply and demand, in which new religious groups and movements emerge to compete for a clientele. Although the Stark and Bainbridge approach is designed to explain the rise and fate of religious *movements*, both cultic and sectarian, it clearly implies a complementary macrosociological approach for studying patterns of conversion to these movements as well. For example, rates of conversion are quite likely to be influenced by rates at which cultic "innovation" and "importation" transpires within a population (Stark and Bainbridge 1985, p. 25). As both the volume and the rate of new religious "commodities" increases in a population, the conversion rate can be expected to increase as well. The macrosocial and cultural factors that promote cultic innovation and importation thereby also promote a higher rate of conversion. Similarly, the demographic characteristics of a population are likely to influence the conversion rate. If, for example, young people are especially structurally available for conversion, and if the population becomes younger, it is reasonable to expect, *ceteris paribus,* that the conversion rate will increase in that population. Or, if the population experiences considerable in-migration by people from a novel religious tradition ("importation"), then the conversion rate may very well rise in response to the increased supply of novel "sacred commodities."

Other approaches to the study of macrosocial contextual influences are nascent in the conversion literature. For example, Kent (1988) recently adopted a Mertonian analysis of the social structural causes of deviance for explaining conversion. Kent advocates the use of a social movements perspective to study conversion as precipitated by a "crisis of means," in the Mertonian sense, rather than a crisis of meaning. This sort of analysis illustrates further the promising novel insights that can derive from attention to the macrolevel processes that may bear on religious conversion.

Today, however, our understanding of macrosocial and demographic contextual influences on conversion remains seriously underdeveloped. Consequently, this represents an aspect of the conversion process that is particularly rich in research opportunities for social scientists interested in macrostructures, macroprocesses, and population dynamics. In fact, we find slightly ironic and inexplicably contradictory the highly developed nature of macrosociology and the disappointingly underdeveloped status of our understanding of macrosocial and demographic influences on conversion.

## WHAT ARE THE CONSEQUENCES OF CONVERSION?

In the eye of the public, the most controversial aspect of cultic conversion pertains to its consequences. For those who subscribe to the view of conversion as "brainwashing," its consequences are a foregone conclusion. Implicit in the very idea of brainwashing is an assumption that conversion inevitably entails a loss of cognitive autonomy, reasoned judgment, and intellectual independence. Consequently, it is hardly surprising that those who subscribe to brainwashing or coercive persuasion models of conversion never fail to find that it yields consequences that are predominantly, if not exclusively, negative. In fact, these consequences are often defined in the language of pathology, such as Conway and Siegelman's (1982) description of cultic conversion as a form of "information disease." Such negative characterizations of alleged consequences of conversion have prompted some social scientists to adduce evidence not only challenging these pathological attributions, but arguing, instead, that cultic conversion confers positive psychological and even therapeutic benefits on converts (Kilbourne 1983). Not surprisingly, these claims and counterclaims have generated debate in the literature that still lacks definitive resolution (Maher and Langone 1985; Kilbourne 1986; Kirkpatrick 1988).

Few social scientists are so confident as to proclaim, as do Clark et al. (1981), that cultic conversion is almost unavoidably destructive. Instead, most researchers challenge the brainwashing model on the grounds that the conditions required for coercive persuasion to be successful simply are not met in the recruitment context available to the vast majority of new religious movements (Anthony 1979-1980; Barker 1984; Robbins 1988). Numerous accounts of high turnover rates among converts to new religious movements cast additional suspicion on the characterization of conversion as brainwashing. For example, Levine (1984) reports that 90 percent of converts leave their groups within two years of their conversion, and Barker (1984) reports that no more than 0.005 percent of prospective converts who visit a Unification Church center will be associated with the movement two years later. If the conversion process actually wrought psychological changes that were as powerful and durable as those implied by the "brainwashing" characterization, we would expect to find a much lower rate of defection from new religious movements than is typically reported.

The very nature of the conversion process appears to militate against reliable assessments of it consequences. Because a conversion is *defined* as self-transforming, converts are strongly motivated both to see and to report themselves as having been profoundly changed by the experience. Typically, converts readily generate claims and accounts about the momentous personal consequences that issue from their conversions. Consequently, such accounts are an unreliable source of information about any real effects of the conversion process in the convert's life. At the same time, these accounts may themselves represent a sociolinguistic phenomenon deserving of analysis and explanatory effort (Beckford 1978; Snow and Machalek 1983, 1984; Kilbourne and Richardson 1988).

Ideally, any attempt to evaluate the consequences of conversion for the individual would involve a comparison of that person's pre-conversion and post-conversion life. In other words, reliable evaluations of the consequences of conversion require the use of longitudinal data. Such data are almost unattainable in principle, because it is not likely that researchers will ever be able to identify those individuals prone to experience conversion, thereby making virtually impossible pre-conversion and post-conversion comparisons. Having acknowledged the problem of separating the effects of preexisting personality conditions from the effects of conversion itself, Ross (1988) settles for a useful compromise by distinguishing long-term from short-term converts to Scientology in order to gauge the effects on personality of the duration of one's status as a convert to Scientology. Contrary to many popular conceptions, Ross fails to find evidence that conversion to Scientology generates negative effects on personality. In fact, he contends that "quite the opposite result was consistently found, with statistically significant improvement in social ease and goal directed behavior being apparent" (Ross 1988, p. 635). Similarly, other researchers such as Galanter (1980) attribute therapeutic benefits to long-standing involvement with new religious movements. More recently, Gordon (1984, p. 41) lists thirteen studies that report that involvement in new religious movements has neutral or beneficial consequences for participants. He also cites three studies that report pathological consequences. Gordon's (1984, p. 42) own research suggests that converts to new religious movements "achieve greater self-control and self-fulfillment by abandoning themselves to the group" to which they become converted.

The study of mental health consequences of conversion to new religious groups has generated considerable literature, and an entire paper in this volume has been devoted to this topic (Saliba). Accordingly, we shall not dwell on it. It is important to note, however, that researchers must take care to specify the type of religious orientation to which a person becomes converted in their efforts to ascertain the consequences of conversion for those individuals. The work of psychologists Batson and Ventis (1982) serves as an excellent model in that regard. They modify and extend Allport's (1959) distinction between intrinsic and extrinsic forms of religiosity to propose the existence of three religious orientations: means, ends, and quest. Their research demonstrates that the social and psychological consequences of being religious depends on the strength with which each orientation is expressed (Batson and Ventis 1982, pp. 173-299). This work is highly suggestive of the sort of conceptual and methodological sophistication that is required if students of conversion to new religious movements are to assess the human consequences of these conversions. It would be useful to characterize the theological/ideological orientations of various cults and sects in terms of the Batson and Ventis means/ends/quest scheme, and then attempt to determine if the consequences of conversion to these cults and sects corresponds to the consequences of different ways of being religious reported by Batson and Ventis.

Finally, it is apparent that any effort to determine the consequences of conversion requires a consideration of the nature and effects of "defection," "apostasy," "deconversion," or "disaffiliation" from new religious movements. Over the past decade, the phenomenon of defection has become one of the most thoroughly researched topics in the study of new religious movements (e.g., Skonovd 1981, 1983; Albrecht and Bahr 1983; Jacobs 1984, 1987, 1989; Wright 1984, 1987, 1988; Beckford 1985; Richardson et al. 1986; Lewis and Bromley 1987; Bromley 1988, 1991; Rochford 1989). As with the mental health consequences of involvement in new religious movements, defection also appears as a paper topic in this volume (Ebaugh and Wright). The proliferation of research and writing on this aspect of conversion consequences may reflect the demise of many new religious movements in the West. In part, this demise may reflect the rapidly dissipating structural availability of those individuals comprising the cohort from which so many converts were drawn in the 1960s and 1970s—the baby boom generation. Adulthood with its attendant occupational, familial, and civic commitments may have deprived new religious movements in the United States of their most valuable resource, a large cohort of potential converts who were born between 1946 and 1964.

As with studies of conversion, students of defection have begun to distinguish among different types of defection and to develop typologies to capture this variation (Richardson et al. 1986). Similarly, other researchers have made advances in specifying the details of various processes comprising defection (Jacobs 1984, 1987; Balch 1985; Ebaugh 1988; Wright 1988; Bromley 1991). Toward that end, scholars have made very fruitful use of general sociological theory in their efforts to "unravel" the nature of the defection process. For example, Jacobs (1984, 1987, 1989) has employed exchange theory, power-dependency theory, and social-psychological insights about the nature of romantic love to account for deconversion. Wright (1984) has shed light on voluntary defection by comparing it to marital separation or divorce, and Lewis and Bromley (1987) successfully employed role theory in order to determine the extent to which the "cult withdrawal syndrome" is attributable to the effects of cult conversion and membership or the processes associated with normal role-exiting and role-transition. They also offer promising theoretical leads about the social psychology of cult withdrawal and defection by invoking the analogy to death and bereavement (Lewis and Bromley 1987, pp. 518-519). Their work is important because it raises the possibility that many of the negative consequences sometimes attributed to cultic conversion and involvement may, instead, be caused by the "normal turbulence" associated with leaving any social role, thereby further de-mystifying popular conceptions of cults as "insidious" forces at work in society. Even more than in the study of conversion, research on defection from new religious movements has begun to demonstrate the analytical promise in venturing beyond the social science literature on religion per se for novel and far-reaching insights about the consequences of involvement in and disengagement from cults and sects. Hopefully, the success of these new inquiries will inspire students of conversion to rethink their established explanatory approaches and to turn to a broader range of social science explanations in order to shed additional light on the conversion process.

## CONCLUSIONS AND RECOMMENDATIONS

In the preceding pages, we have addressed three issues with respect to the study of conversion: its nature, causes, and consequences. We conclude by offering suggestions for subsequent research on these aspects of conversion. While we have noted that progress is evident in social scientific conceptualization of conversion, all too often researchers continue to treat membership as indicative of conversion. Inasmuch as conversion is widely understood to consist of a transformation of consciousness, including self and identity, it is simply no longer admissible for researchers to equate membership with conversion.

We have observed that research on conversion has focused on two broad sets of causes: individual attributes and contextual influences. Individual attributes include physical, psychological, and social status traits; contextual influences consist of temporal (biographical and historical), microsocial, mesosocial, and macrosocial contexts. By far, researchers have focused disproportionately on individual attributes and microsocial factors in their search for the causes of conversion. Although a few studies imply causal significance for the remaining contextual factors, these influences have not been systematically and thoroughly investigated. The result is that much sociological research on conversion has been too heavily reliant on psychological explanation. Consequently, it is somewhat ironic that sociologists have shown little reluctance to subordinate social contextual variables to individual variables in their efforts to explain the causes of conversion. Researchers investigating conversion have made significant gains in advancing our understanding of the sorts of individual characteristics that predispose conversion. But if researchers are to continue to advance our understanding of conversion, the time is nigh to shift analytical focus to the role of temporal, organizational, and macrosocial factors so that we can gain insight about those properties that make sociocultural environments more or less "conversionogenic" (i.e., environments that predispose individuals to experience conversion). Furthermore, it is likely that conversion rates within populations are influenced not only by static characteristics of the sociocultural context, but by changes within that context as well, such as secularization, political and economic revolutions, or migrations. These too deserve much more attention than they have received in the past. In short, there is serious need for a more fully developed macrosociological approach to the study of conversion to new religious movements.

## NOTES

1. This paper is not intended as a comprehensive review and summary of the social scientific literature on religious conversion. Instead, we hope to identify key interpretive themes, analytical approaches, and research findings that have characterized this area of social scientific inquiry. For the reader in search of comprehensive reviews and summaries of this literature, we recommend the following contributions: Robbins (1988), Kilbourne and Richardson (1988), Barker (1986), Greil and Rudy (1983), and Snow and Machalek (1984).

2. According to Stark and Bainbridge, deprivation of "earthly rewards" is more likely to motivate people to join sects rather than cults. Consequently, the "less powerful and more disadvantaged" are more likely to be found in sects than cults (Stark and Bainbridge 1985, p. 404).

3. McAdam (1986) has used the concept "biographical availability" in a similar fashion in his work on social movements.

# REFERENCES

Albrecht, S.L., and H.M. Bahr. 1983. "Patterns of Religious Disaffiliation: A Study of Lifelong Mormons, Mormon Converts and Former Mormons." *Journal for the Scientific Study of Religion* 22: 366-379.

Allport, G.W. 1959. "Religion and Prejudice." *Crane Review* 2: 1-10.

Anthony, D. 1979-1980. "The Fact Pattern Behind the Deprogramming Controversy: An Analysis and an Alternative." *New York University Review of Law and Social Change* 9: 33-50.

Appel, W. 1983. *Cults in America: Programmed for Paradise.* New York: Holt, Rinehart and Winston.

Balch, R.W. 1985. "What's Wrong with the Study of New Religions and What Can We Do About It." Pp. 24-39 in *Scientific Research and New Religions: Divergent Perspectives*, edited by B.K. Kilbourne. San Francisco: Pacific Division of the American Association for the Advancement of Science.

Balch, R.W., and D. Taylor. 1977. "Seekers and Saucers: The Role of the Cultic Milieu in Joining a UFO Cult." *American Behavioral Scientist* 20: 839-860.

Barker, E. 1980. "Free to Choose? Some Thoughts on the Unification Church and Other Religious Movements." *Clergy Review* 65: 365-368, 392-398.

_____. 1984. *The Making of a Moonie: Brainwashing or Choice?* Oxford: Blackwell.

_____. 1986. "Religious Movements: Cult and Anti-cult Since Jonestown." *Annual Review of Sociology* 12: 329-346.

Barker, I.R., and R.F. Currie. 1985. "Do Converts Always Make the Most Committed Christians?" *Journal for the Scientific Study of Religion* 24: 305-313.

Batson, C.D., and W.L. Ventis. 1982. *The Religious Experience: A Social-Psychological Perspective.* New York: Oxford University Press.

Beckford, J.A. 1978. "Accounting for Conversion." *British Journal of Sociology* 29: 249-262.

_____. 1983. "Conversion and Apostasy: Antithesis or Complementarity?" Unpublished paper.

_____. 1985. *Cult Controversies: The Societal Response to New Religious Movements.* London: Tavistock.

Beckford, J.A., and J.T. Richardson. 1983. "A Bibliography of Social Scientific Studies of New Religious Movements in the U.S. and Europe." *Social Compass* 30: 111-135.

Bellah, R. 1975. *The Broken Covenant.* New York: Seabury.

Bromley, D.G., ed. 1988. *Falling from the Faith.* Newbury Park, CA: Sage.

_____. 1991. "Unraveling Religious Disaffiliation: The Meaning and Significance of Falling From the Faith in Contemporary Society." *Counseling and Values* 35: 164-185.

Bromley, D.G., and A. Shupe. 1979. "Just a Few Years Seem Like a Lifetime: A Role Theory Approach to Participation in Religious Movements." Pp. 159-185 in *Research in Social Movements, Conflict and Change*, edited by L. Kriesberg. Greenwich, CT: JAI Press.

_____. 1986. "Affiliation and Disaffiliation: A Role-theory Interpretation of Joining and Leaving New Religious Movements." *Thought* 61: 192-211.

Clark, E.T. 1929. *The Psychology of Religious Awakening.* New York: Macmillan.

Clark, J.G., M.D. Langone, R.E. Schecter, and R. Daily. 1981. *Destructive Cult Conversion: Theory, Research and Treatment.* Weston, MA: American Family Foundation.

Conway, F., and J. Siegelman. 1978. *Snapping: America's Epidemic of Sudden Personality Change.* Philadelphia: Lippincott.

_____. 1982. "Information Disease: Have Cults Created a New Mental Illness?" *Science Digest* 90: 88-92.

Coser, L.A. 1967. "Greedy Organizations." *Archives Europeenes de Sociologie* 8: 196-215.

Crippen, T., and R. Machalek. 1989. "The Evolutionary Foundations of the Religious Life." *Revue Internationale de Sociologie* N3: 61-84.

Dawson, L. 1990. "Self-affirmation, Freedom, and Rationality: Theoretically Elaborating 'Active' Conversions." *Journal for the Scientific Study of Religion* 24: 141-163.

Delgado, R. 1977. "Religious Totalism: Gentle and Ungentle Persuasion Under the First Amendment." *Southern California Law Review* 51: 1-99.

Ebaugh, H.R. 1988. "Leaving Catholic Convents: Toward a Theory of Disengagement." Pp. 100-121 in *Falling From the Faith: Causes and Consequences of Religious Apostasy,* edited by D. Bromley. Newbury Park, CA: Sage.

Enroth, R. 1977. *Youth, Brainwashing, and the Extremist Cults.* Grand Rapids, MI: Zondervan.

Fee, J.L., A.M Greeley, W.C. McCready, and T.A. Sullivan. 1981. *Young Catholics in the United States and Canada.* New York: Sadlier.

Galanter, M. 1978. "The 'Relief Effect': A Sociobiological Model for Neurotic Distress and Large-group Therapy." *American Journal of Psychiatry* 135: 588-591.

————. 1980. "Psychological Induction into the Large-group: Findings from a Modern Religious Sect." *American Journal of Psychiatry* 137: 1574-1579.

————. 1985. "New Religious Movements and Large-group Psychology." Pp. 64-80 in *Scientific Research and New Religions: Divergent Perspectives,* edited by B.K. Kilbourne. San Francisco: Pacific Division of the American Association for the Advancement of Science.

————. 1989. *Cults: Faith, Healing and Coercion.* New York: Oxford University Press.

Galanter, M., and P. Buckley. 1978. "Evangelical Religion and Meditation: Psychotherapeutic Effects." *Journal of Nervous and Mental Disorders* 166: 685-691.

Gartell, C.D., and Z.K. Shannon. 1985. "Contacts, Cognitions and Conversion: A Rational Choice Approach." *Review of Religious Research* 27: 32-48.

Gerlach, L.P., and V.H. Hine. 1970. *People, Power, Change: Movements of Social Transformation.* Indianapolis: Bobbs-Merrill.

Glock, C.Y., and R. Stark. 1965. *Religion and Society in Tension.* Chicago: Rand McNally.

Gordon, D.F. 1974. "The Jesus People: An Identity Synthesis." *Urban Life and Culture* 3: 159-178.

————. 1984. "Dying to Self: Self-control through Self-abandonment." *Sociological Analysis* 45: 41-56.

Greil, A.L., and D.R. Rudy. 1983. "Conversion to the World View of Alcoholics Anonymous: A Refinement of Conversion Theory." *Qualitative Sociology* 6: 5-28.

Harrison, M.I. 1974. "Sources of Recruitment to Catholic Pentecostalism." *Journal for the Scientific Study of Religion* 13: 49-64.

Heirich, M. 1977. "Change of Heart: A Test of Some Widely Held Theories About Religious Conversion." *American Journal of Sociology* 83: 653-680.

Hoge, D.R. 1981. *Converts, Dropouts, Returnees: A Study of Religious Change Among Catholics.* New York: Pilgrim.

Hood, T.C. 1981. "The Uses of Self in the Conversion Ritual." Paper presented at the annual meeting of the Society for the Scientific Study of Religion, Baltimore, MD.

Jacobs, J. 1984. "The Economy of Love in Religious Commitment: The Deconversion of Women from Nontraditional Religious Movements." *Journal for the Scientific Study of Religion* 23: 155-171.

————. 1987. "Deconversion from Religious Movements: An Analysis of Charismatic Bonding and Spiritual Commitment." *Journal for the Scientific Study of Religion* 26: 294-308.

————. 1989. *Divine Disenchantment: Deconverting from New Religions.* Bloomington: Indiana University Press.

James, W. 1902. *The Varieties of Religious Experience.* New York: Longman.

Jones, R.K. 1978. "Paradigm Shifts and Identity Theory: Alternation as a Form of Identity Management." Pp. 59-82 in *Identity and Religion,* edited by H. Mol. Beverly Hills, CA: Sage.

Judah, J.S. 1974. *Hare Krishna and the Counterculture.* New York: Wiley.

Kent, S.A. 1988. "Slogan Chanters to Mantra Chanters: A Mertonion Deviance Analysis of Conversion to Religiously Ideological Organizations in the Early 1970s." *Journal for the Scientific Study of Religion* 49: 104-118.

Kilbourne, B.K. 1983. "The Conway and Siegelman Claims Against Religious Cults: An Assessment of Their Data." *Journal for the Scientific Study of Religion* 4: 380-385.

————. 1986. "A Reply to Maher and Langone's Statistical Critique of Kilbourne." *Journal for the Scientific Study of Religion* 25: 110-123.

Kilbourne, B.K. and J.T. Richardson. 1985. "Social Experimentation: Self Process or Social Role" *The International Journal of Social Psychiatry* 31: 13-22.
_____. 1988. "Paradigm Conflict, Types of Conversion and Conversion Theories." *Sociological Analysis* 50: 1-21.
Kirkpatrick, L.A. 1988. "The Conway-Siegelman Data on Religious Cults: Kilbourne's Analysis Reassessed (Again)." *Journal for the Scientific Study of Religion* 27: 117-121.
Lang, K., and G.E. Lang. 1960. "Decisions for Christ: Billy Graham in New York City." Pp. 415-427 in *Identity and Anxiety,* edited by M. Stein, A. Vidich, and D.M. White. New York: Free Press.
Lenski, G., and J. Lenski. 1982. *Human Societies: An Introduction to Macrosociology.* New York: McGraw-Hill.
Levine, E.M. 1980. "Rural Communes and Religious Cults: Refuges for Middle-class Youth." *Adolescent Psychiatry* 8: 138-153.
Levine, S.V. 1984. "Radical Departures." *Psychology Today* 18: 138-153.
Lewis, J.R., and D.G. Bromley. 1987. "The Cult Withdrawal Syndrome: A Case of Misattribution of Cause?" *Journal for the Scientific Study of Religion* 26: 508-522.
Lifton, R.J. 1961. *Thought Reform and the Psychology of Totalism: A Study of "Brainwashing" in China.* New York: Norton.
Lofland, J., and M. Jamison. 1984. "Social Movement Locals: Modal Membership Structures." *Sociological Analysis* 45: 115-129.
Lofland, J., and J.T. Richardson. 1984. "Religious Movement Organizations: Elementary Forms and Dynamics." Pp. 29-51 in *Research in Social Movements, Conflicts and Change,* edited by L. Kriesbeg. Greenwich, CT: JAI Press.
Lofland, J., and N. Skonovd. 1981. "Conversion Motifs." *Journal for the Scientific Study of Religion* 20: 373-385.
_____. 1983. "Patterns of Conversion." Pp. 1-24 in *Of Gods and Men: New Religious Movements in the West,* edited by E. Barker. Macon, GA: Mercer University Press.
Lofland, J., and R. Stark. 1965. "Becoming a World-saver: A Theory of Religious Conversion." *American Sociological Review* 30: 862-874.
Long, T.E., and J.K. Hadden. 1983. "Religious Conversion and the Concept of Socialization: Integrating the Brainwashing and Drift Models." *Journal for the Scientific Study of Religion* 22: 1-14.
Machalek, R., and D.A. Snow. 1985. "Neglected Issues in the Study of Conversion. Pp. 123-129 in *Scientific Research and New Religions: Divergent Perspectives,* edited by B.K. Kilbourne. San Francisco: Pacific Division of the American Association for the Advancement of Science.
Maher, B.A., and M.D. Langone. 1985. "Kilbourne on Conway and Siegelman: A Statistical Critique." *Journal for the Scientific Study of Religion* 24: 325-326.
McAdam, D. 1986. "Recruitment to High-risk Activism: The Case of Freedom Summer." *American Journal of Sociology* 92: 64-90.
Mead, G.H. 1962. *Mind, Self and Society.* Chicago: University of Chicago Press.
Mills, C.W. 1959. *The Sociological Imagination.* New York: Oxford University Press.
Newport, F. 1979. "The Religious Switcher in the United States." *American Sociological Review* 44: 528-552.
Nock, A.D. 1933. *Conversion.* New York: Oxford University Press.
Nordquist, T. 1978. *Ananda Cooperative Village: A Study of the Values and Attitudes of a New Age Religious Community.* Uppsala, Sweden: Religionhistoriska Institute, Uppsala University.
Ofshe, R. 1980. "The Social Development of the Synanon Cult." *Sociological Analysis* 41: 109-127.
Ofshe, R., and M. Singer. 1986. "Attacks on Peripheral Versus Central Elements of Self and the Impact of Thought Reforming Techniques." *Cultic Studies Journal* 3: 2-24.
Parucci, D.J. 1968. "Religious Conversion: A Theory of Deviant Behavior." *Sociological Analysis* 29: 144-154.

Pilarzyk, T. 1978. "Conversion and Alternation Processes in the Youth Culture." *Pacific Sociological Review* 21: 379-405.

Rambo, L.R. 1982. "Bibliography: Current Research on Religious Conversion." *Religious Studies Review* 8: 146-159.

Richardson, J.T., ed. 1978. *Conversion Careers: In and Out of the New Religions.* Beverly Hills, CA: Sage.

————. 1985. "The Active and Passive Convert: Paradigm Conflict in Conversion/Recruitment Research." *Journal for the Scientific Study of Religion* 24: 119-236.

————. 1989. "The Psychology of Induction: A Review and Interpretation." Pp. 211-238 in *Cults and New Religious Movements,* edited by M. Galanter. Washington, DC: American Psychiatric Association.

Richardson, J.T., and M. Stewart. 1977. "Conversion Process Models and the Jesus Movement." *American Behavioral Scientist* 20: 819-838.

Richardson, J.T., J. van der Lans, and F. Derks. 1986. "Leaving and Labeling: Voluntary and Coerced Disaffiliation from Religious Social Movements." *Research in Social Movements* 9: 97-126.

Robbins, T. 1988. *Cults, Converts and Charisma: The Sociology of New Religious Movements.* Beverly Hills, CA: Sage.

Rochford, E.B. 1982. "Recruitment Strategies, Ideology, and Organization in the Hare Krishna Movement." *Social Problems* 29: 399-410.

————. 1985. *Hare Krishna in America.* New Brunswick, NJ: Rutgers University Press.

————. 1989. "Factionalism, Group Defection, and Schism in the Hare Krishna Movement." *Journal for the Scientific Study of Religion* 28: 162-179.

Roof, W.C., and C.K. Hadaway. 1979. Denominational Switching in the Seventies: Going Beyond Glock and Stark." *Journal for the Scientific Study of Religion* 18: 363-379.

Ross, M.W. 1988. "Effects of Membership in Scientology on Personality: An Exploratory Study." *Journal for the Scientific Study of Religion* 27: 630-636.

Rudin, M. 1984. "Women, Elderly and Children in Religious Cults." *Cultic Studies Journal* 1: 8-26.

Salzman, L. 1953. "The Psychology of Religious and Ideological Conversion." *Psychiatry* 16: 177-187.

Sargant, W. 1957. *Battle for Mind: A Physiology of Conversion and Brainwashing.* London: Heinemann.

Schein, E.H. 1961. *Coercive Persuasion: A Socio-Psychological Analysis of the "Brainwashing" of American Civilian Prisoners by the Chinese Communists.* New York: Norton.

Shinn, L.D. 1983. "The Many Faces of Krishna." Pp. 113-135 in *Alternatives to American Mainline Churches,* edited by J.H. Fichter. New York: Rose of Sharon Press.

Simmonds, R.B. 1977. "Conversion as Addiction: Consequences of Joining a Jesus Movement Group." *American Behavioral Scientist* 20: 909-924.

Skonovd, L.N. 1981. "Apostasy: The Process of Defection from Religious Totalism." Unpublished Ph.D. dissertation, University of California, Davis.

————. 1983. "Leaving the Cultic Religious Milieu." Pp. 91-105 in *The Brainwashing/ Deprogramming Controversy: Sociological, Psychological, Legal and Historical Perspectives,* edited by D.G. Bromley and J.T. Richardson. Lewiston, NY: Edwin Mellen Press.

Snow, D.A. 1976. "The Nichiren Shoshu Buddhist Movement in America: A Sociological Examination of Its Value Orientation, Recruitment Efforts and Spread." Unpublished Ph.D. dissertation, University of California, Los Angeles.

————. 1987. "Organization, Ideology and Mobilization: The Case of Nichiren Shoshu of America." Pp. 153-172 in *The Future of New Religious Movements,* edited by D.G. Bromley and P.E. Hammond. Macon, GA: Mercer University Press.

Snow, D.A., and R. Machalek. 1983. "The Convert as a Social Type." Pp. 259-289 in *Sociological Theory, 1983,* edited by R. Collins. San Francisco: Jossey-Bass.

————. 1984. "The Sociology of Conversion." *Annual Review of Sociology* 10: 167-190.

Snow, D.A., and C.L. Phillips. 1980. "The Lofland-Stark Conversion Model: A Critical Reassessment." *Social Problems* 27: 430-437.

Snow, D.A., L.A. Zurcher, Jr., and S. Ekland-Olson. 1980. "Social Networks and Social Movements: A Microstructural Approach to Differential Recruitment." *American Sociological Review* 45: 787-801.

Somit, A. 1968. "Brainwashing." Pp. 138-143 in *International Encyclopedia of the Social Sciences,* edited by D. Sills. New York: Macmillan.

Sorokin, P.A. 1937-1941. *Social and Cultural Dynamics.* 4 vols. New York: American Book Co.

Staples, C.L., and A.L. Mauss. 1987. "Conversion or Commitment? A Reassessment of the Snow and Machalek Approach to the Study of Conversion." *Journal for the Scientific Study of Religion* 26: 133-147.

Starbuck, E.D. 1915. *The Psychology of Religion.* New York: Scribner's.

Stark, R., and W.S. Bainbridge. 1985. *The Future of Religion: Secularization, Revival and Cult Formation.* Berkeley: University of California Press.

Straus, R.A. 1976. "Changing Oneself: Seekers and the Creative Transformation of Life Experience." Pp. 252-272 in *Doing Social Life,* edited by J. Lofland. New York: Wiley.

————. 1979. "Religious Conversion as a Personal and Collective Accomplishment." *Sociological Analysis* 40: 158-165.

Travisano, R.V. 1970. "Alternation and Conversion as Qualitatively Different Transformations." Pp. 594-606 in *Social Psychology Through Symbolic Interaction,* edited by G.P. Stone and H.A. Faberman. Waltham, MA: Ginn-Blaisdell.

Tucker, R.C., ed. 1978. *The Marx-Engels Reader.* New York: W.W. Norton.

Ungerleider, J.T., and D.K. Wellisch. 1979. "Coercive Persuasion (Brainwashing), Religious Cults, and Deprogramming." *American Journal of Psychiatry* 136: 279-282.

Volinn, E. 1985. "Eastern Meditation Groups: Why Join?" *Sociological Analysis* 46: 147-156.

Wallis, R., and S. Bruce. 1982. "Network and Clockwork." *Sociology* 16: 102-107.

Wenegrat, B. 1989. "Religious Cult Membership: A Sociobiologic Model." Pp. 193-208 in *Cults and New Religious Movements,* edited by M. Galanter. Washington, DC: American Psychiatric Association.

Wilson, J.Q., and R.J. Herrnstein. 1985. *Crime and Human Nature.* New York: Simon and Schuster.

Wilson, S.R. 1984. "Becoming a Yogi: Resocialization and Deconditioning as Conversion Processes." *Sociological Analysis* 45: 301-314.

Wimberley, R.C., T.C. Hood, C.M. Lipsey, D.A. Clelland, and M. Hay. 1980. "Conversion in a Billy Graham Crusade." Pp. 278-285 in *Collective Behavior: A Source Book,* edited by M. Pugh. St. Paul, MN: West.

Wright, S.A. 1984. "Post-involvement Attitudes of Voluntary Defectors from Controversial New Religious Movements." *Journal for the Scientific Study of Religion* 23: 172-182.

————. 1987. *Leaving Cults: The Dynamics of Defection.* Washington, DC: Society for the Scientific Study of Religion.

————. 1988. "Leaving New Religious Movements: Issues, Theory, and Research." Pp. 143-165 in *Falling From the Faith: Causes and Consequences of Religious Apostasy,* edited by D.G. Bromley. Newbury Park, CA: Sage.

Wuthnow, R. 1976. *The Consciousness Reformation.* Berkeley: University of California Press.

Zald, M.N., and R. Ash. 1966. "Social Movement Organizations: Growth, Decay and Change." *Social Forces* 44: 327-341.

# A SOCIAL PSYCHOLOGICAL CRITIQUE OF "BRAINWASHING" CLAIMS ABOUT RECRUITMENT TO NEW RELIGIONS

James T. Richardson

## ABSTRACT

This paper offers a multifaceted critique of so-called "brainwashing theories" which purports to explain recruitment to and participation in new religions, sometimes referred to as "cults." Reasons for the development and widespread acceptance of theories involving claims about brainwashing and "mind control" in religious groups are presented, as is a logical, historical, and data-based critique of such theories. Then alternative explanations are presented using general theories in social psychology, especially some focusing on conformity and changes in behaviors and attitudes. This classical work in social psychology is criticized itself, however, for being somewhat passive and deterministic in its orientation. The paper closes with an application and extension of work on "minority influence" in groups that assumes a much more interactionist perspective. This perspective includes the view that individual recruits are active agents, involved in a negotiation process with potential groups of membership, and even influencing groups that they join.

Large numbers of young people have been involved with new religious groups—sometimes pejoratively called "cults"—over the past two or three decades in American society and other Western countries. These young people have often been from dominant class groups, and among the most affluent

Religion and the Social Order, Volume 3B, pages 75-97.
Copyright © 1993 by JAI Press Inc.
All rights of reproduction in any form reserved.
ISBN: 1-55938-715-7

and better educated of all youth in their societies. Huge controversies have erupted about the meaning of this participation, as parents, friends, and political and opinion leaders have attempted to understand why this "collective desertion" by many of its youth has occurred and as methods are sought to control such involvement.

Joining the groups, some of which appear culturally strange in their beliefs and organizational patterns, has seemed to many to be an act of ultimate rejection of American or even Western culture. The act of participating in new religions has appeared to be an overt rejection of American and Western values and institutions—including religious, economic, and familial. This "culture-rejecting" explanation has been difficult for many to accept, prompting a search for alternative explanations for involvement.

One of the most appealing alternatives has been so-called "brainwashing," "mind control," or "thought reform" theories (Bromley and Richardson 1983). According to those espousing these ideas, youth have not joined the new religions volitionally, but have instead been manipulated or forced into participating by leaders and members of groups using powerful psychotechnology practiced first by communist, anti-Western societies. This psychotechnology allegedly traps or encapsulates young people in the new religions, allowing subsequent control of their behavior by leaders of the groups (see, for example, Shapiro 1977; Delgado 1977; Singer 1979). It was originally developed, according to these claims, in Russian purge trials of the 1930s, and later refined by the Chinese communists after their assumption of power in China in 1949. The techniques also were used against POWs during the Korean War of the 1950s. Now these techniques are allegedly being used by foreign-based and inspired religious leaders against young people in Western countries, who are supposedly virtually helpless before such sophisticated methods.

When questioned about the obvious logical problem of applying these theories to situations without physical coercion, proponents have ready, if problematic, answers. They claim that physical coercion has been replaced by "psychological coercion," which is actually more effective than simple physical coercion (Singer 1979). These ideas are referred to as "second generation" brainwashing theories, which take into account new insights about manipulation of individuals. It is not necessary to coerce recruits physically if they can be manipulated by affection, guilt, or other psychological influences. Simple group pressures and emotion-laden tactics are revealed as more effective than those used by officials in physically coercive Russian, Chinese, and Korean POW situations.

These theories might be thought of as quaint ideas developed for functional reasons by those who have an interest in their being accepted. They plainly are a special type of "account" which "explains" why people join the groups and why they stay in them for a time (see Beckford 1978a; Bromley and Shupe 1979 on conversion accounts; Richardson, Balch, and Melton, this volume, for problems with such accounts). Whatever the origin, and no matter that the veracity of such accounts is questionable, these ideas have become commonly accepted among the general public. For instance, DeWitt (1991) reports that 78 percent of a randomly drawn sample of 383 individuals from an urban county in Nevada said they believed in brainwashing, and 30 percent agreed that "brainwashing is required to make someone join a religious cult." A similar question asked of a random sample of 1,000 residents in New York prior to the tax evasion trial of Reverend Moon (Richardson 1992) revealed that 43 percent agreed "brainwashing is required to make someone change from organized religion to a cult." Latkin (1986) reported on results from a random sample of Oregon residents who were asked about the controversial Rajneesh group centered in Eastern Oregon. Sixty-nine percent of respondents agreed that members of the group were brainwashed. Bromley and Breschel (1992) report that 73 percent of 1,700 randomly drawn respondents in a national survey support legislation prohibiting conversion of teenagers by religious cults. This strong finding may derive from concern about perceived brainwashing-based recruitment techniques allegedly used by new religions.[1]

These notions about brainwashing and mind control have pervaded institutional structures in our society as well. Such views have influenced actions by governmental entities and the media (van Driel and Richardson 1988; Richardson, Kilbourne, and van Driel 1989; Bromley 1984). The legal system has seen a number of efforts to promote brainwashing theories as explanations of why people might participate in new religions (Richardson 1991a; Post 1988; Anthony 1990; Anthony and Robbins 1992). A number of these initiatives have resulted in multimillion dollar judgments against religious groups allegedly using brainwashing techniques on recruits (Bromley 1988b).

Thus it appears that ideas about brainwashing of recruits to new religions have developed momentum of their own in our society and other Western countries (Bromley and Shupe, forthcoming; Beckford 1985; Barker 1984). These notions are impacting society in many ways, including as contributors to a possible severe limitation on religious freedom in American society (Post 1988; Richardson 1991a). Thus, we need to examine the brainwashing thesis more closely, in order to see if it might be a proper explanation of what takes place when people join and participate in a new religion. This paper begins with a critique of brainwashing theories from a social science perspective, followed by an attempt to explain the recruitment process from another point of view—generic social psychological theories developed to explain changes in behavior and attitudes. The paper closes with an application of a more activist perspective of the process of recruitment and participation, building on some creative work by Moreland and Levine (1985) and Levine and Russo (1988).

## CRITIQUE OF "BRAINWASHING" THEORIES

Brainwashing theories serve the interests of those espousing them in a number of ways. Parents can blame the groups and their leaders for what were volitional decisions to participate by their sons and daughters (Shupe and Bromley 1979). Former members can blame the techniques for a decision to participate which the participant later regrets. Deprogrammers can use brainwashing theories as a justification for their new "profession" and as a quasi-legal defense if they are apprehended by legal authorities during their deprogrammings, which often have involved physical force and kidnapping (Bromley 1988a). Societal leaders can blame the techniques for seducing society's "brightest and best" away from traditional cultural values and institutions. Competitive religious leaders as well as some psychological and psychiatric clinicians attack the groups with brainwashing theories, to underpin what are basically unfair competition arguments (Kilbourne and Richardson 1984). The claims that new religions engage in brainwashing thus become powerful, effective social weapons for many partisans in the cult controversy (Anthony and Robbins 1992). Such ideas are used to "label" the exotic religious groups as deviant or even evil (Richardson et al. 1986; Robbins and Anthony 1982). However, the new "second generation" brainwashing theories propounded by a few psychologists, sociologists, and others whose interest such theories serve have a number of problems.

## Misrepresentation of Classical Tradition

Modern brainwashing theories in some crucial ways misrepresent earlier scholarly work on the processes developed in Russia, China, and the Korean POW situation (Anthony 1990; Anthony and Robbins 1992). These misrepresentations are as follows. First, early research by Schein (1959), Schein and associates (1961) and Lifton (1961) revealed that, contrary to some recent claims, the techniques were generally rather ineffective at doing more than modifying behavior (obtaining compliance) for the short term (see Schein et al. 1961, p. 332; Lund and Wilson 1977, p. 348; Scheflin and Opton 1978). Such theories would seem even less useful when trying to explain long-term changes of behavior and belief, which are implied if not explicitly alleged by those propounding brainwashing theories to explain participation in new religions.

Second, the degree of determinism associated with contemporary brainwashing applications usually far exceeds that found in the earlier foundational work of Lifton and of Schein. Anthony (1990) and Robbins (Anthony and Robbins 1992) contrast the "soft determinism" of the work of Lifton and Schein with the "hard determinism" of contemporary proponents of brainwashing theories such as Singer and Ofshe (1990). The hard determinism approach assumes that humans can be turned into robots through application of sophisticated brainwashing techniques. Thus, humans become "Manchurian Candidates," even in spite of great efforts to overcome the techniques. Such a perspective is not acceptable to classical scholars Lifton and Schein, who seem more willing to recognize human beings as more complex entities than do some contemporary brainwashing theorists. Richardson and Kilbourne (1983) also note that extreme determinism of contemporary applications of brainwashing theories.

Third, another major problem for contemporary brainwashing theories is that both scholars (Lifton and Schein) who produced what has come to be called classic work in this field are not comfortable with their work being applied to modern noncoercive situations. Lifton (1985, p. 69) explicitly disclaims use of the ideas concerning brainwashing to attack so-called cults as a legal problem, and earlier (Lifton 1961, p. 4) he had stated: "the term (brainwashing) has a far from precise and questionable usefulness; one may even be tempted to forget about the whole subject and return to more constructive pursuits." The work of Schein and of Lifton both suggest great difficulty in "drawing the line" between acceptable and unacceptable behaviors on the part of those involved in influencing potential subjects for change (Anthony and Robbins 1992). Group-influence processes operate in all areas of life, which makes singling out one area for special negative attention quite problematic. Such a negative focus cannot be adopted on strictly logical or scientific grounds.

### Ideological Biases of Brainwashing Theorists

Richardson and Kilbourne (1983) point out that contemporary applications of brainwashing theories share an ideological bias in opposition to collectivistic solutions to problems of group organization (Richardson 1989). In the 1950s Americans opposed collectivistic communism; in the 1970s and 1980s many Americans shared a concern about communally oriented new religions. Another problematic element of contemporary applications concerns the ethocentrism and even racism which may be related to their use. The fact that a number of new religions are from outside Western culture and were founded and led by foreigners should not be ignored in understanding the propensity to apply simplistic brainwashing theories to explain participation and justify efforts at social control.

### Limited Research Base of Classical Work

Richardson and Kilbourne (1983) as well as Anthony (1990) note that the research on which the classical models are based is quite limited. Small samples were used by both Lifton and Shein, and they were not necessarily representative of the general populations of those societies. Those in the samples were presented using an anecdotal reporting style, derived from clinical settings, especially with Lifton's work. As Biderman (1962) pointed out, Lifton only studied 40 subjects in all, and gave detailed information on only 11 of those. Shein's original work was based on a sample of only 15 America civilians who returned after imprisonment in China.

### Predisposing Characteristics Ignored

Contemporary application of brainwashing theories to recruitment tactics of new religions also ignores important work on predisposing characteristics (Lofland 1978; Anthony and Robbins 1992). The techniques of brainwashing supposedly are so successful that they can transform a person's basic beliefs into sharply contrasting beliefs. This aspect of brainwashing theory is appealing to proponents who have difficulty recognizing that an individual might have been attracted to a new and exotic religion. This potential of brainwashing also allows proponents conveniently to ignore volitional aspects of recruitment to new religions.

## Therapeutic Effects of Participation Ignored

Participation in new religious groups seems to have a generally positive impact on most participants, an often-replicated finding that undercuts brainwashing arguments, but is usually ignored by proponents of such theories. Robbins and Anthony (1982) summarized positive effects that have been found. They list ten different therapeutic effects, including such things as reduced neurotic distress, termination of illicit drug use, and increased social compassion. Richardson (1985b) reviewed a large literature concerning personality effects of participation. He concluded (1985b, p. 221): "Personality assessments of these group members reveal that life in the new religions is often therapeutic instead of harmful." Kilbourne (1989) drew similar conclusions in his assessment of why some therapists ignore positive outcomes from participation.

Psychiatrist Marc Galanter, who has done considerable assessment research on participants in some of the more prominent new religious groups, has even posited a general "relief effect" brought about by participation in such groups (Galanter and Diamond 1981). He is interested in finding out what about participation leads to such consistent positive effects, so that other therapists can use the techniques themselves. McGuire (1988) found that large numbers of ordinary people participate in exotic religious groups and experiences in search of alternatives to modern medicine, and that many apparently think themselves the better for the experience. Brainwashing theorists usually conclude that participation in the new religions is a negative experience, which seems counter to the line of research just cited.

## Voluntaristic Character of Participation Overlooked

Brainwashing theorists such as Delgado (1982) turn predispositions and interest in exotic religions into susceptibilities and vulnerabilities, adopting an orientation toward recruitment that defines the potential convert in completely passive terms. This view ignores an important aspect of classical work in the brainwashing tradition. For instance, Lifton's (1961) work clearly shows the voluntaristic character of much of the thought reform which went on in China. Richardson and Kilbourne (1983) discuss the passive orientation of most brainwashing theories, and Richardson (1985a) discusses the growing use of "active" (versus passive) paradigms in conversion/recruitment research. More activist views of conversion stress the predispositional and volitional character of participation, deriving such a view from research findings that many participants actually seek out the new groups in order to learn about them and try out different lifestyles (Kilbourne 1986).

## Large Research Tradition Ignored

There has been a huge amount of research done on recruitment to and participation in the new religious groups and movements, research which is almost totally ignored by brainwashing theorists. This work, which is summarized in such reviews as Greil and Rudy (1984), Richardson (1985a), and Robbins (1985, 1988), nearly always applies standard theories from sociology, social psychology, and psychology to explain why youth join such groups. The explanations offered by these researchers seem quite adequate to explain participation, without any "black box" of mystical psychotechnology such as offered by brainwashing theorists. Examples of such work include Heirich's (1977) study of the Charismatic Renewal movement, Pilarzyk's (1978) comparison of conversion in the Divine Light Mission and the Hare Krishna, Straus' (1981) "naturalistic social psychological" explanation of seeking religious experiences, and Bromley and Shupe's (1986) role theory approach.

## Lack of Success of New Religions Disregarded

There are a number of other problems in applying brainwashing theories to research data on participation in new religions. One obvious problem with assuming the efficacy of powerful recruitment techniques concerns the *size* of the new religious groups. Most are quite small: the Unification Church probably never had over 10,000 American members, and can now boast only 2,000 to 3,000 members in the United States; the Hare Krishna may not have achieved the size of the Unification Church; and most other groups have had similar problematic experiences in recruiting large numbers of participants. These histories of meager growth and/or rapid decline raise serious questions about the efficacy of brainwashing explanations of participation (Bromley 1991). Such powerful techniques should have resulted in much larger groups.

A related problem concerns attrition rates for the new religions. As a number of scholars have noted, most participants in the new groups remain for only a short time, and most of those who have been recruited simply ignore or rebuff recruiters and go on with their normal lives (Bird and Reimer 1982; Barker 1984; Galanter 1980). Many people leave the groups after being in them relatively short periods (Wright 1983, 1987; Skonovd 1983; Richardson et al. 1986). Recruitment techniques characterized as brainwashing should lead to retention of members if they are as powerful as claimed, but this is not the case.

## Class Origins of Members Not Properly Recognized

A related issue concerns the education level and sophistication of participants. It would seem reasonable to assume that those most susceptible to so-called brainwashing would be less well-educated. However, sizable numbers of "America's finest" in terms of education level and relative affluence have participated in the groups, if only for a short time (Richardson et al. 1979; Kilbourne 1986; Barker 1984). This finding raises questions about application of brainwashing theories as adequate explanations of participation. Both Barker (1984) and Kilbourne (1986) have found that there are predisposing characteristics for participation in the Unification Church—such as youthful idealism that has provoked interest in the Unificationist message. Thus, the brainwashing theorist's argument would seem to be refuted, even if such data are often ignored.[2]

Brainwashing as Its Own Explanation

A last critique of brainwashing theories is that they are self-perpetuating, through "therapy" offered those who leave, especially those who are forcibly deprogrammed. As Solomon (1981) has concluded, those who are deprogrammed often accept the views that deprogrammers use to justify their actions, and which are promoted to the deprogrammee as reasons for cooperating with the deprogramming. These views usually include a belief in brainwashing theories. One could say that a successful deprogramming is one in which the deprogramee comes to accept the view that they were brainwashed, and are now being rescued. Solomon's finding has been collaborated by other research on those who leave, including Lewis (1986), Lewis and Bromley (1987), and Wright (1987). The social psychological truth that such ideas are *learned interpretations or accounts* would seem to undercut truth claims by brainwashing theorists.

# SOCIAL PSYCHOLOGY OF THE RECRUITMENT PROCESS

The preceding critique indicates that brainwashing theories of participation in new religions fail to take into account considerable data about participation in such groups. The theories ignore the small size of the groups, as well as their high attrition rates and motivations for joining of many participants. Also, they are not based on accurate renditions of what classical research revealed about the process of change in coercive situations. And the classical research may itself be built on shaky foundations. However, many people and institutional leaders still accept such theories, which requires that serious attention be paid to developing alternative explanations that demystify the process of recruitment to and participation in the new religions.[3]

The following section presents some rather straightforward applications of theories and research from social psychology to aid in understanding recruitment and participation, relying in major part on a few explicit efforts to apply social psychology to new religions. Following that discussion, the area of "minority influence" from social psychological studies of nonconformity will be reviewed. This latter effort relies on creative work based on an assumption of a more independent and active individual functioning within the group context and influencing group culture through a process of negotiation with the group and its leaders. Such theorizing and research belies many of the claims made by so-called brainwashing theorists.

Coverage of New Religions in Text Books

Two well-known text books in social psychology, in an apparent effort to be current, discuss participation in new religions. Zimbardo, Ebbesen, and Maslach (1977) open their text with discussion of two situations bound to attract readers' attention. They describe in detail the circumstances of the kidnapping of Patty Hearst, and make the point that simplistic claims about "brainwashing" cannot be used to explain her odd behavior. The authors point out that efforts were made to present a brainwashing defense in the Hearst trial (also see Fort 1983), but they did not succeed. Their brief discussion of the classical theorists discussed above is sound.

However, the authors then discuss the Unification Church (sometimes referred to in the text using the negative descriptor, "Moonies"), under the subtitle, "A (Reverend) Moon for the Misbegotten." The authors' description of the Unification Church follows many of the stereotypes about this group, and their treatment suggests that something as sinister as the kidnapping of Patty Hearst occurs in this group. They also include a copy of a very derogatory editorial cartoon about the Unification Church that appeared in a recent *APA Monitor*. The text indicates that a student of theirs who visited a Unification Church training camp came away "shaken...by the brief, two day experience" (Zimbardo et al. 1977, p. 19).

Later in the text Zimbardo et al. (1977, pp. 182-189) offer more detail about the experiences of this student who feigned an interest in the Unification Church. They are making a similar point to the overall thrust of this section— that the influence techniques are actually quite mundane and ordinary. However, the reader cannot help but deduce that Zimbardo and company do not care for the Unification Church or the content of the influence processes being used. Several social psychological concepts are mentioned as being apropos, including deindividuation, social reinforcement, informational control, "foot in the door" techniques, dissonance, personal attraction, and semantic distortion. The following quote about the recruitment process shows the approach being taken in this text (Zimbardo et al. 1977, p. 185):

> (T)here are informational inputs to be listened to uncritically. An "open mind" means a nonevaluative vulnerable mind set of acceptance. A childlike atmosphere filled with simple demands that are easy to satisfy recreates the passivity, dependence, and obedience of childhood (and evokes our elementary school conditioning). Minimal obedience is all that is required at first. Dissonance follows once the foot is in the door, and then attitudes fall into line to justify compliant actions.

Thus Zimbardo et al. have built an excellent and socially acceptable "straw man" to show how useful and powerful social psychological techniques are for changing people.

Another prominent social psychology text that includes discussion of participation in new religions is Cialdini's (1985) widely cited and very readable *Influence: Science and Practice*. Cialdini discusses the Peoples Temple tragedy, using concepts such as social isolation and pluralistic ignorance to explain the 900 plus suicides and murders that occurred in the South American jungle. He refutes the idea that personal attributes of Jim Jones led directly to the tragedy, but gives Jones credit for knowing how to manipulate the situation so that his wishes would be followed.

This text contains as well a fairly lengthy treatment of the famous "new religion" examined by Festinger et al. (1956). The infiltration of this small group by Festinger's colleagues yielded some fascinating detail about how a group prophesying the end of the world can overcome the obstacle of a failed prophecy. Cialdini posits "social proof" as the mechanism of explanation about what happened with this group which managed to talk itself into an acceptable interpretation of why the end did not come. There was no physical proof of the events they have predicted, but an acceptable social account was developed which most members were able to adopt and even propagate rather forcefully to those who wanted to know why the end had not occurred. Cialdini ignores (as do Festinger et al. 1956) the significant impact of the infiltration and subsequent actions of the covert researchers (see Richardson 1991b). However, his discussion is relatively objective and informative, even if it overlooks the importance of the researcher intervention.

Cialdini also uses the Hare Krishna as an excellent example of the power of reciprocity in social affairs. He notes that the Krishna, a stigmatized group, were able to raise large amounts of money from strangers who did not care for them or want to talk with them, simply by offering them a token (usually a flower or book) in exchange for a donation. This example relates to participation and thus is germane to an examination of brainwashing theories explaining such activities.

### Other Applications of Social Psychology to New Religions

Solomon (1983) has done the most thorough job of analyzing recruitment to new religions from a social psychological perspective. Her analysis begins by offering a provocative comparison of Russian and Chinese brainwashing techniques, which she claims differ in important ways. Her analysis reveals that the Chinese approach allegedly is more similar to the practices of new religions in the United States. Unlike the earlier Russian model, the objective of the Chinese approach was a person who was usable after the process. Chinese methods thus seek "conversion," which implies a change of attitude, instead of just compliance, and uses persuasion instead of physical coercion as a major tool. The approach is "evangelistic" instead of "scientific" in orientation, uses a social group as the change agent instead of an individual interrogator, and practices "overstimulation" as contrasted to the "understimulation" (through isolation) of the Russian model. With its emphasis on group processes and on making the convert a functioning member of the group through focused interaction, the Chinese model is obviously social psychological in orientation.

Solomon (1983, p. 169) then launches into a discussion two major issues in social psychology:

> (1) how and under what circumstances can social influence processes impact upon individual participants, and (2) what is the nature of the relationship and direction of causality between attitudinal and behavioral changes.

These issues demonstrate the problematic nature of simplistic views of social influence. Individual behavior can be modified through group pressure, as the classic studies of Asch (1960) and Sherif (1936) demonstrated long ago. However, it is not clear why this occurs or what conditions cause some people to appear to conform to group pressures while others do not. The relationship of attitudes and behavior also remains unspecified. Were peoples' minds actually changed in the classic experiments on social influence, or were those who gave incorrect answers simply conforming to avoid conflict or to get along with their fellow subjects? If their minds were changed, did this occur before or after the incorrect behavioral response? These questions are, of course, important to understanding what happens when an individual is in a recruitment situation with a new religious group.

Solomon focuses her analysis of the process of recruitment on three general factors: (1) isolation from contact with other environments; (2) group pressures that seem to influence attitudinal and behavioral changes; and (3) coercion of a physical nature, including food and sleep deprivation. Her discussion gives extended treatment to some topics covered briefly in the two texts just mentioned, and thus her delineation will be used to offer detail needed to flesh out our assertion that social influence processes in new religions are easily understood.

## Isolation

Isolation of recruits can be found in a number of new religions, as efforts are made to reduce potential recruits' ties with family and friends, and "encapsulate" them in the new milieu (Greil and Rudy 1984). In some groups, such as the Unification Church, this effort is often quite systematic, whereas in others, particularly noncommunal groups, facilities do not exist for much isolation from normal life. Whatever efforts the groups make are often complemented by actions and predispositions of the recruits. Considerable research has shown that many potential recruits already had weak ties with their family and former friends. Indeed, many were "on the road," looking for alternative lifestyles and belief structures (Straus 1976, 1979; Lofland and Skonovd 1981; Long and Hadden 1983; Richardson 1985a). The combination of group efforts at isolation and individual willingness to become isolated sometimes has produced a situation in which few or weak ties remain to anyone outside the recruiting group. Such a circumstance allows a greater impact from various group pressures which might develop within the group.

New religions are not the only groups seeking to influence behavior which have encouraged isolation and the weakening of ties with former friends and with family. Parental restriction of dating partners or otherwise monitoring contact with other youth exemplify the technique of isolation. College sororities and fraternities which discourage contact with home or with certain groups of students on campus are also implementing isolation techniques. Marine boot camp or juvenile detention halls are less benign examples of organizations which isolate "recruits" to improve chances of modifying behavior and belief.

*Group Pressures*

Group pressures can take many forms, including repetition, monopolization of time, and positive reinforcement of desired behaviors and beliefs (Solomon 1983, p. 170). The combination of such techniques can influence behavior and perhaps beliefs. The classic experiments of Asch clearly show that a significant minority of people will, under certain conditions, change their behavioral response to one which is obviously incorrect but nonetheless conforming. It is not clear, however, whether attitudes and beliefs were actually impacted in these experiments. Social psychology assumes that beliefs and attitudes can be modified through group processes, but there are competing theories to explain this phenomenon.

Treatments such as Solomon, Zimbardo et al., and Cialdini generally assume a cognitive perspective with the person actively seeking an understanding of what they encounter. Solomon discusses cognitive theories that have been developed to explain attitude changes in individuals, including Festinger's (1957) dissonance theory and Bem's (1972) self-perception theory. Both theories place emphasis on the primacy of behavior. Festinger suggests that when cognitions and behavior differ, there is a tendency to alleviate the dissonance that occurs (the actual occurrence of dissonance is a key but untestable assumption of dissonance theory). It is usually easier to modify beliefs than behaviors, or, more accurately, to align beliefs with the behaviors in which a person has engaged.

In contrast to Festinger's ideas, Bem argues that a person's self-perception develops from observing his or her own behavior, which is the same way that individuals make sense of other peoples' behaviors. Individuals attribute beliefs and attitudes to others by observing them, and Ben claims they do the same with themselves.

Both these theories assume that getting a person to act can lead to changes of belief. Thus, the theories suggest that getting potential recruits to participate in the round of group activities is the best way to begin the process of changing their belief structures to ones more closely aligned with those of the group. A number of new religions and some traditional ones as well seem to understand this concept at least intuitively, and seek to involve the potential recruit in many activities from fundraising to proselytizing. The groups welcome the recruit, and reinforce behaviors fitting the group lifestyle and values.

One example of such actions would be Mormon Church encouragement of participation by young people in the two-year volunteer mission program of the church. Whether this and similar practices are cynical manipulation or the actions of a group concerned about demonstrating a caring atmosphere to recruits and others depends in significant measure on the intentionality of the actors. In the case of highly controversial groups, manipulation may be "in the eye of the beholder," and nowhere else.

One criticism that can be made about the phenomenon group pressure and about the classic experiments which undergird this approach is that the experiment occurs in an artificial and relatively nonsalient situation in which subjects are usually only passive recipients of actions by a majority. In Asch's classic experiment the subjects were not allowed to interact with the confederate majority, to question them, or seek information about why they were giving incorrect responses. In a situation with a task of low saliency to most individuals, many who responded with incorrect answers probably just conformed to avoid conflict. In later refinements of this and similar experiments, when even one confederate was instructed to give a correct response, the conforming responses of the subjects plummeted from over 30 percent to around five percent (van Avermaet 1988).

The recruitment situation for most new religions more closely resembles a situation in which interaction is possible between recruits and between recruits and recruiters, with questions being raised by recruits. Recruitment is often an active interaction situation, with the possibility of dissenters from group views being present. Social support would typically be available from other potential recruits who are present. Most importantly, potential recruits were usually present because they chose to be there, and they could leave if they desired.

This is not to say that every recruitment situation allows maximum conditions for dissent. Indeed, new religious groups and other types of recruiting organizations are usually attempting to discourage contacts with dissenters and to "make the sale" without being impeded by other influences. Few used car salespersons deliberately introduce a client to someone who just refused to buy a car from them. Instead, for obvious reasons, they want to have the client interact with other satisfied customers. The salesperson wants to monopolize the time of the client and to have them hear positive repetitions about the value of the car they are considering. And positive behaviors, such as wanting to take a test drive, are reinforced. A less mundane example might be actions taken by members of a convent when interacting with potential recruits. Interactions with defectors would usually be kept to a minimum, while repetitions of positive experiences would be demonstrated, and actions which signaled interest in becoming a nun would be reinforced by the group of already committed nuns and their leaders.

## Coercion

This concept has already been discussed in the context of examining assumptions about how brainwashing occurs in new religions. There is little evidence that actual physical coercion occurs in recruitment situations, although there have been a limited number of reports of food and sleep deprivation in a few groups. Food deprivation may be a function of limited group resources, however, and sleep deprivation may be the result of a very full round of group activities designed to accomplish group tasks rather than to tire potential recruits deliberately (see, e.g., Richardson, Stewart, and Simmonds 1979).

It should be noted, however, that if physical coercion did occur, social psychological research would predict that it would not have long-term effects on attitudes and beliefs. Indeed, forced behavioral change may lead to a backlash against the beliefs of those forcing the behavior. As dissonance theory suggests, only when behaviors are freely chosen will they lead to a commensurate change in attitudes about the object of the behavior. Only when the person chooses to behave in a certain fashion will there be an aligning of cognitions with behaviors, according to this line of thought. Cialdini (1985, pp. 60-63) makes a similar point in his examination of the ways in which Chinese captors manipulated the behavior of Korean POWs. He focuses on a kind of "foot in the door" approach, coupled with subsequent labelling of the prisoner as a collaborator to explain behavior changes which occurred.

It bears repetition that most scholars dealing with recruitment into new religions or other groups would not agree that psychological coercion can be equated with physical coercion in terms of impact on recruits (see Anthony 1990). Psychological coercion of various types is simply a fact of life with which contemporary people have to deal. Most handle psychological coercion by ignoring it and going about their business. Only a rare and unique set of circumstances would call for serious concern about the impact of psychological coercion in our society. Solomon includes physical coercion in her analysis because she is also analyzing the social psychology of "deprogramming," and those situations often do involve direct physical coercion (Solomon 1983, pp. 181-182).

### Recruitment as an Interaction/Negotiation Situation

As indicated above in the discussion of group pressure phenomena, there are some difficulties with the paradigm adopted in most majority influence research, starting with the classical studies of Sherif and of Asch. A key metatheoretical assumption of most such work is that the subject is relatively passive in the face of majority pressures, with the majority acting upon the individual subject with relative impunity. Such a perspective cannot be sustained in the face of considerable evidence that people in real recruitment situations not involving physical coercion are quite active, seeking out opportunities to engage in personal change (Straus 1976, 1979; Richardson 1985a).

In order to understand this different, more activist perspective, one must recast the recruitment situation. Instead of conceiving of a group or organization acting upon an individual who is relatively helpless in the face of unwelcome group pressures, the situation should be thought of as one in which recruits are seeking alternatives, find one in which they are tentatively interested, and then engage in open interaction with the group to "feel them out." If the results of the initial contact are positive for the recruits and the group as well, then negotiations are opened to determine what the recruits *as well as the group* must do in order for a longer-term relationship to be agreed upon.

Such a perspective implies relative autonomy on the part of individual potential recruits, and it assumes that the group is not all-powerful. The individual can decide to withdraw from the interaction situation, and the group must allow this autonomous act, unless force is used. In short, the relative power of the group and the recruit(s) is not as highly asymmetrical as assumed by proponents of brainwashing theories. There is rough symmetry, simply because the individual recruits can withdraw. In fact, either side in the negotiations can withdraw. The group can decide that the potential member is not worth the effort of recruitment, and individual recruits may decide that the group is simply too strange or too demanding to be worth the effort to meet entrance requirements; see Galanter (1980) for examples of the Unification Church deciding that some potential recruits were not acceptable, and Richardson et al. (1986) for a general discussion of "expulsion" by new religions.

## The Moreland/Levine Model of Socialization to Small Groups

The more subject-centered perspective on recruitment just described has been best delineated in the work of Moreland and Levine (1985) and Levine and Russo (1988). The Moreland/Levine theory of socialization into small voluntary groups is replete with ideas germane to recruitment to new religions. Indeed, they cite some of the research that has been conducted by scholars on new religious conversion as a part of their supporting data.

The Moreland/Levine model assumes three psychological and social psychological processes as crucial to any recruitment situation: evaluation, commitment, and role transition. The authors assume that decisions are made by the individual and the recruiting group on the basis of evaluations of the "rewardingness" of the relationship. If evaluations result in a positive assessment, then both the individual and the group make commitments to each other. These levels of commitment rise and fall over time and with different circumstances, leading to transitions from one role to another for the individual recruits.

Individual recruits pass through five different phases or roles vis-à-vis the group: investigation, socialization, maintenance, resocialization, and remembrance. The *investigation phase* involves the group looking for individual members who can contribute to group goals, while individual potential recruits look for groups which can help meet personal needs and goals. If both the group and an individual finds that the interaction meets minimum levels of satisfaction, then commitment levels for both to each other may rise to that level allowing the individual recruit to enter the *socialization phase*. In this crucial testing phase, the group attempts to change recruits so that they will make a maximum contribution toward group goals, while the individual recruits attempt to modify the group so that it will better meet their goals. If this negotiation process is successful, then mutual commitment levels may rise again, this time moving the recruit into a *maintenance phase*.

In maintenance a specialized role is sought by the individual which will maintain a high level of personal satisfaction, while the group wants to find a role for the individual which will maximize the ongoing contribution of the individual to group goals. If rewards remain high for both the group and the individual, then the maintenance phase can be prolonged indefinitely. However, if something happens to lower the rewardingness for either the individual or the group, the person may shift into a *resocialization phase*. During this phase an effort is made to renegotiate a mutually satisfactory agreement between the individual and the group. If this outcome occurs, then the person re-enters the maintenance phase. If the rewardingness remains below a criterion level for either the group, the individual, or both, then the individual exits the group and enters the *remembrance phase*. In this phase the group and the individual engage in retrospective evaluations of each other in an effort to "explain" to each other and to outsiders why the individual left or was forced out involuntarily.

Moreland and Levine (1985, p. 153) offer a diagram which relates level of commitment in each of the five phases to passage of time. They posit a bell-shaped curve, with commitment lowest at either end of the curve during the investigation and remembrance phases, while commitment is highest during the maintenance phase. This diagram offers an informative visual for those seeking to understand recruitment to any group, including new religions.

However, the diagram perhaps misleads a bit on two counts—first, by assuming that the remembrance phase leaves the person in a neutral position vis-à-vis evaluation of and commitment to the group. As is well known, sometimes a person leaving a group does so with animosity on the part of the person, the group, or both. Such situations can involve much recrimination and self-justification. Richardson, van der Lans, and Derks (1986) discuss the use of labeling in such situations, as self-justificatory accounts are developed by internal and external parties alike.

Another misleading aspect of the diagram is that the curve depicting level of commitment seems to assume a mutual level of commitment occurring simultaneously for the individual and the group. Plainly, levels of commitment of the individual to the group do not always match levels of commitment of the group to the individual. When such mismatches occur in level of commitment, there obviously may be difficulties with the relationship. Indeed, one could speculate that certain methods of leaving might be preceded by systematic differences in levels of mutual commitment.

For instance, if the group valued the individual more than the individual valued the group and the group could not satisfy the personal needs of the individual, then we might predict more voluntary exiting by such individuals. By contrast, if the group did not value a member highly despite a high level of commitment of the member toward the group, then the group might eventually expel the member from the group. One might also predict that there would be greater "success" in forced disaffiliation through deprogramming ("extraction" in Richardson et al. 1986) in phases other than "maintenance," when commitment is usually highest for both the individual and group.

Speculation could be developed, as well, about ways to characterize specific groups in terms of the relationship of mutual commitment between the group and individual recruits. For instance, some groups seeking large numbers of recruits might have a high level of apparent commitment initially, which would yield a group commitment curve higher than the individual commitment curve in initial phases of recruitment. But once the person became a member, the group commitment curve could rapidly drop to a minimum required to maintain some loyalty from recruits. Beckford's (1978b) discussion of people leaving the Unification Church suggests that this group's approach to recruitment might illustrate this interesting pattern. The strategy of high apparent initial commitment by the group but lower commitment once the person expresses commitment illustrates that the process of recruitment is variable and involves interaction and negotiation.

Another variation indicating differences in level of group and individual recruit commitment would be a group which was hard to enter as a new member, but which was in high demand. Individual commitment might be quite high initially, but the group level would remain cautiously low until the individual had clearly proved him/herself. Once this was accomplished, then, the group commitment level might rapidly approach the individual commitment level.

These illustrations suggest that examining the interaction of mutual commitment curves could lead to some interesting insights into who might stay or leave (or be encouraged to remain or to leave). The mutual commitment curves might also be useful in characterizing different groups and different individual potential recruits. Moreland and Levine's social psychology of mutual commitment therefore seems a very fruitful area to develop as their ideas relate to recruitment to new religions.

## Minority "Conversion" and Innovation

One significant area of research which most clearly demonstrates the value of an interactive approach to social influence in new religious group recruitment derives directly from the earlier classical studies of majority influence done by Sherif and Asch. We refer to what is called "minority influence" research, first given impetus by Moscovici and his colleagues (see Moscovici and Faucheux 1972; Moscovici 1985). Moscovici decided that the majority influence paradigm was too sterile because it assumed a completely asymmetrical power distribution and usually involved little interaction between participants. He posited a more realistic situation in which there could be mutual influence of the majority over the minority *and* the minority over the majority. He also assumed that the processes of influence differed significantly in the two situations. Moscovici set about attempting to discern situations in which a minority could "convert" members of the majority to their views.

This line of research has revealed that indeed there are situations in which the minority can influence the majority. Such circumstances usually involve consistency on the part of the minority, with its views being displayed in a nonrigid and reasonable way. Moscovici asserts that a consistent, nonrigid, reasonable minority will focus attention on the substance of the minority arguments, and over time this strategy can lead to modifications of belief by the majority, *even if behaviors are not modified*. This situation is, of course, quite different from the majority influence situation which may lead to compliance but not necessarily with any concomitant shift in beliefs.

Levine and Russo (1988) and Moreland and Levine (1985) have been among the leaders in developing this line of research. They have sought the source of innovation in small groups through an incorporation of ideas imported by new recruits who subsequently were successful in spreading their ideas within the group.

This fascinating line of research has not been focused directly on new religions as yet, but it plainly is applicable. It is discussed here, if only briefly, to drive home the point that when individuals choose to participate in any group, including religious ones, there is an interaction and an exchange that takes place. Group culture changes with each new member, even if the change is small, and even if the process of change is not overt or perceived by group leaders or the members doing the influencing. Sometimes the change is open and dramatic, as when a large group of new recruits are welcomed into membership even though they differ significantly from the regular members already present. Such a situation occurred with a number of new religions when their "target populations" of itinerant youth contracted, and the groups were forced to start recruiting from the ranks of married couples or college students. The incorporation of different types of new members led directly to change in the groups, sometimes quickly as the new members expressed their disagreements with group policies (see Richardson et al. 1979). There also are instances of new members rapidly becoming leaders in their new group, which allowed them considerable opportunity to change a group's beliefs and practices over time.

## CONCLUSIONS

This analysis of the brainwashing metaphor has demonstrated its ideological foundation, as well as its lack of scientific support. The simplistic perspective inherent in the brainwashing metaphor appeals to those attempting to locate an effective social weapon (Robbins, Anthony, and McCarthy 1983) to use against disfavored groups. The fact that such efforts at social control have been relatively successful should not detract from the lack of scientific basis for such opinions.

A much more fruitful way to view recruitment processes into new religions is to treat them as small groups making use of well-known social psychological techniques to gain recruits. The classical studies of Sherif and Asch give some hints about how this view might be developed, and the work of several social psychologists, particularly Solomon (1983), offers systematic application of the classical tradition of social influence research to new religions' recruitment practices.

The classical work on conformity, however, suffers from metatheoretical assumptions which may mislead scholars somewhat. The traditional paradigm in social influence assumes a relatively passive subject and seems quite anti-interactionist. The work of Moreland and Levine (1985) attempted to develop a more interactionist general theory of socialization into small groups which seems quite valuable when applied to recruitment into new religions. Their perspective emphasizes the reciprocal influences of the group and individual recruit have on one another, as well as assuming that the relationship between the individual recruit and the group is constantly changing.

The follow-up research done by Moreland and Levine (1985) and Levine and Russo (1988) on minority influence over majorities within a small group setting adds another element to the understanding of what happens when recruits participate in new religions. Recruits can and do influence the group, sometimes in dramatic ways. Such situations of minority "conversion" of the majority offer evidence that the process of recruitment into religious groups should not be characterized as situations of majoritarian influence in which the majority always wins totally and dominates all recruits. Such a view misleads, and it detracts from fruitful lines of research which might be pursued by more knowledgeable researchers willing to admit that recruits can and do seek participation, and that they can also influence the groups which they join.

## NOTES

1.  Why the general public might hold such views is an interesting question. As Fort (1985) has noted, the Patty Hearst trial made the world aware of the "brainwashing defense" attempted in that case. Also, other media have promoted the use of terms like brainwashing, mind control, and associated ideas. Popular movies such as *Manchurian Candidate* have perhaps convinced viewers of the efficacy of psychotechnological techniques in changing and controlling people's behavior. Media have also used such ideas in reporting stories about new religions and their recruitment practices. Thus, the stories can be framed in simple "good versus evil" or "stealing of children" motifs which belie the usual complexities of such situations. Van Driel and Richardson (1988) noted that psychological manipulation (including brainwashing) was a common theme found in their large content analysis study of print media coverage on new religions in the United States.

2.  This argument has been "turned on its head" somewhat by brainwashing theorists, who argue that because the subjects are relatively well-educated they should not be so susceptible. Therefore, the fact that large numbers of youth have shown such susceptibility is interpreted to mean that the psychotechnological techniques must be powerful indeed!

3.  Before proceeding with demystification of recruitment to new religions one caveat is in order. It is not true, of course, that no problems exist with any new religions, or that no laws are ever broken by leaders and members of new religions. It would be astonishing if some such actions did not occur, even if rarely. As Balch (1991) has noted, sometimes a "corruption of power" develops and groups go awry. Law-breaking associated with the Rajneesh group in Oregon is a case in point, as is the mass murder and suicide of Peoples Temple in the jungle of Guyana (but see Richardson 1980). When such actions do occur, "brainwashing" is seldom useful as an explanatory device. No magical psychological "black boxes" are needed to explain most of what happens in human societies and groups, including recruitment to religious groups.

## REFERENCES

Anthony, D. 1990. "Religious Movements and Brainwashing Litigation: Evaluating Key Testimony." Pp. 295-344 in *In Gods We Trust,* edited by T. Robbins and D. Anthony. New Brunswick: NJ: Transaction Books.

Anthony, D., and T. Robbins. 1992. "Law, Social Science and the 'Brainwashing' Exception in the First Amendment." *Behavioral Sciences and the Law* 10: 5-30.

Asch, S. 1960. "Effects of Group Pressure Upon the Modification and Distortion of Judgments." Pp. 189-200 in *Group Dynamics,* edited by D. Cartwright and A. Zander. New York: Harper and Row.

Balch, R. 1991. "Religious Totalism and the Corrupting of Religious Power." Paper presented at annual meeting of the Society for the Scientific Study of Religion, Pittsburgh, PA.

Barker, E. 1984. *The Making of a Moonie: Choice or Brainwashing?* Oxford: Blackwell.

Beckford, J. 1978a. "Accounting for Conversion." *British Journal of Sociology* 29: 249-262.

_____. 1978b. "Through a Looking Glass and Out the Other Side: Withdrawal from Reverend Moon's Unification Church." *Archives de Sciences Sociales des Religions* 45: 95-116.

_____. 1985. *Cult Controversies: The Societal Response to the New Religious Movements.* London: Tavistock.

Bem, D. 1972. "Self-Perception Theory." Pp. 2-62 in *Advances in Experimental Social Psychology,* edited by L. Berkowitz. Vol. 6. New York: Academic Press.

Biderman, A. 1962. "The Image of 'Brainwashing'." *Public Opinion Quarterly* 26: 547-563.

Bird, F., and W. Reimer. 1982. "A Sociological Analysis of New Religious and Para-religious Movements." *Journal for the Scientific Study of Religion* 21: 1-14.

Bromley, D. 1984. "Conservatorships and Deprogramming: Legal and Political Prospects." Pp. 267-294 in *The Brainwashing/Deprogramming Controversy: Sociological, Psychological, Legal and Historical Perspectives,* edited by D.G. Bromley and J.T. Richardson. Lewiston, NY: Edwin Mellen Press.

_____. 1988a. "Deprogramming as a Mode of Exit from New Religious Movements: The Case of the Unificationist Movement." Pp. 166-184 in *Falling From the Faith,* edited by D.G. Bromley. Newbury Park, CA: Sage.

_____. 1988b. "ISKCON and the Anti-Cult Movement." Pp. 252-289 in *Krishna Consciousness in the West,* edited by D.G. Bromley and L. Shinn. Lewisburg: Bucknell University Press.

_____. 1991. "Unraveling Religious Disaffiliation: The Meaning and Significance of Falling from the Faith." *Counseling and Values* 36: 164-185.

Bromley, D., and E. Breschel. 1992. "General Population and Institutional Elite Support for Social Control of New Religious Movements: Evidence from National Survey Data." *Behavioral Sciences and the Law* 10: 39-52.

Bromley, D.G., and J. Richardson, eds. 1983. *The Brainwashing/Deprogramming Controversy: Sociological, Psychology, Legal, and Historical Perspectives.* Lewiston, NY: Edwin Mellen Press.

Bromley, D., and A. Shupe. 1979. "Atrocity Tales, the Unification Church, and the Social Construction of Evil." *Journal of Communication* 29: 42-53.

_____. 1986. "Affiliation and Disaffiliation: A Role Theory Approach to Joining and Leaving New Religious Movements." *Thought: A Review of Culture and Ideas* 61: 197-211.

_____. Forthcoming. *Strange Gods and Cult Scares.* Boston: Beacon Press.

Cialdini. R. 1985. *Influence: Science and Practice.* Glenview, IL: Scott, Foresman.

Delgado R. 1977. "Religious Totalism: Gentle and Ungentle Persuasion Under the First Amendment." *Southern California Law Review* 51: 1-99.

_____. 1982. "Cults and Conversion: The Case for Informed Consent." *Georgia Law Review* 16: 533-574.

DeWitt, J. 1991. "Novel Scientific Evidence and the Juror: A Social Psychological Approach to the *Frye/*Relevancy Controversy." Ph.D. dissertation in Social Psychology, University of Nevada, Reno.

Festinger, L. 1957. *A Theory of Cognitive Dissonance.* Evanston, IL: Row, Peterson.

Festinger, L., H. Riecken, and S. Schachter. 1956. *When Prophecy Fails.* New York: Harper.

Fort, J. 1985. "What is Brainwashing and Who Says So?" Pp. 57-63 in *Scientific Research and New Religions: Divergent Perspectives,* edited by B. Kilbourne. San Francisco: American Association for the Advancement of Science, Pacific Division.

Galanter, M. 1980. "Psychological Induction in the Large-Group: Findings from a Modern Religious Sect." *American Journal of Psychiatry* 137: 1574-1579.

Galanter, M., and C. Diamond. 1981. "'Relief' of Psychiatric Symptoms in Evangelical Religious Sects." *British Journal of Hospital Medicine* 26: 495-498.

Greil, A., and D. Rudy. 1984. "What Have We Learned About Process Models of Conversion? An Examination of Ten Studies." *Sociological Analysis* 54: 115-125.

Heirich, M. 1977. "Change of Heart: A Test of Some Widely Held Theories About Religious Conversion." *American Journal of Sociology* 85: 653-680.

Kilbourne, B. 1986. "Equity or Exploitation? The Case of the Unification Church." *Review of Religious Research* 28: 143-150.

――――. 1989. Psychotherapeutic Implications of New Religious Affiliation." Pp. 127-144 in *Cults and New Religions,* edited by M. Galanter. New York: American Psychiatric Association.

Kilbourne, B., and J. Richardson. 1984. "Psychotherapy and New Religions in a Pluralistic Society." *American Psychologist* 39: 237-251.

Latkin, C. 1986. "Rajneeshpuram, Oregon—An Exploration of Gender and Work Roles, Self-Concept, and Psychological Well-Being in an Experimental Community." Ph.D. dissertation in Psychology, University of Oregon, Eugene.

Levine, J., and E. Russo. 1988. "Majority and Minority Influence." Pp. 13-54 in *Group Processes,* edited by C. Hendrick. Newbury Park, CA: Sage.

Lewis, J. 1986. "Reconstructing the Cult Experience: Post-Involvement Attitudes as a Function of Mode of Exit and Post-Involvement Socialization." *Sociological Analysis* 46: 151-159.

Lewis, J., and D. Bromley. 1987. "The Cult Withdrawal Syndrome: A Case of Misattribution of Cause?" *Journal for the Scientific Study of Religion* 26: 508-522.

Lifton, R. 1961. *Thought Reform and the Psychology of Totalism.* New York: Norton.

――――. 1985. "Cult Processes, Religious Liberty and Religious Totalism." Pp. 59-70 in *Cults, Culture and the Law,* edited by T. Robbins, W. Shepherd, and J. McBride. Chico, CA: Scholars Press.

Lofland, J. 1978. "'Becoming a World-saver' Revisited." Pp. 805-818 in *Conversion Careers,* edited by J. Richardson. Beverly Hills, CA: Sage.

Lofland, J., and N. Skonovd. 1981. "Conversion Motifs." *Journal for the Scientific Study of Religion* 20: 375-385.

Long, T., and J. Hadden. 1983. "Religious Conversion and Socialization." *Journal for the Scientific Study of Religion* 24: 1-14.

Lund D., and T. Wilson. 1977. "Brainwashing as a Defense in Criminal Liability." *Criminal Law Bulletin* 13: 341-382.

McGuire, M. 1988. *Ritual Healing in Suburban America.* New Brunswick, NJ: Rutgers University Press.

Moreland, R., and J. Levine. 1985. "Socialization in Small Groups: Temporal Changes in Individual-Group Relations." Pp. 143-169 in *Advances in Experimental Social Psychology,* edited by L. Berkowitz. New York: Academic Press.

Moscovici, S. 1985. "Innovation and Minority Influence." Pp. 9-51 in *Perspectives on Minority Influence,* edited by S. Moscovici, G. Mugny, and E. van Avermaet. Cambridge: Cambridge University Press.

Moscovici, S., and C. Faucheux. 1972. "Social Influence, Conformity Bias, and the Study of Active Minorities." Pp. 149-202 in *Advances in Experimental Social Psychology,* edited by L. Berkowitz. Vol. 6. New York: Academic Press.

Pilarzyk, T. 1978. "Conversion and Alienation Processes in the Youth Culture." *Pacific Sociological Review* 21: 379-405.

Post, S. 1988. The *Molko* Case: Will Freedom Prevail?" *Journal of Church and State* 31: 451-464.

Richardson, J.T. 1980. "Peoples' Temple and Jonestown: A Corrective Comparison and Critique." *Journal for the Scientific Study of Religion* 19: 239-255.

――――. 1985a. "Active versus Passive Converts: Paradigm Conflict in Conversion/Recruitment Research." *Journal for the Scientific Study of Religion* 24: 163-179.

――――. 1985b. "Psychological and Psychiatric Studies of New Religions." Pp. 209-223 in *Advances in the Psychology of Religion,* edited by L. Brown. New York: Pergamon Press.

――――. 1989. "The Psychology of Induction: A Review and Interpretation." Pp. 211-238 in *Cults and New Religious Movements,* edited by M. Galanter. New York: American Psychiatric Association.

————. 1991a. "Cult/Brainwashing Cases and Freedom of Religion." *Journal of Church and State* 33: 55-74.

————. 1991b "Reflexivity and Objectivity in Research on Controversial New Religions." *Religion* 21: 305-318.

————. 1992. "Public Opinion and the Tax Evasion Trial of Reverend Moon." *Behavioral Sciences and the Law* 10: 53-64.

Richardson, J.T., and B. Kilbourne. 1983. "Classical and Contemporary Brainwashing Models: A Comparison and Critique." Pp. 29-45 in *The Brainwashing/Deprogramming Controversy,* edited by D. Bromley and J. Richarson. Lewiston, NY: Edwin Mellen Press.

Richardson, J.T., B. Kilbourne, and B. van Driel. 1989. "Alternative Religions and Economic Individualism." Pp. 33-56 in *Research in the Social Scientific Study of Religion,* edited by M. Lynn and D. Moberg. Vol. 1. Greenwich, CT: JAI Press.

Richardson, J.T., M. Stewart and R. Simmonds. 1979. *Organized Miracles: A Study of the Contemporary Youth, Communal, Fundamentalist Organization.* New Brunswick, NJ: Transaction.

Richardson, J., J. van der Lans, and F. Derks. 1986. "Leaving and Labeling: Voluntary and Coerced Disaffiliation from Religious Social Movements." Pp. 99-126 in *Research in Social Movements, Conflict and Change,* edited by M. Lang and G. Lang. Vol. 9. Greenwich, CT: JAI Press.

Robbins, T. 1985. "Government Regulatory Powers and Church Autonomy." *Journal for the Scientific Study of Religion* 24: 237-251.

————. 1988. *Cults, Converts and Charisma: The Sociology of New Religious Movements.* Newbury Park, CA: Sage.

Robbins, T., and D. Anthony. 1982. "Deprogramming, Brainwashing, and the Medicalization of Deviant Religious Groups." *Social Problems* 29: 283-297.

Robbins, T., D. Anthony, and J. McCarthy. 1983. "Legitimating Repression." Pp. 319-328 in *The Brainwashing/Deprogramming Controversy,* edited by D. Bromley and J. Richardson. Lewiston, NY: Edwin Mellen Press.

Scheiflin, A., and E. Opton. 1978. *The Mind Manipulators.* New York: Paddington.

Schein, E. 1959. "Brainwashing and Totalitarianization in Modern Society." *World Politics* 2: 430-441.

Schein, E., I. Schneier, and C. Becker. 1961. *Coercive Persuasion.* New York: Norton.

Shapiro, E. 1977. "Destructive Cultism." *American Family Foundation* 15: 80-87.

Sherif, M. 1936. *The Psychology of Social Norms.* New York: Harper and Row.

Shupe, A., and D. Bromley. 1979. "The Moonies and the Anti-Cultists: Movement and Counter-Movement in Conflict." *Sociological Analysis* 40: 325-334.

Singer, M. 1979. "Coming Out of the Cults." *Psychology Today* 12: 72-82.

Singer, M., and R. Ofshe. 1990. "Thought Reform Programs and the Production of Psychiatric Casualties." *Psychiatric Annals* 20: 188-193.

Skonovd, N. 1983. Leaving the Cultic Religious Milieu." Pp. 91-105 in *The Brainwashing/Deprogramming Controversy,* edited by D. Bromley and J. Richardson. Lewiston, NY: Edwin Mellen Press.

Solomon, T. 1981. "Integrating the 'Moonie' Experience: A Survey of Ex-members of the Unification Church." Pp. 275-295 in *In God We Trust,* edited by T. Robbins and D. Anthony. New Brunswick, NJ: Transaction.

————. 1983. "Programming and Deprogramming the 'Moonies': Social Psychology Applied." Pp. 163-181 in *The Brainwashing/Deprogramming Controversy,* edited by D. Bromley and J. Richardson. Lewiston, NY: Edwin Mellen Press.

Straus, R. 1976. "Changing Oneself: Seekers and the Creative Transformation of Life Experience." Pp. 252-272 in *Doing Social Life,* edited by J. Lofland. New York: Wiley.

————. 1979. "Religious Conversion as a Personal and Collective Accomplishment." *Sociological Analysis* 40: 158-165.

————. 1981. "A Social-Psychology of Religious Experience: A Naturalistic Approach." *Sociological Analysis* 42: 57-67.

van Avermaet, E. 1988. "Social Influence in Small Groups." Pp. 350-380 in *Introduction to Social Psychology,* edited by M. Hewstone, W. Stroebe, J. Codol, and G. Stephenson. New York: Basil Blackwell.

van Driel, B., and J. Richardson. 1988. "Print Media Coverage of New Religious Movements: A Longitudinal Study." *Journal of Communication* 36: 37-61.

Wright, S. 1983. "Defection from New Religious Movements: A Test of Some Theoretical Propositions." Pp. 106-121 in *The Brainwashing/Deprogramming Controversy,* edited by D. Bromley and J. Richardson. Lewiston, NY: Edwin Mellen Press.

————. 1987. *Leaving the Cults: The Dynamics of Defection.* Washington, DC: Society for the Scientific Study of Religion.

Zimbardo, P., E. Ebbesen, and C. Maslach. 1977. *Influencing Attitudes and Influencing Behavior.* Reading, MA: Addison-Wesley.

# THE NEW RELIGIONS AND MENTAL HEALTH

John A. Saliba

## ABSTRACT

The debate on the effects of cult membership on mental health has dominated psychological and psychiatric literature on NRMs. Most research so far has concentrated on converts to several Eastern movements, members of Pentecostal and fundamentalist sects and practitioners of meditation, particularly Transcendental Meditation. In general, studies on active members of NRMs tend to find membership beneficial, while those on deprogrammed members conclude that cultic lifestyle has devastating effects on personality. Adoption of better theoretical frameworks and methodological procedures is necessary before any definite conclusions are reached on the effect of cult membership.

The effects that cults might have on their members have long been the subject of debate in psychological and psychiatric literature (Richardson 1980). In spite of the continuing disagreement, the latest edition of the *Diagnostic and Statistical Manual of Mental Disorders* (American Psychiatric Association 1987) has endorsed the position that cultic beliefs and lifestyles contribute to mental illness and are an obstacle to the development of a healthy personality. In this major reference work in psychiatric literature leaders of cults and other fringe religions are cited as examples of the paranoid personality (1987, p. 338). Trance states and/or altered states of consciousness, which many of the new religious movements promote, are held to be indicators of dissociative disorders (1987, p. 277). Magical thinking and euphoric and ecstatic states are linked with immaturity and defective personality traits (1987, p. 401). Most

**Religion and the Social Order, Volume 3B, pages 99-113.**
**Copyright © 1993 by JAI Press Inc.**
**All rights of reproduction in any form reserved.**
**ISBN: 1-55938-715-7**

significantly, the DSM-III-R still favors the brainwashing theory of conversion to the new religions, a theory which makes cult recruits unwilling victims of cult propaganda, manipulation, and indoctrination.[1]

The major problem with this negative appraisal of cults is that it relies heavily on the psychiatric evaluation of ex-cult members, the majority of whom have been forced or pressured out of their newly-found faith communities.[2] Recent studies have shown that psychologists and psychiatrists differ sharply on both the method and theory that should be adopted in the study of the new religions (Kilbourne 1985; Galanter 1989). Further, studies of cult members lean toward a more cautiously favorable assessment of the consequences of cult membership.

## PSYCHOLOGICAL AND PSYCHIATRIC STUDIES OF MEMBERS OF NEW RELIGIONS

The debate on the impact of cults on the mental health of their members centers around two main issues: Are recruitment methods and socialization processes so inflexible and forceful that the converts are more likely to be harmed than helped? And do the spiritual practices and lifestyles endorsed by the cults stagnate, inhibit, or warp personality development? Three types of studies are relevant to the discussion of these questions: (1) *converts to Eastern religious movements*, (2) *members of Pentecostal and fundamentalist sects*, and (3) *individuals who have taken up the practice of meditation*.

### Studies of Eastern Religious Groups

Many psychological studies on new religions imported from the East deal with three controversial groups: the Unification Church (UC), the International Society for Krishna Consciousness (ISKCON), and the Divine Light Mission (DLM).[3] Galanter and his colleagues have conducted one of the most comprehensive psychiatric studies of the members of the Unification Church. They have correlated the religious qualities of these members with their psychological characters. Neurotic distress, religiosity, general well-being, level of belief, sense of purpose in life, and feelings of being coerced were explored through questionnaires and personal interviews. Borrowing models from various disciplines (attribution theory and cognitive dissonance from psychology, systems theory from sociology, and sociobiology from anthropology), Galanter and his associates conclude that those individuals who join a new religious movement are usually experiencing psychological distress more intensely than their peers and that cult membership tends to bring relief. Participation in a well-organized and meaningful lifestyle contributes to the well-being of the cult member, who might abandon the use of drugs and alcohol. The experience of conversion to a charismatic sect or cult, rather than being an indication of mental illness, is a means to social adaptation and has a "potentially restitutive function" (Galanter 1982, p. 1542).

Accordingly, cults do not cause mental or psychological aberrations, but rather alleviate the stress of life, enhance the feeling of well-being, and resolve conflicts. They can, therefore, make a positive contribution to personality development. Without denying that some UC members might still need traditional therapy, Galanter and his associates maintain that membership tends to function as a comfort system (Galanter et al. 1979, p. 169) and/or an alternative therapy (Galanter and Buckley 1978, pp. 689-690). Galanter (1986), who conducted an extensive study of the church's distinctive sexual mores and marital customs, reports that the mental and psychological state of its married members is not impaired and remains comparable to that of the population as a whole.

Psychologists have also been interested in why individuals join one particular religious movement rather than another. Poling and Kenney (1986) have endeavored to pinpoint the exact personality traits that attract young adults to the Hare Krishna Movement. In a unique study they suggest that the Hare Krishna devotees share the same basic features common to all would-be cult members—they are deprived, alienated, and religiously inclined people in a state of crisis. They observe, however, that one specific trait characterizes those who become members of ISKCON, namely they have a "sensate personality." Pre-converts to this movement tend to seek sensual pleasure, but are afraid of becoming victims of sense gratification for its own sake. ISKCON promotes a sensate orientation in, for instance, the centrality of food in its elaborate system of ritual and its belief that the deities are contained in clay images. It validates its members' natural orientation in religious terms, provides mechanisms for controlling their sensual inclinations, and offers a Hindu alternative for coping with life situations. Other studies (Poling 1980; Ross 1983) show that the personality types attracted to the Hare Krishna Movement occur frequently in the general population.

Comprehensive studies by Weiss and Comrey (1987a, 1987b, 1987c), while not confirming the "sensate" personality theory, agree with Poling and Kenney's basic conclusion that the devotee's personality is not much different from that of the average young adult in the West. They hold that the distinguishing trait of ISKCON members is their compulsivity, which is consonant with their highly structured lifestyle. "Compulsivity may also lead them to hold narrowly focused world and personal views, dogmatic reasoning, and to attempt to live to their idealized standards under unnecessary stress and pressure as well as to try to induce others to their ways"(Weiss and Comrey 1987c, p. 411). Such compulsivity, however, does not necessarily indicate mental illness. Weiss and Mendoza (1990) point out that the rate of mental disorder and psychological distress of ISKCON members are statistically equivalent to the rest of the population. Ross's (1985) study of Hare Krishna members in Australia not only corroborates the view that the ISKCON lifestyle does not induce mental illness, but also establishes that long-term membership has salutary effects on its members.

One of the few lengthy sociopsychological monographs on an Eastern religious movement is Downton's (1979) study of members of the Divine Light Mission. Though intended primarily as an analysis of the conversion process to this group, Downton's work provides several insights into the psychology of those who join this movement. Downton explains that the "premies" (as initiates in the DLM are called) do not go through a sudden conversion, a kind of personality snapping which has been linked with mental illness. Rather, instead of experiencing a radical and instantaneous personality transformation, they undergo, in many stages, an evolutionary change in their egos. Though the author warns that prolonged dependence on the guru creates serious psychological problems, he still assures his readers that DLM members "are less alienated, aimless, worried, afraid, and more peaceful, loving, confident, and appreciative of life" (Downton 1979, p. 210).

Galanter and Buckley (1978) confirm that the conversion experience of DLM members is a mystical experience similar to that of the Quakers and of Christian saints like Augustine and Ignatius of Loyola. It has a beneficial function and can be seen as "a regression in the service of the ego that resolved their immediate and intrapsychic and social conflicts" (1979, p. 286). Membership in the DLM and UC are similar in that they both have a "relief effect" and act, to some degree, as alternative forms of psychotherapeutic treatment (Galanter and Diamond 1981).[4]

Some studies that compare the mental and psychological states of the members of several new religious groups, including the UC, ISKCON, DLM, and Transcendental Meditation (TM), are less optimistic in their appraisal. Hopkins (1978), for instance, asserts that membership always results in some deterioration in social and intellectual functioning. Johnson (1977) thinks that members of the new movements are characterized by a rejection or avoidance of the adult world through a regressive, narcissistic retreat from reality. More specific psychopathologies have been ascribed to members of particular groups. Magaro et al. (1984) theorize that the Hare Krishna devotees (like the members of InterVarsity Christian Fellowship) exhibit a depressive personality, while Transcendental Meditators and DLM premies suffer from catatonia. Some scholars (Kriegman and Solomon 1985) have argued that the DLM caters to the needs of a narcissistic personality. Members of this mission develop a relationship to the guru similar to the idealizing transference that arises between some narcissistic patients and their group therapist. The opinion that narcissism is typical of cult leaders is common.[5]

The view that the new religious movements are detrimental to one's psychological and mental health is corroborated by those mental health specialists[6] who have interviewed and/or counseled ex-cult members, many of whom had been pressured or forced to abandon their new commitment. The cult environment itself is said to cause psychiatric symptoms. In the words of Langone (1990, p. 194), "atypical dissociative disorder and even occasionally post-traumatic stress disorder have been used to describe cult-related psychopathology." Others (Sirkin and Wynne 1990) see cult involvement as a "relational disorder," by which they mean that the psychological problem lies in the quality of the relationship between the individual cult member and the group. Cults diminish or completely remove the member's ability to function independently from the group.

In more general terms cults are seen as totalistic institutions that use thought reform methods to change the personalities and worldviews of their members (Hockman 1990; Singer and Ofshe 1990). Halperin (1990, pp. 212-213), for instance, warns that "the psychiatrist should alert the potential cult member to the reality that cult affiliation is potentially self-destructive and may, in many circumstances, severely limit the individual's further growth and development," even though he admits that "a few individuals whose needs for structure are so great might benefit from affiliation." This general view of cult membership as harmful to one's psychological well-being is applied not only to Eastern religious movements, but also to many Christian fundamentalist sects.

## Studies on Neo-Pentecostal/Fundamentalist Sects

Concerns about the mental health of individuals who have joined a new religious movement have not been restricted to members of Eastern groups, but have included the neo-pentecostal (charismatic) and fundamentalist Christian churches that have probably attracted more people than their Eastern counterparts. Such Christian churches are often lumped with Eastern religious groups and labeled "destructive cults."[7]

Several Christian religious groups are of interest to psychologists and psychiatrists because many of their beliefs and lifestyles have been linked in clinical practice to various kinds of mental, emotional, or personality disorders. The following features are particularly subject to a negative evaluation by psychiatrists: the dogmatic stance that tolerates no dissent or variety; the narrow-mindedness and exclusiveness that are the hallmarks of membership; the authoritarian attitudes that typically dictate the behavior of the members in both spiritual and secular matters; the mistreatment of women and children based on what are believed to be biblical injunctions; and the occasional refusal to have recourse to what is considered to be routine medical practice in Western culture.

The tendency to regard members of these religious groups as suffering from some psychological weakness or mental disorder still dominates psychiatric counseling. Charismatic and fundamentalist movements are said to attract the emotionally disturbed and mentally ill and do nothing to better their conditions. Many of the psychological problems of ex-fundamentalists have been attributed to their former religious orientation (Moyers 1990). The practice of charismatic healing, although it has some analogies with traditional psychotherapy, "is not without difficulties and drawbacks even for the population it serves" (Csordas 1990, p. 88). Glossolalia, which is so commonly encouraged in these groups, is particularly subject to a negative psychiatric evaluation. There is still no agreement as to whether speaking in tongues is a form of trance, an altered state of consciousness, a cathartic expression of one's emotions, a sign of hysteria or neurosis, or just a form of improvised religious language. In clinical practice, however, it is rarely taken as a sign of a balanced, healthy, and mature personality.[8]

There is evidence, however, that some researchers of pentecostal movements have made a theoretical shift from viewing their members from a perspective of pathology to assessing their personality and social learning variables (Gritzmacher et al. 1988). Such an approach has led to a reassessment of sect involvement as salutary, rather than detrimental, to one's psychological well-being. Charismatic movements could help people in distress, curing them of mild emotional and functional disorders and enabling them to cope with the problems of life. According to some researchers, there is little empirical evidence to support the contention that fundamentalism produces or exacerbates mental problems because of its authoritarianism (Hartz and Everett 1989; cf. Hood et al. 1986). On the contrary, fundamentalist faith-healing groups operate as coping mechanisms for the externalization and explanation of anxiety, misfortune, and illness (Pattison et al. 1973). Glossolalia might itself be a form of therapy, because it tends to relieve the individual's emotional stress and anxiety. Many of those who speak in tongues are practically indistinguishable from the average individual, except when they are in a ritual context that both endorses and instigates glossolalic utterances.

## Studies on the Effects of Meditation

Various forms of meditation, especially Transcendental Meditation, Yoga, and several forms of Buddhist meditation, have been subjected to intensive studies under controlled experimental conditions (Murphy and Donovan 1988; Saliba 1987). The question raised in psychiatry is whether the practice of meditation is a useful relaxing technique that produces beneficial psychological effects or whether it fosters trance-like or mystical states and altered states of consciousness that are a hindrance to personality development and promote psychotic behavior. Four main points of view dominate current psychiatric literature.

The first proposes the opinion that the technique of meditation, detached from its religious and/or cultic roots, can be a useful auxiliary tool in psychotherapy. Benson (1976) was among the first researchers who developed a form of meditation, similar to TM, without, however, the spiritual and ideological components that accompany the teachings of Maharishi Mahesh Yogi and the mystique of a personal mantra and secret initiation ritual. Carrington (1984) has applied noncultic meditation extensively in her clinical practice and firmly holds that it can be used as an adjunct to traditional psychotherapy.

Innumerable experiments have shown that the practice of noncultic meditation is often conducive to many positive results. It has, consequently, been recommended as a form of relaxation that reduces stress and elicits mental catharsis, with consequent psychological growth and development.[9] Several experiments have demonstrated that those who meditate on a daily basis register an intensification of performance and endurance in their tasks. The following are said to be the main psychological advantages of meditation: reduced anxiety; heightened awareness; increased self-knowledge, self-control, and self-acceptance; reduction of the level of hostility and aggression; and the cure of alcohol and drug addiction.

The second position holds that a particular type of meditation is the ideal tool for the development of personality and for the solution of all personal and/

or social problems within the context of the religious movement that dispenses it. This view has been advanced largely by those who had adopted the practice of a particular meditation, whether this happens to be TM or some type of Yoga or Buddhist concentration. Followers, for instance, of Maharishi Mahesh Yogi (founder of TM), Muktananda (founder of Siddha Yoga Dham), and Guru Maharaji Ji (founder of the DLM) contend that the meditation passed on to them by their respective guru is qualitatively superior to all others and has the power of transforming one's spiritual, mental, and psychological abilities.

An overwhelming proportion of meditation research deals with the positive effects of TM (Orme-Johnson and Farrow 1977; Murphy and Donovan 1988). Many researchers of TM, several of whom teach at Maharishi International University in Iowa, have vigorously pursued their experiments aimed at extolling the merits of TM and the TM-Sidhi program. Their conclusions have remained practically unchanged over a period of 15 years: the practice of TM is a simple, safe, nonreligious method that can be employed to tackle almost all human problems. Besides the good qualities of meditation mentioned above, TM is held to further the individual's self-development, fulfillment, and actualization. It improves one's work, creativity, and independence. It is advertised as an unfailing cure for those struggling with academic deficiency, sexual problems, and marital conflicts. Attempts have been also made to market it as a novel and effective approach to rehabilitate prison inmates. Moreover, because it cultivates empathy, it has been suggested that it should be incorporated in the training programs of counselors. In glowing terms, supporters of the TM and of the TM-Sidhi program insist that the meditation of Maharishi Mahesh Yogi helps the individual achieve pure awareness which, in turn, leads to "heaven on earth." Many of the results attributed to TM have also be ascribed to those who practice one of the many forms of Eastern meditation. Yoga and Zen are sometimes said to be reliable forms of therapy that can be compared to, if not substituted for, modern psychotherapy.

The third follows from the previous positive assessments of the practice of meditation, be it cultic or noncultic. It proposes that meditation is a suitable and sometimes desirable replacement for, or alternative to, Western psychotherapy. Two rationales are behind this position: Western psychotherapy is inadequate to deal with many of the human problems (particularly those that stem from spiritual values and existential issues) and Asian psychologies and psychotherapies are broader and more comprehensive systems that might furnish a complement and corrective balance to Western psychotherapy (Claxton 1986).

A much more radical approach claims that Western psychology is "proving itself fundamentally futile."

> Individuals are turning to Eastern meditative practices because Western psychotherapy (be it the traditional type, like psychoanalysis, or the more outside-the-mainstream variety, such as Reichian breath therapy or Rolfian bodywork) has largely failed. Eastern meditation's current popularity might be based on the fact that it is an ideal method for improving the individual by transcending the mind, an approach neglected in the West (Coleman 1989/1990, p. 22).

Proponents of a fourth perspective have tried to show that meditation, in whatever form it is practiced, is more likely to bring about damage and distress than provide cure and comfort. The traditional perspective in psychotherapy evaluates trances and mystical experiences as pathological forms involving split or dissociated personalities. In spite of recent studies that look on these states more positively (Tart 1990a), there is still a strong tendency in the psychological disciplines to consider any attempt to induce them a dangerous practice that might result in psychopathology and be a hindrance to the psychotherapeutic process itself.

Critics have argued that the enthusiastic claims that make TM the ultimate solution to all human ills are largely unfounded. They insist that research on TM has been hampered by both theoretical and methodological problems. Further, they observe that expectancy, suggestibility, and other personal and social factors may be playing a crucial role in the positive outcomes of most of the tests given to meditators (Saliba 1987, pp. 400-403).

Moreover, several studies have reported negative behavioral patterns associated with the practice of TM, which could engender or precipitate, rather than solve, a person's difficulties. People with emotional troubles may actually get worse by meditating. Because this type of meditation is a method of stilling the mind, it may evoke into one's consciousness compelling, and possibly damaging, fantasies and primitive distressing thoughts. The end result could be pathological regression. Further, because supervision of meditation is not required (except during the relatively short initiation period), those who practice TM may have to face on their own any unconscious material that regular practice might unearth. The prolonged practice of TM could cause serious problems, among which are anxiety, tension, confusion, depression, frustration, neurotic dependency, and psychotic behavior (e.g., Heide 1984). Similar concerns have been raised about Yoga and Buddhist meditation, the practice of which could aggravate the symptoms of neurosis or lead to psychotic behavior. Intense meditation could result in insularity, self-centeredness, and acquisitiveness.

## DISCUSSION

The majority of psychological and/or psychiatric studies on members of new religions are based on the testing and interviewing either of current members or of those who have been pressured to leave. More than 75 percent of studies of the former type tend to show that the psychological profiles of individuals tested fall well within "normal" bounds. Studies of the latter type generally conclude that ex-members suffer from serious mental and emotional dysfunctions that have been directly caused by cultic beliefs and practices. So few psychological studies have been made on the large number of ex-members who left the groups voluntarily that few reliable generalizations can be formulated.[10]

The divergent conclusions reached on the effects of cult membership are obviously influenced by the methodological procedures and theoretical assumptions of the scholars who conduct the tests. Studies that begin with the premise that the effects of cult life are best measured by an examination of active participants have at least one overriding advantage—they are based on the examination of, and interviews with, individuals who are experiencing, and apparently benefiting from, the full effects of cult membership. The conclusion that the lifestyles and practices of many new religions could have the same goal and outcome as traditional therapies is an original and constructive perspective for evaluating the psychological impact of involvement. This does not mean, however, that religious cults function as therapeutic institutions. The fact that cult members unequivocally attest to their improved condition and enhanced quality of life cannot be advanced as indisputable evidence that their new lifestyles have cured them of their psychological and mental ailments. The most that can be concluded is that some individuals find membership rewarding. The "relief effect" could be temporary and/or superficial.

Psychologists and psychiatrists who have limited their research largely to deprogrammed and/or disgruntled ex-members are correct in their assessment that these individuals are psychologically distressed and need professional counseling. However, the assertion that such problems are directly created by participation in the instruction programs and lifestyles of new religions does not follow logically. It is equally plausible and consistent with the data that the impaired mental and psychological condition of these ex-members existed prior to entry into the cult or is the result of the deprogramming methods themselves. In other words, the negative psychological evaluations of former members who have been coerced to abandon their group affiliations reveals little about the alleged harmfulness of cultic beliefs and practices. On the other hand, it is also possible that individuals who have left the new religions on their own initiative may have done so because they became aware that membership was too confining and demanding to have any lasting benefits and therapeutic value.

The need to have reliable psychological profiles and diagnostic data of cult members prior to their involvement is thus imperative. Converts' claims to well-being, disillusioned members' anti-cult statements, and parental assessments that their offspring have psychologically deteriorated or regressed are all insufficient for an accurate assessment of the mental and psychological implications of cultic lifestyles. Given the likelihood that many of those who join new religions have been experiencing some degree of heightened stress or anxiety and that a substantial percentage of cult members do not persevere in their new commitments, the question of whether membership invariably creates new psychological problems or augments, resolves or simply suspends already existing ones remains unsolved.

The theoretical tools used to study the impact of new religions on mental health require careful scrutiny. While borrowing various models from different disciplines is recommended, several theories appear to add little to our understanding of the new religions and even less to our ability to diagnose the mental state of their members. The brainwashing model begs the questions it purports to ask and has generated little productive research. Some traditional approaches that on their face value are appealing, like the deprivation theory of cult formation, not only tend to be inherently pejorative and reductionistic but also fail to explain the complexity of the conversion process. Because not all religiously deprived individuals join new religions, the deprivation theory of cult formation is unable prospectively or retrospectively to distinguish between those who join new religious movements and those who do not.

Another unresolved issue is the validity of the psychological tests to which both cult members and ex-members have been subjected. It is safe to state that the standard psychological tests were not designed to resolve the complex issues raised by the controversy over the new religions. Further, the assumptions and values implicit in these tests may be culturally biased. Western customs and attitudes, such as the romantic form of marriage and the pursuit of personal independence that often gives the family a secondary role, should not be taken as absolute proof of mental health and psychological maturity. Individuals, who for ideological reasons and emotional satisfaction prefer an arranged marriage and/or a communal style of living in which their individuality is subordinated, are not necessarily suffering from a personality disorder, as psychiatric diagnostic manuals infer or assert. In this respect, it might be instructive to compare the communal lifestyles of several of the new religions with those traditional monastic institutions that have flourished particularly in Christianity and Buddhism.

While studies of several religious groups (such as the Hare Krishna devotees and the Unificationists) provide the kind of adequate and solid data needed to avoid the sweeping conclusion that involvement in some Eastern religions is a major source of psychopathology, those on meditation are more problematic. Rao (1989), for instance, quite categorically asserts that methodologically deficient experiments, conceptually confused discussions, and largely unsubstantiated claims mar the many studies on meditation.

The results of experiments carried out to determine if meditation, whether it is linked with a religious group or not, has unique therapeutic qualities are inconclusive and largely unconvincing. It would appear that some claims, particularly about the physiological and psychological effects of meditation, have been substantiated. Reber (1985, p. 428) sums up the matter accurately and succinctly: "a few aspects of the meditational state have been documented: the EEG pattern generally shows alpha waves, oxygen consumption drops, energy expenditure is lowered, and subject reports are consistent in describing the experience as relaxing and salutary." But these results could probably be replicated by other practices. Further, evidence that meditation is a well-tested substitute for traditional psychotherapy or that one particular form of meditation is the panacea for all individual and social problems is simply lacking.

## FUTURE PROSPECTS FOR THE PSYCHIATRIC STUDY OF NEW RELIGIONS

The study of the relationship between new religious movements and mental health is in its infancy. Several areas of investigation need to be vigorously pursued both to resolve contested issues and to establish a knowledge base for generalizations about how cults affect their members.

First, more studies of individual religious groups are necessary. At present there are few in-depth psychological and psychiatric studies on individual movements, especially when compared with the sociological research in the field. Larger samples (similar to those of Galanter and Weiss and Comrey) are a must for any definitive assessment of the mental and psychological state of the membership of one particular group. In like manner, there is an urgent need for comparative studies, if for no other reason than to avoid the error of applying to all groups statements or judgments reached after studying one particular movement.

The same reflection is applicable to meditation research. There are few studies of techniques of meditation in groups like Siddha Yoga Dam, DLM, and Ananda Marga. Meditation research needs to be broadened to include not only a wider variety of meditation forms but also their relationship to the ideological system in which they are embedded. Comparative experiments might generate more productive theoretical models. With few exceptions the published research on meditation repetitively examines the same issues without yielding new insights, an indication that new theoretical and methodological approaches are necessary to achieve fresh insights on the meditation process.

Second, the psychological health of cult members cannot be assessed adequately by testing cult members and those ex-cult members who have been deprogrammed. It is imperative to conduct studies of the large number of ex-members who have exited voluntarily. Further, ways of generating baseline data on the mental health condition of cult members prior to their membership must be devised. Any meaningful evaluation of the intellectual and emotional influence cults might have on their members requires knowledge of their state of mind prior to membership. To affirm, for example, that those attracted to the new movements are alienated does not shed much light on the issue. Many alienated individuals never join a new religion. Why is it that only relatively few of these young adults end up in a cult and what distinguishes joiners from nonjoiners?

Third, studies by transpersonal and humanistic psychologists on the various Asian psychologies and psychotherapies (e.g., Tart 1990b) might shed light on the recent success of Eastern religious groups. Although psychological anthropology, and more recently transcultural psychiatry, have significantly increased our knowledge of mental disorder and its treatment in various cultural settings (cf. Saliba 1987, pp. 185 ff.), traditional psychiatrists continue to evaluate members of Eastern cults from a Western cultural perspective. The psychological tests to which members of new religions have been subjected by these clinicians may well be too culture-bound to yield meaningful results. Asian theories of personality might be more fruitful in explaining both the change that cult members experience and their psychological states.

## CONCLUSION

There obviously are cultural and social factors that must be taken into consideration before the effects cults might have on mental health can be fully determined. The contribution of the psychological disciplines lies particularly in the analysis of religious experience and its influence on personality, in the examination of the conversion process itself, and in the exploration of the consequences of cultic lifestyle on personal growth and development. The complex issues that these disciplines have raised, however, concern not only the individual's psychological and mental health but also legal, social, and moral questions that need to be resolved.

Contemporary research does not offer an unequivocal answer to the intriguing question of whether the cults are adverse or beneficial to individual mental health. Like commitment to any religion, cult membership can give the kind of meaning and direction in one's life that leads to contentment, maturity, and well-being.

For some persons new religious group affiliation could be associated with emotional disorder, a form of escape from one's personal problems, which are camouflaged rather than confronted and treated. For others, it might create such an exacting and narrow environment that it generates or augments, rather than eliminates or alleviates, psychological disorder. There is little doubt as well that the psychological repercussions of new religious movements have been felt not only by those who joined them but also by many of their concerned relatives. Whatever stand one takes on the relationship between the new religions and mental health, it is becoming increasingly clear that psychiatrists, psychotherapists, and counselors will assume an important role in the study and evaluation of the impact these movements are having on individuals, family members, and society as a whole (Galanter 1990, p. 550).

## NOTES

1. The revised version of the manual (American Psychiatric Association 1987) makes some important changes. Unlike its predecessor (American Psychiatric Association 1980), it admits that deviant behavior, be it political or religious, is not necessarily a symptom of personality dysfunction. It also omits the mention of meditation as a predisposing factor of depersonalization disorder (1980, p. 276).

2. West and Singer (1980) have articulated the negative stance on cultism without much reference to studies on cult members. The same arguments have been reiterated with little modification in a more recent publication (Singer and Ofshe 1990).

3. It should be noted that the DLM has undergone substantial changes during the 1980s and has adopted the new name of Elan Vital. There has been, to our knowledge, no published research on the psychology of the DLM members that takes into consideration recent developments.

4. Preliminary studies on members of the Church of Scientology (Ross 1988) and on American Zen monks (MacPhillamy 1986) attest to the same positive psychological effects of membership.

5. A good example of such an interpretation is Clarke's (1988) short essay on Bhagwan Shree Rajneesh. The view that there is some connection between the rise of new religions and contemporary narcissistic culture is also found in sociological literature. Neitz (1987), for instance, maintains that the Catholic Charismatic Movement, while being a part of the culture of narcissism, enables its members to transcend it. Involvement in the movement might, therefore, have some therapeutic value.

6. The April 1990 issue of Psychiatric Annals is dedicated to the issue of contemporary cults. All the main contributors (Halperin 1990; Hockman 1990; Langone 1990; Singer and Ofshe 1990; Sirkin and Wynne 1990) agree that cults have a deleterious effect on those individuals who join them, though they debate the kind of psychiatric illness that membership causes.

7. See, for example, *Cultic Studies Journal,* vol. 2(3), 1985, which is dedicated to "Cults, Evangelicals, and the Ethics of Social Influence."

8. For an overview of various theories of glossolalia, see Samarin (1970). For references to the many studies on glossolalia in different cultural settings, consult Saliba (1987).

9. This view is sometimes expressed in medical journals. Consult, for instance, Kunz and Finkel (1987, pp. 19-21), where the technique of noncultic meditation is briefly described and listed, together with muscle-relaxation and breathing exercises, as an effective way of relieving tension.

10. Most of the studies of voluntary defections have been made by sociologists (Bromley 1988; Wright 1987). Wright found that over 65 percent of voluntary defectors claimed that they were wiser for their experience. This leads one to conclude that membership did not lead to any serious mental and/or psychological damage. Wright, however, did not use the standard psychological tests in his research.

# REFERENCES

American Psychiatric Association. 1980. *Diagnostic and Statistical Manual of Mental Disorders* (DSM-III). Washington, DC: American Psychiatric Press.

————. 1987. *Diagnostic and Statistical Manual of Mental Disorders [DSM-III-R].* Revised ed. Washington, DC: American Psychiatric Press.

Benson, H. 1976. *The Relaxation Response.* New York: Avon Books.

Bromley, D.G., ed. 1988. *Falling from the Faith: Causes and Consequences of Religious Apostasy.* Beverly Hills, CA: Sage.

Carrington, P. 1984. "Meditation Techniques in Clinical Practice." Pp. 60-78 in *The New Therapies: A Sourcebook,* edited by L.E Apt and I.R. Stewart. New York: Van Nostrand.

Clarke, R.O. 1988. "The Narcissistic Guru: A Profile of Bhagwan Shree Rajneesh." *Free Inquiry* 8: 33-35.

Claxton, G.L., ed. 1986. *Beyond Therapy: The Impact of Eastern Religious on Psychological Theory and Practice.* London: Wisdom Publications.

Coleman, R. 1989/1990. "From the Id to the Aum: Psychology Takes a Backseat to Meditation." *Critique* 32: 21-24.

Csordas, T.J. 1990. "The Psychotherapy Analogy and Charismatic Healing." *Psychotherapy* 27: 79-90.

Downton, J.V. 1979. *Sacred Journeys: The Conversion of Young Americans to the Divine Light Mission.* New York: Columbia University Press.

Galanter, M. 1982. "Charismatic Religious Sects and Psychiatry: An Over-View." *American Journal of Psychiatry* 139: 1539-1548.

————. 1986. "'Moonies' Get Married: A Psychiatric Follow-up Study of a Charismatic Religious Sect." *American Journal of Psychiatry* 143: 1245-1248.

————, ed. 1989. *Cults and New Religious Movements: A Report of the American Psychiatric Association.* Washington, DC: American Psychiatric Association.

————. 1990. "Cults and Zealous Self-help Movements: A Psychiatric Perspective." *American Journal of Psychiatry* 147: 543-551.

Galanter, M., and P. Buckley. 1978. "Evangelical Religion and Meditation: Psychotherapeutic Findings." *Journal of Nervous and Mental Disease* 166: 685-691.

Galanter, M., and L.C. Diamond. 1981. "Relief of Psychological Symptoms in Evangelical Sects." *British Journal of Hospital Medicine* 26: 495-497.

Galanter, M. et al. 1979. "The 'Moonies': A Psychological Study of Conversion and Membership in a Contemporary Religious Sect." *American Journal of Psychiatry* 136: 165-170.

Gritzmacher, S.A., B. Bolton, and R.H. Dana. 1988. "Psychological Characteristics of Pentecostals: A Literature Review and Psychodynamic Synthesis." *Journal of Psychology and Theology* 16: 233-245.

Halperin, D.A. 1990. "Psychiatric Perspectives of Cult Affiliation." *Psychiatric Annals* 20: 204-218.

Hartz, G.W., and H.C. Everett. 1989. "Fundamentalist Religion and Its Effect on Mental Health." *Journal of Religion and Health* 28: 107-117.

Heide, F.J. 1984. "Relaxation-induced Anxiety: Mechanisms and Theoretical Implications." *Behavior Research and Therapy* 22: 1-12.

Hockman, J. 1990. "Miracle, Mystery, and Authority: The Triangle of Cult Indoctrination." *Psychiatric Annals* 20: 179-187.

Hood, R.W., R.J. Morris, and P.J. Watson. 1986. "Maintenance of Religious Fundamentalism." *Psychological Reports* 59: 547-559.

Hopkins, R.P. 1978. "The Hospital Viewpoint: Mental Illness or Social Maladjustment." *National Association of Private Psychiatric Hospitals Journal* 9: 19-26.

Johnson, A.B. 1977. "A Temple of Last Resorts: Youth and Shared Narcissism." Pp. 27-65 in *The Narcissistic Condition,* edited by M.C. Nelson. New York: Human Sciences Press.

Kilbourne, B.K., ed. 1985. *Scientific Research and New Religions: Divergent Perspectives.* San Francisco: American Association for the Advancement of Science.

Kriegman, D., and L. Solomon. 1985. "Psychotherapy and the 'New Religions': Are They the Same?" *Cultic Studies Journal* 2: 2-16.

Kunz, J.R.M., and A.J. Finkel, eds. 1987. *The American Medical Association Family Medical Guide.* Revised ed. New York: Random House.

Langone, M.D. 1990. "Working with Cult-affected Families." *Psychiatric Annals* 20: 94-98.

MacPhillamy, D.J. 1986. "Some Personality Effects of Long-term Zen Monasticism and Religious Understanding." *Journal for the Scientific Study of Religion* 25: 304-319.

Magaro, P.B., I.W. Miller, and T. Sesto. 1984. "Personality Style in Post-traditional Religious Organizations." *Psychology: A Journal of Human Behavior* 21: 10-14.

Moyers, J.C. 1990. "Religious Issues in the Psychotherapy of Former Fundamentalists." *Psychotherapy* 27: 42-45.

Murphy, M., and S. Donovan. 1988. *The Physical and Psychological Effects of Meditation: A Review of Contemporary Meditation Research with a Comprehensive Bibliography, 1931-1988.* San Raphael, CA: Esalen Institute.

Neitz, M.J. 1987. *Charisma and Community: A Study of Religious Commitment within the Charismatic Renewal.* New Brunswick, NJ: Transaction Books.

Orme-Johnson, D.W., and J.T. Farrow, eds. 1977. *Scientific Research on the Transcendental Meditation Programs.* Collected papers, vol. 1. Seelisberg, Switzerland: Maharishi Research University Press.

Pattison, E.M., N.A. Lapin, and H.A. Doerr. 1973. "Faith Healing: A Study of Personality and Function." *Journal of Nervous and Mental Disease* 157: 397-409.

Poling, T.H. 1980. "Personality Profiles in Krishna Consciousness." Pp. 158-160 in *Proceedings of the Southwest Conference on Asian Studies,* edited by E.J. Lazzerini. New Orleans: University of New Orleans Press,.

Poling, T.H., and J.F. Kenney. 1986. *The Hare Krishna Character Type: A Study of the Sensate Personality.* Lewiston, NY: Edwin Mellen Press.

Rao, K.R. 1989. "Meditation: Secular and Sacred: A Review and Assessment of Some Recent Research." *Journal of the Indian Academy of Applied Psychology* 15: 51-74.

Reber, A.S. 1985. *Dictionary of Psychology.* New York: Penguin.

Richardson, H., ed. 1980. *New Religions and Mental Health.* Lewiston, NY: Edwin Mellen Press

Ross, M.W. 1983. "Clinical Profiles of Hare Krishna Devotees." *American Journal of Psychiatry* 140: 416-420.

_____. 1985. "Mental Health in Hare Krishna Devotees." *American Journal of Social Psychiatry* 4 : 65-67.

_____. 1988. "Effects of Membership in Scientology on Personality: An Exploratory Study." *Journal for the Scientific Study of Religion* 27: 630-636.

Saliba, J.A. 1987. *Psychiatry and the Cults: An Annotated Bibliography.* New York: Garland.

Samarin, W.J. 1970. *Tongues of Men and Angels: The Religious Language of Pentecostalism.* New York: Macmillan.

Singer, M.T., and R. Ofshe. 1990. "Thought Reform Programs and the Production of Psychiatric Casualties." *Psychiatric Annals* 20: 189-193.

Sirkin, M.I., and L.C. Wynne. 1990. "Cult Disorder as Relational Disorder." *Psychiatric Annals* 20: 199-203.

Tart, C.T., ed. 1990a. *Transpersonal Psychologies.* 3rd ed. San Francisco: Harper and Row.

————. 1990b. *Altered States of Consciousness.* Revised ed. San Francisco: Harper and Row.

Weiss, A.S., and A.L. Comrey. 1987a. "Personality Factor Structure among Hare Krishnas." *Educational and Psychological Measurement* 47: 317-328.

————. 1987b. "Personality and Mental Health Care of Hare Krishnas Compared with Psychiatric Outpatients and 'Normals'." *Personality and Individual Differences* 8: 721-730.

————. 1987c. "Personality Characteristics of Hare Krishnas." *Journal of Personality Assessment* 51: 399-413.

Weiss, A.S., and R.H. Mendoza. 1990. "Effects of Acculturation into the Hare Krishna Movement on Mental Health and Personality." *Journal for the Scientific Study of Religion* 29: 173-180.

West, L.J., and M.T. Singer. 1980. "Cults, Quacks, and Non-professional Psychotherapies." Pp. 3245-3258 in *Comprehensive Textbook of Psychiatry, III,* edited by H. Kaplan, A.H. Freedman, and B.J. Sadock. Baltimore: Williams and Wilkins.

Wright, S.A. 1987. *Leaving the Cults: The Dynamics of Defection.* Washington, DC: Society for the Scientific Study of Religion.

Section B

EMERGING ISSUES

# LEAVING NEW RELIGIONS

## Stuart A. Wright and Helen Rose Ebaugh

## ABSTRACT

A growing corpus of studies of defection from new religions signals an important shift in research in the last decade. Many new movements have encountered organizational change, stagnation, or decline. Subsequent high turnover rates have afforded researchers expanded opportunities to investigate the causes and consequences of apostasy. This paper examines and evaluates the current state of knowledge regarding defection or disaffiliation from new religions. It is organized around three fundamental issues: (1) the conceptualization of defection, (2) methodological issues, and (3) theoretical perspectives.

Only a decade ago, one could scarcely find any social science research on defection or disaffiliation from new religious movements. The bulk of attention was focused on conversion of youth to highly controversial new religions or "cults," such as the Unification Church or Hare Krishna. Even the research on apostasy among mainline religions was notably thin (Bromley 1991). A survey of the sociological literature revealed only four studies that dealt with cult disaffiliation, wholly or in part, prior to 1980 (Beckford 1978; Downton 1979; Kim 1979; Skonovd 1979). An inspection of the clinical and psychological literature turned up only three studies (Singer 1978, 1979; Ungerleider and Wellisch 1979). In contrast, the body of research literature on conversion up to this point has a long and illustrious history dating back to the 1902 publication of William James' seminal work, *The Varieties of Religious Experience* (Snow and Machalek 1984). Rambo (1982) reports 256 behavioral

Religion and the Social Order, Volume 3B, pages 117-138.

science entries on conversion, 62 percent of which have been published since 1973. The research record on conversion to new religions is even more revealing. A bibliography by Beckford and Richardson (1983) shows a rapid increase in conversion studies of new religions. They identify 145 entries, 95 percent of which had appeared since 1973. Not surprisingly, Snow and Machalek (1984, p. 168) conclude from their study that conversion "appears to be the phenomenon that students of new religious movements examine most frequently." Yet the intense research activity on conversion evidently stimulated few studies of defection during this same period.

As the growth of the new religious movements began to slow or stagnate in the late 1970s and early 1980s, many social scientists turned their attention to defection. Some hint of high turnover rates made by observers of the new religions was gradually confirmed as studies began to accumulate. In addition, it appeared that the purported growth rates in previous years claimed by partisan movement leaders and echoed by the media were exaggerated. Focusing only on converts entering these movements, few were aware of a steady flow of disaffected members exiting by the back door at the same time. Popular conceptions of cult brainwashing most likely precluded any suspicions of mass voluntary defections. Consequently, the public assumed erroneously that most members were destined to remain in these movements for long periods of time. The emergent anti-cult movement promoted this view and the subsequent need for intervention and deprogramming (Bromley and Shupe 1987; Robbins 1984, 1988; Robbins and Anthony 1982; Shupe and Bromley 1980).

The decade of the 1980s witnessed an outpouring of studies on defection from new religions. A survey of the research literature since 1980 reveals 42 entries on cult withdrawal, a substantial increase over the previous decade. By our calculations, then, we can account for approximately 83 percent of the studies on cult defection between 1980 and 1990. These studies reflect a wide range of research objectives and questions. Clinical and psychological studies have tended to focus on the emotional and behavioral effects of participation (e.g., Galanter 1983, 1984, 1989; Levine 1984; Maleson 1981). A select number of these have been concerned primarily with the narrower issues of brainwashing and deprogramming or clinical intervention (Clark et al. 1981; Eichel et al. 1984; Verdier 1980). Sociological studies of defection have targeted issues such as social movement dynamics, interactional factors, ideology or belief systems, social and demographic correlates, attrition rates, and exiting modes. Sociologists have also concerned themselves with the brainwashing controversy as the research documenting high turnover rates has raised serious questions about claims of psychological coercion and "destructive cult" influences. But even aside from the polemics of this controversy, many research questions remain to be explored. The ledger is far from balanced, and the rapidly expanding body of literature on defection requires sustained attention from scholars before it can begin to rival the massive volume of literature on conversion.

The purpose of this paper is to examine and evaluate the current state of knowledge regarding disaffiliation from new religions. We contend that this is an important exercise precisely because the field of study is growing so rapidly. We examine important works in various fields such as psychology and psychiatry, but we focus primarily on sociological contributions. The paper is organized around three fundamental issues related to disaffiliation: (1) the conceptualization of defection, (2) methodological issues, and (3) theoretical perspectives. As a burgeoning topic in the sociology of religion, it is our conviction that a greater understanding of exiting processes depends on our ability to identify and clarify such key issues and questions.

## CONCEPTUALIZING DEFECTION

Conceptualization and operationalization of defection raise some of the same problems as defining conversion (see Lofland and Skonovd 1981; Snow and Machalek 1984). Just as the terms "adhesion," "consolidation," "radical transformation," "reaffirmation," and "affiliation" reflect the complexity of conversion, so the terms "disaffection," "deconversion," "withdrawal," "disaffiliation," and "apostasy" reflect the complexity of defection. Different perspectives typically emphasize particular components over others (affective, cognitive, situational, social) in the disengagement process. But most likely, it points to the fact that defection is multidimensional in a manner not unlike Bohannon's (1970) classic analysis of divorce. Indeed, the comparison of divorce and apostasy is a fitting one (see Wright 1991). Bohannon suggests that divorce occurs at various levels (emotional, legal economic, community, psychic, co-parental). Similarly, we posit that defection involves multidimensional detachment. At the very least, we can identify the following components of defection: (1) *affective* (disaffection), (2) *cognitive* (disillusionment), and (3) *social organizational* (disaffiliation). It follows from this logic that defection is a *process* because it is not likely that the individual will experience detachment at these various levels simultaneously. It is not often clear which of these components begins the disengagement process, but it does seem clear that our conceptualization of defection must be broad enough to encompass all of these. In other words, unidimensional detachment is not sufficient to explain defection.

For example, a member may be disillusioned when the prophetic visions of a charismatic leader fail to materialize. Yet disillusionment does not necessarily culminate in defection. The adherent's disillusionment may be rationalized or explained away in light of new events or revelations, resulting in reintegration or rededication. Research indicates that cognitive dissonance resulting from prophetic failure is often successfully dispelled through reinterpretation by leaders and followers alike so as to deter defection (Festinger et al. 1964; Gager 1975; Wallis 1982; Wilson 1987; Zygmunt 1972). Thus, while disillusionment may result in defection, it is by no means inevitable.

Briefly then, we observe that defection involves minimally three aspects of detachment. We offer the following analytical distinctions for purposes of conceptual delineation and understanding: disaffection, disillusionment, and disaffiliation.

Disaffection refers to emotional withdrawal and detachment from the group. Deterioration of affective bonds undermines a powerful component of commitment. Feelings of oneness, solidarity, communion, love, and shared religious experience serve to enhance loyalty to the group. In fact, studies show that converts may be sustained in their commitment by strong interpersonal ties even when there is little evidence of cognitive assent or theological understanding (Bromley and Shupe 1979). That some new religions, particularly communal movements, are able to cultivate intimate, primary group relations amidst an increasingly impersonal, bureaucratic society accounts for some of their appeal. When interpersonal relationships are perceived as indifferent, uncaring, or unloving, however, disaffection may arise.

Disillusionment refers to disbelief and doubts that arise from cognitive dissonance. It suggests that the interpretive framework by which the believer defines and orders the world has come apart. The truth value of the movement's ideology or doctrine is questioned, removing the moral authority of the organization and its leaders. While the true believer is willing to endure innumerable sacrifices to further the message and mission of the group, the disillusioned member is immobilized by disappointment and confusion. Disillusionment increases the likelihood of critical re-evaluation of one's faith and the investigation of alternative belief-systems or interpretive frameworks.

Disaffiliation refers to the severance of organizational ties and membership. Individuals disaffiliate when they discontinue participation in a specific movement organization (MO), though not necessarily the "general social movement" (see McCarthy and Zald 1977; Blumer 1946, p. 199). This may involve relinquishment of official duties, resignation, or generally just one's disinvolvement with the organization in any formal capacity. Disaffiliation is analytically distinct from disaffection and disillusionment in that it points to disavowal of an MO. Thus, while disaffected or disillusioned members may remain affiliated with the movement, at least temporarily, the disaffiliated individual has quit the organization.

This delineation makes clear what is often not stated or is even misunderstood. Because conversion is a dynamic process that must be continually reinvigorated, the religious group constantly faces the prospect of waning commitment and defection. Dissatisfaction, disagreements, and doubts arise on a regular basis. Disillusionment or disaffection may surface leading the adherent either to redouble his/her commitment or to withdraw. Recognizing the various dimensions of defection facilitates seeing how individuals must disengage themselves at several points of attachment in order to complete the act of leaving.

This delineation also explains why there appears to be some confusion over terms such as deconversion and exiting (is deconversion the same as disaffiliation?). We suggest that the confusion often reflects a failure to account for the multidimensionality of the event. Further studies should enhance our ability to make these distinctions and broaden the social scientific understanding of defection.

# METHODOLOGICAL ISSUES: THE VIABILITY OF APOSTATE ACCOUNTS AND THE RHETORIC OF CHANGE

Data on both conversion to new religious movements and defection from them are derived primarily from retrospective reports of those who have gone through the experience. While direct observation and longitudinal analysis would yield more objective and firsthand information of the events themselves, such techniques have their limitations—time constraints, inability to know when and where such events will occur, and the subjective interpretations of events by those experiencing them. While there are those who argue that such verbal accounts should be accepted as valid and reliable records of past events (Bruce and Wallis 1983; Wallis and Bruce 1983), many researchers studying both commitment and defection from religious groups argue that such accounts reveal more about the current status and self-identity of the individual than the situation being recalled. Taylor's (1978) comment regarding accounts of conversion is equally applicable to defectors—what the respondent chooses to tell the researcher is that which requires explanation, and it does not of itself constitute that explanation.

There are three major issues that impact the validity of accepting accounts of previous events and experiences at face value: (1) retrospective reporting, (2) social and organizational factors influencing reconstruction, and (3) temporal variability of accounts.

## Retrospective Reporting

As Mead (1934), Berger and Luckmann (1967), Scott and Lyman (1968) and numerous ethnomethodologists and everyday life sociologists (Garfinkel 1967; Cicourel 1964; Sacks 1972) remind us, personal biographies and identities are constantly being redefined in the light of current experiences. The validity of retrospective accounts, therefore, is what they tell us about the person's present situation and interpretation of past events. Both conversion and defection represent dramatic shifts in personal identity and events that beg causal explanation, both to others and to oneself. In an effort to understand and make sense of past decisions, defectors reconstruct their pasts in ways that fit in with their present lives. One aspect of this biographical reconstruction is the need to justify why one joined in the first place.

An exiter's family and friends frequently berate the group and rejoice in the apostate's freedom while the individual himself/herself experiences ambivalent feelings about the events (Beckford 1985; Barker 1984; Wright and Piper 1986). One reason for this ambivalence is the need to understand and justify to oneself and others the reasons for participation and commitment. To admit to being brainwashed or pressured into membership is to admit vulnerability and lack of integrity; to claim weakness and need for group support is also humiliating. Either admission is associated with guilt and failure. The fact of abandoning previous convictions is a threat to personal character and stability.

Someone who has left a religious movement is also likely to have become disillusioned and may well regret joining. One way to explain one's membership to others, and to oneself, is to blame the movement's persuasive influence rather than accepting responsibility for having joined. Leaving is therefore explained in terms of enlightenment and the recognition of external pressures. In an attempt to incorporate past experience with current identity, apostates reflect back on and reinterpret the exiting process in a framework that fits in with their present self-conception.

In his study of ex-Moonies, Beckford (1985) describes the reluctance of many defectors to denigrate their former group while significant others, such as family members, were often anti-cultists eager to show the harm of a "destructive cult." In addition to the struggle to justify conversion and commitment, many ex-Moonies also had pleasant memories of friends and events in the movement. In fact, Beckford (1984) observes that some informants wanted to preserve their memories of the rewarding experiences in the group. Many missed the camaraderie of the group at a time when they were laboring to reenter family and peer situations.

Barker (1984) argues that retrospective reporting is especially distorted in the case of defectors who have been deprogrammed. Part of the deprogramming process is to convince members that they have been brainwashed and to challenge them with contradictory evidence about the group. Part of the deprogramming process is to encourage ex-members to verbalize the atrocities and negative experiences with the group. Skonovd (1983) also makes the point that deprogrammers promote the social reintegration of the ex-devotee by insisting on the brainwashing model of conversion which absolves the individual of responsibility for participation and enhances the possibility of a healthy existence independent of the group. The deprogramee is urged to see the group as a controlling agent that destroys personal and intellectual freedom. Such deprogramming inevitably colors the way ex-members recall their exiting process (see also Solomon 1981; Lewis 1986; Wright 1984).

## Social and Organizational Factors of Reconstruction

In addition to the biographical reconstruction of past events that are influenced by new situations and identities, organizations themselves provide ideologies and frameworks within which apostates construct accounts of their exits. A number of studies demonstrate ways in which organizations influence the accounts ex-members give of the factors causing and the process of leaving. Ebaugh's (1977) research on ex-nuns found that many women who had left religious orders in the years after the Second Vatican Council verbalized their reasons for leaving in terms that were legitimated by renewal in the orders. In other words, they expressed the realization that "they no longer had a vocation" or the fact that organizational change was either too slow or too rapid to suit their individual needs. Likewise, in his study of the Rajneesh colony in Eastern Oregon, Carter (1987) describes variations in the accounts given by defectors contingent upon the progression of events that were taking place in the political turmoil of the commune at the time of defection. Rochford (1985) describes the failure of "ideological work" by ISKCON amidst policy changes regarding "sankirtana," effectively alienating some devotees.

While there is much evidence of the interplay between conversion accounts and organizational ideology in the extensive literature on entering religious movements (Barker 1984; Beckford 1978; Preston 1981; Snow 1976; Snow and Rochford 1983), corresponding research on defection is just beginning to grow. As accounts of exiting accumulate, hopefully researchers will be better attuned to the dynamics of organizational factors and personal interpretations.

### Temporal Variability

Accounts of why apostates leave and descriptions of their exiting process vary over time. The further removed from the exiting experience, the more leavers tend to reconstruct the event in light of what has happened to them in the interim. San Giovanni (1978), for example, found that the longer ex-nuns were out of the convent, the less they felt compelled to reveal and justify their previous role as nuns. Moreover, as ex-nuns gained confidence in their ability to move into secular life and successfully entered new roles, their accounts became less negative and emotionally charged.

A number of studies (Judd et al. 1970; Ebaugh 1977; San Giovanni 1978; Beckford 1985) have found that those ex-members who experience success in their post-exit roles are less likely to regret leaving and to verbalize either their group membership or exit process as negative. The longer individuals have been out of the group, the more likely they have been involved in a number of successful roles and therefore the less likely they will be to harbor strong negative feelings about their prior experience in the group.

In summary, retrospective accounts of the exiting process need to be treated as topics of analysis, not just objective data of past events. They provide valuable evidence of ways in which exiters have integrated their previous group experiences with current biographies, how ideological and structural aspects of groups can influence accounts, and the impact of time factors on interpretive frameworks.

## PERSPECTIVES ON DEFECTION

A variety of theoretical models and perspectives characterize studies of leaving new religions. This section of the paper briefly outlines the major theoretical orientations that have emerged in the literature. They are condensed into the following categories: (1) role theory, (2) causal process models, and (3) social movement theory.

### Role Theory: Defection as Role Exiting

While most of the early work on new religious movements utilized a motivational framework to explain why individuals were attracted to these groups (Festinger et al. 1964; Lofland 1977; Lofland and Stark 1965; Zygmunt 1972), more recent studies (Balch and Taylor 1978; Barker 1984; Bromley and Shupe 1979; Richardson and Stewart 1977) have adopted a role theory model to explain both conversion and defection. Though motivational theories focus on predisposing conditions and needs of potential seekers and connections between these needs and appeals of religious movements (Zygmunt 1972), role theory conceptualizes recruitment, membership, and defection as socially structured events embedded in role relationships. The assumption of role theory is that needs and behavior are shaped by normative expectations that are a part of the social structure of groups. Individual actions, therefore, are influenced and shaped by the expectations which significant others have and which are internalized by the individual.

From a role theory perspective, leaving is a process of role-exiting in which an individual disengages from role behaviors associated with belonging to a particular group and establishes an identity as an ex-member. As Ebaugh (1988b) points out, being an ex is uniquely different from never having been a member of the group and presents unique role challenges. There are four major issues that ex-members have to negotiate in the process of disengaging from the group and reestablishing identity as an ex-group member: (1) incorporating an ex-status, (2) role residual, (3) societal sanctions, and (4) shifting friendship networks.

*Incorporating An Ex-status*

The process of role exiting is two-fold, namely, disengagement from a role that has been meaningful to an individual's self-identity and the re-establishment of identity in a new role that takes into account one's previous role (Ebaugh 1977, 1988a). Disengagement, or the process of separation from a group, is only part of the process of becoming an ex. The defector is faced with incorporating the expectations associated with once having been a member. In addition to justifying to oneself the fact of recruitment and membership in the group for a time, ex's constantly face both challenges and expectations of other people related to their former group affiliation. Many ex-members spend months and years trying to understand and make sense of why and how they were caught up in the group which they now reject. As Wright (1991) points out, withdrawing and learning to incorporate an ex-status into self-identity is similar to that experienced by divorce(e)s. Both the marital dyad and totalistic religions are high commitment groups that socialize individuals to establish close affective ties and intense moral (even sacred) obligations. Defection and disavowal, therefore, are challenges to self-identity that entail incorporating one's previous beliefs and involvement into a current self-definition.

*Role Residual*

Even after leaving a group, many ex's struggle with aspects of "role residual," that is, the identification that they maintain aspects of the role long after they are no longer members. Role residual is a kind of "hangover identity" which makes it difficult to chart the passage to a new role. Rather than making a clean break with previous role expectations, they continue to identify with prescriptions appropriate to members of the group. Beckford (1985) reports that many ex-Moonies expressed lingering support for various aspects of their group and clung to the movement's literature and to their notebooks dating from their initial entry. These materials represented something precious but ambiguous. They amounted to a last tie with their former companions and indicated an emotional ambivalence about totally disavowing the group.

Role residual may also take the form of dreams and psychic phenomena. Ebaugh (1988b) found that among the ex's she studied dreams were related to exit decisions that were difficult and anxiety provoking rather than to ambivalence or regrets about leaving the group. In Beckford's (1985) study, ex-Moonies interpreted their own dreams as symptoms of guilt about abandoning a would-be Messiah who required their help. Most of the ex-Moonies who experienced dreams reported similar episodes when they were in the group, but they were easier to handle in the context of group support. Interestingly, those who reported dreams after leaving the church experienced frightening or threatening themes even though they recalled group membership as pleasant and inspiring. They tended to find life unsettling and dissatisfying after exiting and felt fear, guilt, and sadness at losing better times and friends in the group. Wright (1987a) also reports that many of the ex-cult members he studied experienced periods of personal anxiety and confusion resulting from incomplete transitions to a new role and identity. Jacobs' (1989, p. 112) study of disaffected female devotees also finds that they "often feel adrift, unsure of what they believe in, and uncomfortable with the outside world after leaving the cloistered environment of the religious group."

*Societal Reactions*

One of the most important dynamics in becoming an ex-member of any group is the social reaction of other people to one's having been a member. This is particularly the case for exits out of new religious movements which many define as destructive, autocratic, and malevolent. In addition to the curiosity about why anyone would join such a group, the exiter constantly has to deal with the embarrassment that results from negative evaluations of having been a part of such a devious enterprise. Beckford (1985) reports two patterns among ex-Moonies he interviewed, those who were too ashamed to go out of their parents' homes to be seen in the neighborhood and those who spent as much time as possible away from home in public places. He maintains that both patterns are based on the desire to avoid having to give account of their past actions and suffering the stigma that others attach to having once been a Moonie.

*Shifting Friendship Networks*

Besides adjusting to new role expectations, the exiter also experiences shifts in the people who are important to them. Studies show that it is relatively rare for an ex-member to maintain close ties with members (Beckford 1985; Ebaugh 1977; Jacobs 1989; San Giovanni 1978; Skonovd 1981; Wright 1987a). Defection is threatening to the group in some instances, and then the exiter is likely to be defined as a traitor. Group norms forbid contact with apostates. Even in cases in which exiting is not viewed negatively, it is difficult for ex-members to sustain relationships when interests and daily activities begin to diverge from those of group members.

Most ex's develop new friendship networks over time based on emergent interests, jobs, marital situations, and social activities. While it is sometimes hard to cultivate new networks, they frequently serve as a bridge or asset in helping the exiter reestablish a new identity apart from previous role expectations. Though some ex-members may continue to have limited contact with friends still in the group, the intensity of the relationships tends to change.

A role theory approach to defection has sensitized researchers to a number of crucial issues, especially the normative expectations that influence and shape individual predispositions to join, belong, and disengage from religious movements. Individual actions are seen in the context of broader social structures that define norms, values, and self-definitions internalized by persons experiencing various social processes such as recruitment into and withdrawal out of religious movements.

## Causal Process Models: Defection as Sequential Disengagement

An essential part of conversion research has involved efforts to model the sequence of causal factors that culminate in conversion. Lofland and Stark's (1965) seminal work on conversion to the DP cult laid the groundwork for this type of approach. It is not surprising that a former student of Lofland pioneered the causal process model of defection (Skonovd 1979, 1981, 1983). Skonovd's research is based on a study of 60 former members of nine "totalistic" religious groups, including the Unification Church, the Church of Scientology, and several Buddhist sects. Skonovd (1979) outlines a stage-like process of deconversion involving the following sequence: (1) crisis, (2) review and reflection, (3) disaffection, (4) withdrawal, (5) cognitive transition, and (6) cognitive reorganization.

One critical flaw in Skonovd's research is the failure to distinguish between deprogrammed and voluntary leavers. The two groups of defectors are treated as an undifferentiated sample, making generalization about features of the disengagement process strained. Research clearly shows that deprogramming involves a distinctly different set of circumstances, sequence of events, or episodes and certainly different emotional responses on the part of defectors (Galanter 1983, 1989; Levine 1984; Lewis 1986; Lewis and Bromley 1988; Solomon 1981; Wright 1984, 1987a).

Wright (1983, 1984, 1986, 1987a, 1988) has conducted a study of purely voluntary defectors utilizing matched samples of leavers and stayers of three new religious movements (Unification Church, Hare Krishna, Children of God).

This research also attempts to construct a causal process model of disengagement, building on the work of Skonovd and others. By introducing a comparison group in the research design, Wright is able to formulate and test a set of hypotheses. He isolates four sources of disruption ("precipitating factors") among leavers that "set the disengagement process into motion" (1987a, p. 50). These are (1) a breakdown in members' insulation from the outside world, (2) the development of unofficial or unregulated dyadic relations, (3) the perceived lack of success in achieving world transformation, and (4) inconsistencies between the actions of leaders and the ideals they symbolically represent.

At a second stage of disengagement, individuals gravitating toward defection seek to arm themselves with additional justification for withdrawal. These are identified as ancillary factors and include the affective pulls of parents and family (Wright and Piper 1986), returning to school, and the discovery of alternative religious belief systems. It is argued that ancillary factors by themselves are not likely to be regarded as valid reasons to defect. They are effective only in the wake of powerful triggering episodes or precipitating factors.

At still another stage, individuals are shown to select different modes of exit. While Skonovd suggests that some deliberate planning is present in the actions of leavers, his findings do not reveal much diversity in exiting modes. He finds that an overwhelming majority leave stealthily and that a "public leave-taking is extremely difficult, if not impossible, for most" (1981, p. 122). However, Wright's study uncovers three distinct exiting modes: covert, overt, and declarative. Covert departures (42 percent) refer to clandestine exits deployed to circumvent resistance or interference by members. Overt departures (the most common, 47 percent) are conducted openly but without fanfare and typically involve some unsuccessful negotiation efforts with leaders. Declarative exits (11 percent) are dramatic announcements of departure often incorporating displays of anger and vented frustration. A significant correlation is shown between exiting strategy and length of membership. The vast majority (92 percent) of covert defectors were "novices" (less than 1 year of involvement) while 79 percent of overt and declarative defectors were "veterans" (more than 3 years). These findings suggest that the latter group exhibited greater willingness to confront, make demands, and carefully weigh their decisions to leave.

The final stage of disengagement involves social relocation. Relocation and reintegration are accomplished through the adoption of a new plausibility structure (Berger and Luckmann 1966), helping to seal or finalize the legitimation sequence. Families, college campuses, the workplace, and fundamentalist/evangelical groups are primary channels of reentry for defectors.

In assessing defectors' attitudes toward their former groups, Wright (1987a, p. 87) finds that most are able to assimilate their experiences in a constructive manner and learn from them. Most of the sample (67 percent) said they were "wiser for the experience." Relatively few invoked a "brainwashing" explanation of conversion (9 percent), suggesting that self-initiated withdrawal requires markedly different responses and rationales than for those who are deprogrammed. Disengagement is likened to marital dissolution, both of which are characterized by preparation for departure, the formulation of independent goals and objectives prior to leaving and the struggle with "mixed emotions' and the "management of ambivalence."

A variety of other studies have developed causal process models. Jacobs (1984) has recently proposed a three-stage model of deconversion from nontraditional religious movements. Jacobs conducted in-depth interviews with 40 defectors representing 16 different religious organizations. Approximately half of her respondents came from Hindu-based groups such as the Divine Light Mission. Some studies of causal processes have been conducted in the form of "natural histories" of defection from a single group or movement. Downton (1979, pp. 211-220) describes the evolution of doubt and disaffection of three "premies" (Divine Light Mission) who eventually defect. Balch (1982) identifies a sequence of nine stages of defection in a study of a UFO cult, extending and elaborating on Skonovd's model.

Causal process models are useful analytical schemes, but there remains some debate as to whether they are amenable to theoretical generalization (Beckford 1985). The debate echoes the same arguments generated around causal processes of conversion (Austin 1977; Beckford 1978; Lofland 1977; Richardson and Stewart 1977; Seggar and Kunz 1972; Snow and Machalek 1984). Snow and Machalek (1984) caution against confusing the natural history of a single group as an adequate gauge of causal process. Because conversion (or deconversion) patterns differ from group to group, "the natural history of one group will by no means necessarily record the natural history of another" (1984, p. 184). This helps to "explain divergences reported by those who have tried to apply the Lofland-Stark model to groups for which it was never intended" (1984, p. 184). For example, the application of this model to groups such as Alcoholics Anonymous (Greil and Rudy 1984) or a communal experiment sponsored by Campus Crusade for Christ (Austin 1977) might be inappropriate because they are not "deviant" groups (Richardson 1978). However, some applications that do qualify still raise questions about particular features of the model (Snow and Phillips 1980), if not the empirical generalizability of causal processes. Snow and Machalek do not think conversion is a result of idiosyncratic processes that are not amenable to empirical generalizations. They contend the mere labeling of stages does not specify the causal relationships responsible for conversion.

### Social Movement Theory: Defection as a Consequence of Movement Transformation, Decline, or Failure

New religions are social movements that fluctuate in their development, variously experiencing growth, decline, and change. In these processes, a wide range of internal and external pressures affects the success and failure of social movements over time. By focusing on social movement organizations (MOs) as units of analysis, important information can be learned about factors that facilitate or promote attrition.

Zald and Garner (1987) suggest that members may be lost through three types of changes that occur in movement transformation. The first is "goal transformation," referring to pragmatic leadership's replacement of unattainable goals with more diffuse goals so that the organization can pursue a broader range of targets. Goal transformation typically moves the organization in a more rational and conservative direction of accommodation to dominant societal consensus. The second type of change is "organizational maintenance," described as a special form of goal transformation "in which the primary activity of the organization becomes the maintenance of membership, funds and other requirements of organizational existence" (Zald and Garner 1987, p. 121). The third type of change is "oligarchization," defined as the narrow concentration of power into the hands of a minority in the organization (this type assumes a democratic decision-making structure).

For our purposes, the first two types of movement transformation identified by Zald and Garner are relevant to new religious movements. Goal transformation is evident in studies of ISKCON as the organization in recent years has moved away from the previous objective of building a legion of monastic priests (sannyasin) and toward establishing a congregational membership among middle-class, Hindu immigrants from India (Gelberg 1987, 1988; Rochford 1985, 1987, 1989). Rochford observes that most Indian members will not commit to the more austere demands of discipleship designed and instituted by the movement's founder, possibly contributing to fragmentation and the disaffection of purists. Other developments of goal transformation may be found in ISKCON, the Unification Church and a number of other new religions. Accommodation of organizational goals to the dominant societal consensus is readily apparent in the Unification Church's shift away from unconventional methods of fundraising (street soliciting) in favor of the placement of members in full-time employment in church-sponsored businesses (Bromley 1985; Richardson 1982, 1985, 1988). Such developments reflect the inherent problems of aging memberships with full-blown families and increased economic needs (Barker 1987). Many local centers or temples lack the financial base to support families, forcing members to find secular jobs and become self-supporting. Outside the insulated confines of the communal centers, many devotees experience weakened ties to the organization and lose interest.

Organizational maintenance, a special form of goal transformation, is evident in the benign preoccupation with organizational existence and survival in a changing cultural climate. Many new religious movements gained their popularity during the height of the youthful counterculture, the late 1960s and early 1970s. But the decade of the 1980s did not provide the cultural milieu conducive to cult growth. Consequently, many new religions moved toward explicit strategies of amelioration and accommodation, attempting to soften their public images. ISKCON lobbied for legitimacy as an "ethnic church" (Gelberg 1988), and the Unification Church attempted to give Reverend Moon a low public profile after the tax evasion case by promoting Dr. Mose Durst to President and financing national tours to "share the new image of the church"

(Wright 1987b). Groups such as the Children of God and the Church of Scientology de-emphasized "exclusivity" and intolerance, claiming to accept others who did not maintain all their beliefs and loyalties (Wallis 1987). Nonetheless, most of these movements witnessed high attrition rates as they became entrenched in organizational maintenance. This condition or state is similar to what Zald and Garner (1987, p. 130) call a "becalmed movement." A becalmed movement is one that has found a niche in society, but its growth has slowed or stagnated. Research shows that members may be lost to becalmed movements because of unrealized claims of a new social order or world transformation, leading to deep disillusionment (Wright 1987a). Institutional entrenchment may signal a stage in the "natural history" of social movements moving toward decline (Mauss 1975), though it is not inevitable.

Problems of attrition may rise also in response to organizational shifts or restructuring. Toch (1965, p. 168) has argued that shifts within a social movement may have the effect of "reshuffling ...sustaining forces." Because members come to rely on the familiarity and security of the congenial group, sudden changes or disruptions can be catalysts of disaffection and withdrawal. Skonovd (1981, p. 53) asserts that abrupt changes within routine activities of members are highly correlated with defection. Wallis (1982) contends that a major shift in the organizational structure of the Children of God in 1978 resulted in a wave of defections. Moses David Berg, the charismatic leader and founder of the movement, dismantled the top leadership positions in an effort to defuse a potential power struggle. Wallis (1982, pp. 92-93) reports that many senior leaders left in bitter disappointment and many rank and file members "were lost to the movement entirely."

Defection may simply be a result of movement decline or failure in some cases. Balch and Cohig (1985) have conducted a study of the collapse of the Love Family/Church of Armageddon in Seattle. They found that the dissolution of the group was precipitated by major organizational changes requiring socially insulated members to work outside the community in secular jobs. As these members became financially independent, they demanded a greater voice in decisions and policies, creating conflicts between the charismatic leader (Love Israel) and a growing contingent of disgruntled followers. Love Israel resisted any concessions of power to dissidents and eventually the conflict grew to insurmountable proportions. By the end of 1983, Balch and Cohig estimate that 85 percent of the membership had defected (see also Balch et al. 1983).

Carter (1987) has chronicled the demise of Rajneeshpuram in Oregon after the deportation of the commune's leader, Bhagwan Shree Rajneesh. Carter (1987, p. 162) observes that the "commune maintained it would continue, but frozen bank accounts and the absence of the Bhagwan soon made it apparent that the commune would be closed." Most of the residents of Rajneeshpuram have "returned to the world" except for a small core of maintenance staff. Some have returned to prior occupations while others have been aided in finding "appropriate jobs through Rajneesh networks" (1987, p. 163).

## Psychosocial Disruption: Expulsion and Extraction

Defection may be the result (direct or indirect) of the intervening actions of social others. The religious organization to which the convert belongs may take actions to expel the individual under specified circumstances. In other cases, parents or family members may employ deprogrammers or "exit counselors" to dissuade the member from continuing.

### Expulsion

Expulsion is an important form of disaffiliation though it has not received adequate attention from scholars. While not a common practice in new religions (or old religions), we do have some record of expulsion. Galanter (1983) has observed that several individuals in a Unification Church training center were asked to leave because they exhibited signs of "psychological instability." Stoner and Parke (1977, p. 211) describe the case of a Krishna devotee who was expelled because of a mother's dogged efforts to report building code violations in a Brooklyn temple. Zablocki (1980) records several accounts of expulsion among recent communal movements. Beckford (1985, p. 159) reports that some members of the Unification Church in Britain "were forced to leave" because "(t)hey were accused of being lazy, insubordinate or disruptive." Barker (1988) echoes these findings in her study of the Unification Church.

Richardson et al. (1986) offer an informative discussion of expulsion within a typology of disaffiliation. They argue that expulsion is the easiest type of disaffiliation to accomplish for the communal organization and the most difficult for the member to resist. The inverse is held to be true for noncommunal organizations. Noncommunal groups typically have fewer ties with members making forced disaffiliation problematic unless the organization has the cooperation of the individual. The member may refuse to relinquish claims of identification, challenge organizational authorities, and even successfully mobilize a schismatic faction. Communal groups, by contrast, can literally push the dissident out the door. Or if this type of physical coercion is not approved, the group can implement "shunning" to effectively isolate the dissident and thereby bring social and psychological pressures to bear on the situation. Because communal organizations are more highly regulated than noncommunal groups, exercising control over membership and participation is a distinct advantage.

Richardson et al. (1986) also suggest that the likelihood of expulsion is correlated with the life-cycle of the movement. In the formative stage, its leaders may be less concerned about who is allowed to affiliate. The movement can ill afford to be selective in this important stage of mobilization, and efforts of intensive socialization are deployed to countermand the lack of selectivity (see Bromley and Shupe 1979). After the movement has become established, however, greater selectivity is exercised in allowing people to share limited resources and power, and less tolerance may be shown toward recreants.

According to Robbins (1988, p. 98), issues regarding expulsion from new religious movements generally involve the following: (1) dissidence, insubordination, and challenges to authority; (2) rule violations; and (3) the incapacity of those devotees who cannot care for themselves, or who may embarrass the group or be unable to contribute to enhancing the movement's resources (see also Rochford 1985; Straus 1986; Wallis 1977). The few studies available indicate support for Robbins' observation. In any case, more research is needed for a full understanding of the role of expulsion.

*Extraction*

Extraction refers to techniques of intervention that induce defection. Some common methods include deprogramming, rehabilitation, exit counseling, and so-called exit therapies, such as Promoting Voluntary Reevaluation (see Clark et.al. 1981; Galper 1982; Goldberg and Goldberg 1982; Hassan 1988; Ross and Langone 1988; Singer 1978, 1979; Schwartz and Kaslow 1982; Solomon 1981). Studies of the anti-cult movement reveal that in the early stages, most efforts of extraction were cases of coercive deprogrammings (Bromley and Shupe 1987). The movement more recently has experienced increased "professionalization...in which research and the roles of psychiatrists, psychologists and social workers have become more salient" (Robbins 1988, p. 6). The techniques of extraction thus may be coercive or voluntary depending on the practitioner and the willingness of the devotee to participate in the dissuasion effort. It appears that some forms of exit counseling take place after disaffection or disaffiliation has already occurred (Rothbaum 1988). In these instances, the counseling is not a form of extraction at all. In other cases, however, the imposition of the therapy is clearly foisted on the committed but unsuspecting convert in a manner that belies the meaning and intent of the term "counseling" (e.g., Hassan 1988, pp. 123-124).

Richardson et al. (1986) recognize extraction as a type of disaffiliation from new religious movements. They divide extraction into two types, re-evaluation (noncoercive) and coercive deprogramming. These are broken down into a four-cell typology and analyzed according to type of organization (communal vs. noncommunal). They report that coercive extractions in communal groups are the most difficult to accomplish (i.e., have the lowest success rates) because communal organizations exercise greater control over the time and activities of their members and tend to build stronger social ties. On the other hand, noncoercive extractions in noncommunal groups are said to be the easiest to accomplish, facing fewer social controls and weaker group ties.

An important component in the process of extraction is the use of labeling the potential defector as a "victim." Deprogrammers and exit counselors typically frame the conversion process as a form of brainwashing or mind control which releases the "victim" from responsibility and facilitates a rapid adoption of an alternative perspective. Redefinition of conversion events and stigmatization of "cult servitude" in the context of deprogrammings are analogous to what Garfinkel (1956) calls "degradation ceremonies." Successful extraction depends on the subject's acceptance of the victimization account, which he or she may do to simply relieve themselves from the barrage of degradation (Galanter 1989, pp. 166-170).

The line of demarcation between coercive and voluntary techniques of intervention is not always clear because pressures by parents, friends, or anti-cult groups, who become part of the process, are often intense. The ethical contradiction of using techniques that involve manipulation and deception—the techniques for which they condemn cults—is not lost on exit counselors who express real ambivalence about them (e.g., Ross and Langone 1988, p. 69).

Some exit therapists seek to justify the use of these techniques claiming benevolent motives, which amounts to a means-justifies-the-end argument. "Covert interventions involve using deception," says one exit counselor, "something I accuse cults of doing, which makes me uncomfortable. However, I am not trying to make someone into my follower (Hassan 1988, p. 124). A similar justification based on higher motives is offered by exit therapists Ross and Langone (1988, p. 69): "The parents' goal is to protect and advance their child's well-being; the cult's goal is to fulfill the leader's desires." Most exit counselors believe that they are providing a service to help families in trouble, and thus are able to reconcile the apparent inconsistencies in their practices.

However, there is contravening clinical evidence which suggests that extraction may cause *more* emotional and psychological harm to the convert than parental inaction (Levine 1984; Galanter 1989). Levine, who studied more than 800 joiners of radical religious and political cults, argues that youth who join these types of groups are engaged in a desperate attempt to establish post-adolescent identity and autonomy. They are often individuals who are unable to create an identity independent of their parents. By engineering a "radical departure," youth actually exploit the cult in the service of growing up. In other words, these groups function to aid the separation and establishment of an independent self. He finds that forced intervention is damaging to the individual because it disrupts the process of post-adolescent separation from one's parents, a necessary prerequisite to adult independence and decision making. Levine cautions against coercive deprogramming. He states that over 90 percent of these radical excursions end in a voluntary return home within two years. Perhaps more important, most defectors "are able to find gratification and significance in the middle-class world they had totally abjured" (Levine 1984, p. 15). Life-cycle and age-specific effects play an important role in explaining youthful experimentation, a finding firmly supported by others (Beckford 1985; Wallis 1987; Wilson 1987; Wright and Piper 1986).

## SUMMARY AND FUTURE RESEARCH

The research on disengagement from new religious movements has grown substantially over the last decade so that we now have a modest, but rapidly growing, corpus of studies. To date, there is an impressive convergence of findings indicating marked progress in understanding the factors and conditions that contribute to disaffection and withdrawal. Nonetheless, there is still much work to be done.

Future research should be able to benefit from problems and findings identified in previous studies affecting apostate accounts. Several conditions and variables appear to have a significant influence on reports and require attention, including (1) mode of exit (voluntary vs. coercive), (2) length of time between exit and account/interview, (3) defector's ability to achieve successful role transition, and (4) attitudes of family and friends in the post-involvement stage. Careful attention to these factors should increase the viability of apostate accounts by giving the researcher some clearly defined limits or parameters of the data.

More attention needs to be focused on differential defection patterns by age, sex, length of membership, type of conversion (e.g., Lofland and Skonovd, 1981) and type of organization (communal vs. noncommunal, totalistic vs. "normative" [Etzioni 1975], charismatic vs. bureaucratic, inclusive vs. exclusive). Existing studies require replication and refinement of theoretical models and methods, as well as specified causal factors, exiting modes, and reentry and readjustment patterns.

A major challenge to sociologists will lie in forging a stronger linkage between exiting and mainstream sociological concepts and theory. While the particular study of cult defection has merit in its own right, the value it has for deepening our understanding of key interactional and structural processes cannot be disregarded. The study of cult withdrawal has important implications and offerings for organizational change and attrition, work overload and "burnout," desocialization, status passage, role transition, and social movement theory.

## REFERENCES

Austin, R.L. 1977. "Empirical Adequacy of Lofland's Conversion Model." *Review of Religious Research* 18: 282-287.
Balch, R.W. 1982. "When the Light Goes Out Darkness Comes: A Study of Defection from a Totalistic Cult." Paper presented at the Third International Conference on Religious Movements, Orcas Island, WA.
Balch, R.W., and J. Cohig. 1985. "The Love Family: Disintegration of Utopia." Paper presented at the annual meetings of the Society for the Scientific Study of Religion, Savannah, GA.
Balch, R.W., G. Farnsworth, and S. Wilkins. 1983. "Reactions to Disconfirmed Prophecy in a Millennial Sect." *Sociological Perspectives* 26: 137-158.
Balch, R.W., and D. Taylor. 1978. "Seekers and Saucers: The Role of Cultic Milieu in Joining a UFO Cult." Pp. 43-64 in *Conversion Careers: In and Out of the New Religions,* edited by J.T. Richardson. Beverly Hills, CA: Sage.
Barker, E. 1984. *The Making of a Moonie.* London: Basil Blackwell.
————. 1987. "Quo Vadis? The Unification Church." Pp. 141-152 in *The Future of New Religious Movements,* edited by D.G. Bromley and P.E Hammond. Macon, GA: Mercer University Press.
————. 1988. "Defection From the Unification Church: Some Statistics and Distinctions." Pp. 166-184 in *Falling From the Faith: Causes and Consequences of Religious Apostasy,* edited by D.G. Bromley. Newbury Park, CA: Sage.
Beckford, J.A. 1978. "Through the Looking-Glass and Out the Other Side: Withdrawal from Reverend Moon's Unification Church." *Archives De Sciences Sociales des Religions* 45: 95-116.

————. 1984. "Holistic Imagery and Ethics in New Religious and Healing Movements." *Social Compass* 31: 259-272.

————. 1985. *Cult Controversies: The Societal Response to New Religious Movements.* London: Tavistock.

Beckford, J.A., and J.T. Richardson. 1983. "A Bibliography of New Religious Movements in the U.S. and Europe." *Social Compass* 30: 111-135.

Berger, P.L., and T. Luckmann. 1967. *The Social Construction of Reality.* Garden City, NY: Doubleday.

Blumer, H. 1946. "Collective Behavior." Pp. 167-219 in *New Outline of the Principles of Sociology,* edited by A.M. Lee. New York: Barnes and Noble.

Bohannon, P. 1970. *Divorce and After.* Garden City, NY: Doubleday.

Bromley, D.G. 1985. "Financing the Millennium: The Economic Structure of the Unificationist Movement." *Journal of the Scientific Study of Religion* 24: 253-275.

————. 1991. "Unraveling Religious Disaffiliation: The Meaning and Significance of Falling From the Faith in Contemporary Society." *Counseling and Values* 35: 164-185.

Bromley, D.G., and A.D. Shupe. 1979. *"Moonies" in America: Cult, Church and Crusade.* Beverly Hills, CA: Sage.

————. 1987. "The Future of the Anticult Movement." Pp. 221-234 in *The Future of New Religious Movements,* edited by D.G. Bromley and P.E. Hammond. Macon, GA: Mercer University Press.

Bruce, S., and R.L. Wallis. 1983. "Accounting For Action: Defending the Common Sense Heresy." *Sociology* 17: 97-105.

Carter, L.F. 1987. "The 'New Renunciates' of the Bhagwan Shree Rajneesh: Observations and Identification of Problems of Interpreting New Religious Movements." *Journal for the Scientific Study of Religion* 26: 148-172.

Cicourel, A. 1964. *Method and Measurement in Sociology.* New York: Free Press.

Clark, J., M.D. Langone, R. Schacter, and R. Daly. 1981. *Destructive Cult Conversion: Theory, Research and Practice.* Weston, MA: American Family Foundation.

Downton, J.V. 1979. *Sacred Journeys: The Conversion of Young Americans to Divine Light Mission.* New York: Columbia University Press.

Ebaugh, H.R. 1977. *Out of the Cloister: A Study of Organizational Dilemmas.* Austin: University of Texas Press.

————. 1988a. "Leaving Catholic Convents: Toward a Theory of Disengagement." Pp. 100-121 in *Falling From the Faith,* edited by D.G. Bromley. Newbury Park, CA: Sage.

————. 1988b. *Becoming an Ex: The Process of Role Exit.* Chicago: University of Chicago Press.

Eichel, S.K., L.D. Eichel, and R. Eisenberg. 1984. "Mental Health Interventions in Cult-Related Cases: Preliminary Investigations of Outcomes." *Cultic Studies Journal* 1: 156-166.

Etzioni, A. 1975. *A Comparative Analysis of Complex Organization: On Power, Involvement and Their Correlates.* New York: Free Press.

Festinger, L., H.W. Riecken, and S. Schachter. 1964. *When Prophecy Fails.* New York: Harper Torchbooks.

Gager, J.G. 1975. *Kingdom and Community.* Englewood Cliffs, NJ: Prentice-Hall.

Galanter, M. 1983. "Unification Church ('Moonie') Dropouts: Psychological Readjustment After Leaving a Charismatic Religious Group." *American Journal of Psychiatry* 140: 984-989.

————. 1984. "Moonies Get Married: A Psychiatric Follow-Up of a Charismatic Religious Sect." *American Journal of Psychiatry* 143: 1245-1249.

————. 1989. *Cults: Faith, Healing and Coercion.* New York: Oxford University Press.

Galper, M. 1982. "The Cult Phenomenon: Behavioral Science Perspectives Applied to Therapy." Pp. 141-150 in *Cults and Family,* edited by F. Kaslow and M.B. Sussman. New York: Haworth.

Garfinkel, H. 1956. "Conditions of Successful Degradation Ceremonies." *American Journal of Sociology* 61: 420-424.

————. 1967. *Studies in Ethnomethodology.* Englewood Cliffs, NJ: Prentice-Hall.

136 STUART A. WRIGHT and HELEN ROSE EBAUGH

Gelberg, S.J. 1987. "The Future of Krishna Consciousness in the West: An Insider's Perspective."
    Pp. 187-209 in *The Future of New Religious Movements,* edited by D.G. Bromley and
    P.E. Hammond. Macon, GA: Mercer University.
_____. 1988. "The Fading of Utopia: ISKCON in Transition." Paper presented at the annual
    meetings of the Society for the Scientific Study of Religion, Chicago, IL.
Goldberg, L., and W. Goldberg. 1982. "Group Work with Former Cultists." *Social Work* 27: 165-
    170.
Greil, A.L., and D. Rudy. 1984. "Social Cocoons: Encapsulation and Identity Transformation
    Organizations." *Sociological Inquiry* 54: 260-278.
Hassan, S. 1988. *Combatting Cult Mind Control.* Rochester, VT: Park Street Press.
Jacobs, J.L. 1984. "The Economy of Love in Religious Commitment: The Deconversion of Women
    From Non-Traditional Religious Movements." *Journal for the Scientific Study of Religion*
    23: 155-171.
_____. 1989. *Divine Disenchantment: Deconverting form New Religions.* Bloomington:
    Indiana University Press.
Judd, G., G. Burch, and T. Mills. 1970. *Ex-Pastors: Why Men Leave the Ministry.* Philadelphia:
    Pilgrim Press.
Kim, B. 1979. "Religious Deprogramming and Subjective Reality." *Sociological Analysis* 40: 197-207.
Levine, S. 1984. *Radical Departures: Desperate Detours to Growing Up.* New York: Harcourt
    Brace Jovanovich.
Lewis, J. 1986. "Reconstructing the 'Cult' Experience." *Sociological Analysis* 47: 151-159.
Lewis, J., and D.G. Bromley. 1988. "The 'Cult Information Disease': A Misattribution of Cause?"
    *Journal for the Scientific Study of Religion* 26: 508-522.
Lofland, J. 1977. *Doomsday Cult: A Study of Proselytization, Conversion and Maintenance of
    Faith.* Enlarged ed. New York: Irvington.
Lofland, J., and N.L. Skonovd. 1981. "Conversion Motifs." *Journal for the Scientific Study of
    Religion* 20: 373-385.
Lofland, J., and R. Stark. 1965. "Becoming a World Saver: A Theory of Conversion to a Deviant
    Perspective." *American Sociological Review* 30: 862-875.
Maleson, F.G. 1981. "Dilemmas in Evaluation and Management of Religious Cultists." *American
    Journal of Psychiatry* 138: 925-929.
Mauss, A.L. 1975. *Social Movements as Social Problems.* Philadelphia: Lippincott.
McCarthy, J.D., and M.N. Zald. 1977. "Resource Mobilization and Social Movements: A Partial
    Theory." *American Journal of Sociology* 82: 1212-1241.
Mead, G.H. 1934. *Mind, Self and Society.* Chicago: University of Chicago Press.
Preston, D.L. 1981. "Becoming a Zen Practitioner." *Sociological Analysis* 42: 47-55.
Rambo, L.R. 1982. "Bibliography: Current Research on Religious Conversion." *Religious Studies
    Review* 8: 146-159.
Richardson, J.T. 1978. *Conversion Careers: In and Out of the New Religions.* Beverly Hills, CA:
    Sage.
_____. 1982. "Financing the New Religions: Comparative and Theoretical Considerations."
    *Journal for the Scientific Study of Religion* 21: 255-268.
_____. 1985. "The 'Deformation' of New Religions: Impacts of Societal and Organizational
    Factors." Pp. 163-175 in *Cults, Culture and the Law,* edited by T. Robbins, W. Shepherd,
    and J. McBride. Chico, CA: Scholars Press.
_____, ed. 1988. *Money and Power in the New Religions.* Lewiston, NY: Edwin Mellen.
Richardson, J.T., and M. Stewart. 1977. "Conversion Process Models and the Jesus Movement."
    *American Behavioral Scientist* 20: 24-42.
Richardson, J.T., J. van der Lans, and F. Derk. 1986. "Leaving and Labeling: Voluntary and
    Coerced Disaffiliation from New Religious Social Movements." *Research in Social
    Movements* 9: 97-126.
Robbins, T. 1984. "Constructing Cultist 'Mind Control'." *Sociological Analysis* 45: 241-256.
_____. 1988. *Cults, Converts and Charisma.* Newbury Park, CA: Sage.

Robbins, T., and D. Anthony. 1982. "Deprogramming, Brainwashing and the Medicalization of New Religious Movements." *Social Problems* 29: 283-297.

Rochford, E.B. 1985. *Hare Krishna in America.* New Brunswick, NJ: Rutgers University Press.

————. 1987. "Dialectical Processes in the Development of Hare Krishna: Tension, Public Definition and Strategy." Pp. 109-122 in *The Future of New Religious Movements,* edited by D.G. Bromley and P.E. Hammond. Macon, GA: Mercer University Press.

Ross, J.C., and M.D. Langone. 1988. *Cults: What Parents Should Know.* Boston: American Family Foundation.

Rothbaum, S. 1988. "Between Two Worlds: Issues of Separation and Identity after Leaving a Religious Community." Pp. 205-228 in *Falling from the Faith: Causes and Consequences of Religious Apostasy,* edited by D.G. Bromley. Newbury Park, CA: Sage.

Sacks, H. 1972. "An Initial Investigation of the Usability of Conversational Data for Doing Sociology." Pp. 31-73 in *Studies in Social Interaction,* edited by D. Sudnow. Englewood Cliffs, NJ: Prentice-Hall.

San Giovanni, L. 1978. *Ex-Nuns: A Study of Emergent Role Passage.* Norwood, NJ: Ablex.

Scott, M.B., and S. Lyman. 1968. "Accounts." *American Sociological Review* 33: 46-62.

Schwartz, L.L., and F.W. Kaslow. 1982. "The Cult Phenomenon: Historical, Sociological and Familial Factors Contributing to their Development and Appeal." Pp. 3-30 in *Cults and the Family,* edited by F. Kaslow and M.B. Sussman. New York: Haworth.

Seggar, J., and P. Kunz. 1972. "Conversions: Evaluation of a Step-Like Process for Problem-Solving." *Review of Religious Research* 13: 178-184.

Shupe, A.D., and D.G. Bromley. 1980. *The New Vigilantes: Deprogrammers, Anti-Cultists and The New Religions.* Beverly Hills, CA: Sage.

Singer, M.T. 1978. "Therapy with Ex-Cult Members." *Journal of the National Association of Private Psychiatric Hospitals* 9: 15-19.

————. 1979. "Coming Out of the Cults." *Psychology Today* (January): 72-82.

Skonovd, N.L. 1979. "Becoming Apostate: A Model of Religious Defection." Paper presented at the annual meetings of the Pacific Sociological Association, Anaheim, CA.

————. 1981. *Apostasy: The Process of Defection from Religious Totalism.* Ann Arbor, MI: University Microfilms.

————. 1983. "Leaving the Cultic Religions Milieu." Pp. 91-105 in *The Brainwashing/Deprogramming Controversy,* edited by D.G. Bromley and J.T. Richardson. Lewiston, NY: Edwin Mellen.

Snow, D.A. 1976. "The Nichiren Shoshu Buddhist Movement in America: A Sociological Examination of its Value Orientation, Recruitment Efforts and Spread." Ph.D dissertation, University of California, Los Angeles.

Snow, D.A., and R. Machalek. 1984. "The Sociology of Conversion." *Annual Review of Sociology* 10: 167-190.

Snow, D.A., and C. Phillips. 1980. "The Lofland-Stark Conversion Model: A Critical Reassessment." *Social Problems* 27: 430-447.

Snow, D.A., and E.B. Rochford. 1983. "Structural Availability, the Alignment Process and Movement Recruitment." Paper presented at the annual meetings of the American Sociological Association, Detroit, MI.

Solomon, T. 1981. "Integrating the 'Moonie' Experience: A Survey of Ex-Members of the Unification Church." Pp. 275-294 in *In Gods We Trust,* edited by T. Robbins and D. Anthony. New Brunswick, NJ: Transaction.

Stoner, C., and J.A. Parke. 1977. *All God's Children.* Radner, PA: Chilton.

Straus, R.A. 1986. "Scientology 'Ethics': Deviance, Identity and Social Control in a Cult-Like Social World." *Symbolic Interaction* 9: 67-82.

Taylor, B. 1978. "Recollection and Membership: Converts' Talk and the Ratiocination of Commonality." *Sociology* 12: 316-324.

Toch, H. 1965. *The Social Psychology of Social Movements.* Indianapolis: Bobbs-Merrill.

Ungerleider, J.T., and D.K. Wellisch. 1979. "Coercive Persuasion (Brainwashing), Religious Cults and Deprogramming." *American Journal of Psychiatry* 136: 279-282.

Verdier, P. 1980. *Brainwashing and the Cults.* North Hollywood, CA: Wilshire.

Wallis, R.A. 1977. *The Road to Total Freedom: A Sociological Analysis of Scientology.* New York: St. Martins.

_____. 1982. "Charisma, Commitment and Control in a New Religious Movement." Pp. 73-140 in *Millenialism and Charisma,* edited by R. Wallis. Belfast: Queens University Press.

_____. 1987. "Hostages to Fortune: Thoughts on the Future of Scientology and the Children of God." Pp. 80-90 in *The Future of New Religious Movements,* edited by D.G. Bromley and P.E. Hammond. Macon, GA: Mercer University Press.

Wallis, R.A., and S. Bruce. 1983. "Accounting for Action: Defending the Commonsense Heresy." *Sociology* 17: 97-111.

Wilson, B. 1987. "Factors in the Failure of New Religious Movements." Pp. 30-45 in *The Future of New Religious Movements.* edited by D.G. Bromley and P.E. Hammond. Macon, GA: Mercer University.

Wright, S.A. 1983. "Defection From New Religious Movements: A Test of Some Theoretical Propositions." Pp. 106-121 in *The Brainwashing/Deprogramming Controversy,* edited by D.G. Bromley and J.T. Richardson. Lewiston, NY: Edwin Mellen.

_____. 1984. "Post-Involvement Attitudes of Voluntary Defectors From New Religious Movements." *Journal for the Scientific Study of Religion* 23: 172-182.

_____. 1986. "Dyadic Intimacy and Social Control in Three Cult Movements." *Sociological Analysis* 47: 151-159.

_____. 1987a. *Leaving Cults: The Dynamics of Defection.* Washington, DC: Society for the Scientific Study of Religion.

_____. 1987b. "Cults in the 80s: Social Movement Transformation and Decline." Paper presented at the annual meetings of the Southwestern Social Science Association, Dallas, TX.

_____. 1988. "Leaving New Religious Movements: Issues, Theory and Research." Pp. 143-165 in *Falling From the Faith,* edited by D.G. Bromley. Newbury Park, CA: Sage.

_____. 1991. "Reconceptualizing Cult Coercion and Withdrawal: A Comparative Analysis of Divorce and Apostasy." *Social Forces* 70: 125-145.

Wright, S.A., and E.S. Piper. 1986. "Families and Cults: Familial Factors Related to Youth Leaving or Remaining in Deviant Religious Groups." *Journal of Marriage and the Family* 48: 15-25.

Zablocki, B. 1980. *Alienation and Charisma.* New York: Free Press.

Zald, M.N., and R.A. Garner. 1987. "Social Movement Organizations: Growth, Decay and Change." Pp. 121-142 in *Social Movements in an Organizational Society,* edited by M.N Zald and J.D. McCarthy. New Brunswick, NJ: Transaction.

Zygmunt, J.F. 1972. "When Prophecies Fail." *American Behavioral Scientist* 16: 245-268.

# HEALTH AND HEALING IN
# NEW RELIGIOUS MOVEMENTS

Meredith B. McGuire

## ABSTRACT

Concerns for health and healing are prominent among many new religious and quasi-religious movements. These movements emphasize images of health and the healing process in which emotional, physical, spiritual, social, and ecological aspects are fundamentally interconnected. This paper outlines some analytical foundations for a sociological interpretation of these concerns and reviews recent empirical studies that have begun to document this little-researched phenomenon. The health and healing focus of these new religious and quasi-religious movements may be understood in the context of several broader social developments: the professional dominance of medicine, the medicalization of deviance and other aspects of life, and the place of religion in modern society.

A common feature of many new religious and quasi-religious movements is the special attention they devote to health and healing. Central to many groups are the beliefs and practices they hold about the prevention of illness as well as the strategies of healing they employ when illness does occur. Most of the these groups hold adamantly holistic images of health, and it is thus impossible to separate their attention to individual bodily health from their concern for emotional, spiritual, social, or ecological health. In most instances these beliefs and practices are very different from those promulgated by orthodox medicine.

In recent decades, attention to health and healing has been particularly prominent in New Age groups, but it is also widely evident in Christian

**Religion and the Social Order, Volume 3B, pages 139-155.**
**Copyright © 1993 by JAI Press Inc.**
**All rights of reproduction in any form reserved.**
**ISBN: 1-55938-715-7**

pentecostal as well as some evangelical groups. For example, "charismatic renewal" movements have arisen within established denominations, and because their approach to health and healing differs dramatically from their parent organizations, these groups also belong in an analysis of alternative healing beliefs and practices.

In order to better understand the linkage between alternative religious movements and alternative healing, it will be useful to encompass a wide range of religious movements. For this reason the analysis presented here will compare the beliefs, practices, and recent developments of older "new religious movements." In addition, several nineteenth- and early twentieth-century movements that devoted special attention to health and healing and that are still part of the American religious scene will be discussed. Some of these earlier groups have historical links with newer movements.

This paper will also address important methodological and epistemological issues that are important for developing a less ethnocentric view of nonmedical healing systems. Further, the analysis presented here will emphasize how an understanding of alternative religions' conceptions of health and healing sheds light on larger sociocultural issues.

Examination of new religious groups' interpretations of health and healing is useful not only for an understanding of contemporary groups themselves but also for an understanding of the societies in which alternative healing systems arise. Some observers have assumed that the use of nonmedical healing in modern industrialized societies is due to lack of education or financial resources to pay for medical treatment. In a similar vein, alternative forms of healing are sometimes regarded as simply remnants of rural or old-country folkways, which presumably will disappear as people become urbanized and acculturated. Further, many observers have assumed that in a society with accessible medical care the primary pool of potential recruits to nonmedical healing systems consists of sick persons for whom conventional medical approaches have been unsuccessful.

In fact, many of these religious movements are attracting educated, economically comfortable individuals. Research reveals that many people are attracted first to a religious group's larger belief system and interpersonal associations and only later "try on" and apply its alternative healing beliefs and practices as the need arises (McGuire 1988). That such fully acculturated persons are attracted to nonmedical approaches to health and healing suggests we should examine our assumptions about the larger society and its biomedical system.

## KEY ISSUES FOR ANALYZING HEALING SYSTEMS

The very idea of *health* is a cultural ideal: Each culture defines a set of norms (i.e., desirable, expected conditions and behaviors) as "healthy" and considers serious deviation from those norms to be "unhealthy" or "illness" (see Freund and McGuire 1991). U.S. society's concepts of health and illness are very different from those of, for instance, peoples of Latin America or Africa. Our own culture has, over time, greatly changed its definitions of "health" and "illness." Conditions and behaviors defined as evidence of illness only decades ago are now considered normal or even desirable. Somatic (body) norms have also changed. In different eras our culture has held very different ideals for bodies: How fat or thin (pale or tanned, dainty or muscular, etc.) a body is considered healthy? The following issues are a minimal research agenda for appreciating the place of health and healing in religious movements.

## Definitions of Health, Illness, and Healing

Because conceptions of health and illness are cultural ideals, they can tell us much about the social group which holds them; thus, they are linked with that group's other norms and ideals, such as gender roles or spiritual values. Alternative healing systems, such as those promulgated by recent religious movements, differ significantly from the biomedical healing system in their basic ideas about the nature of health and illness, ways of knowing about illness, health and healing practices, how healing works, and the nature of the power to heal. Especially important are the group's beliefs about people's responsibility—for illness or for therapeutic failure, because these ideas are linked with the groups' larger moral system and sources of guilt, blame and shame.

From a sociological perspective, however, the biomedical system which holds dominance in our society is merely one, among many, competing healing systems. Because it too is a socially constructed system of ideas and practices, it cannot be used to explain or evaluate other healing systems. A preliminary issue that a study of *any* healing system must address, therefore, is: What are the underlying notions of health, illness, healing, and the nature of the body and the person?

## Specific Health and Healing Practices

What practices does each group pursue to maintain health and prevent illness, as well as to heal? These practices are closely linked with each group's particular ideas about health and illness, because these practices derive from their understanding about the causes of illness, the sources of healing power, how health comes about, and how healing works.

For comparison, these same analytical questions should also be applied to modern biomedicine as a healing system. For example, most biomedical notions of illness-causation are focused on the specific etiology of diseases— the idea that each disease is brought about by bodily effects of a discrete, potentially discernible, agent (such as a virus or bacteria). From this belief follow certain practices, such as emphasis on identifying each disease-causing agent (thus, diagnostic practices involving, for example, lab work) and developing interventions to counteract each agent's effects on the body (thus, healing practices of, for example, inoculations, antibiotics, and surgery). Also from this medical belief about illness causation follows medicine's relative inattention to general disease syndromes (which may have multiple causal factors) and to environmental and other factors that may account for why some persons exposed to disease-causing agents do not become diseased (Dubos 1959; Gordon 1988).

The healing beliefs and practices of many new religious movements are tightly interwoven with other aspects of group structure, ritual, and values. Because these movements are often adamantly holistic, it is sometimes difficult to separate health maintenance and healing practices from other group activities, such as prayer and meditation, childcare, art and music, cooking and eating, exercise, and recreation. Healing is also often linked with the group's measures for social control of its members and with the exercise of authority in the organization.

## The Place of Health and Healing in the Group

Attention to health and healing varies from group to group; some groups give little emphasis to health matters or relegate them to peripheral arenas of group life, while other groups make health and healing central themes. The location of these themes may also change over time; some groups may start out emphasizing health issues, but later turn to other focuses, while other groups may increase their attention to health and healing.

A related question is: How is the theme of health articulated with the groups' larger spiritual concerns? Many new religious movements connect the notion of health with holiness, healing with salvation. This linkage is an important contrast with the dominant biomedical healing system, which virtually completely segregates spiritual concerns from physical health; accordingly, each set of concerns should be addressed by separate institutional arrangements: religion and medicine. One of the ways that new religious movements differ from most established denominations is that they are less likely to accept the appropriateness of this separation of spiritual concerns from other arenas of life such as health and healing.

## Societal Responses

Because many new religious movements represent alternatives to both the established religious organizations and the medical establishment, they are sometimes perceived as a challenge or a problem to which the larger society responds. If they are somewhat successful competitors in the religious or medical marketplaces, their mainstream competition may try to mobilize courts, media, and public policy to control or eliminate these alternatives. Due to constitutional restrictions, the state is typically more hesitant to limit religious competition than medical competition. The state has generally supported the monopoly of the medical profession over the domain of health and illness. Indeed, much of the legislative and juridical consideration of new religious movements in recent decades has been couched in terms of medical and psychiatric domains of "expertise," thereby sidestepping issues of religious liberty and religious establishment. On the one hand, the state has legitimate interests in protecting the health and well-being of its citizens; on the other hand, policy and legislative measures are often based on ideas/ideologies that serve powerful interest groups.

These legal and public policy issues for alternative healing approaches, such as practiced in these religious movements, shed light on a number of important features of modern society. An appreciation of these issues is linked with sociological theories about professionalization, medicalization of deviance, help seeking, and broader social change, discussed further below.

## EMPIRICAL KNOWLEDGE: A CRITICAL REVIEW AND RESEARCH AGENDA

A number of recent studies have documented that religious forms of nonmedical healing are relatively widespread in the United States. In one Virginia sample, 14 percent of adults responding affirmed experiencing "healing of a serious disease or physical condition" as a result of prayer (Bromley et al. 1986); this study did not ask about nonphysical healings experienced. An Indiana survey found that some 30 percent of the respondents used prayer for healing and health maintenance (Trier and Shupe 1991). A third study in Ohio (Poloma and Pendleton 1991) found that 72 percent of respondents believed that prayer sometimes results in physical healing; 44 percent had participated in some form of healing ritual, and 32 percent reported experiences of being healed. One large exploratory study, using ethnographic field methods, found numerous religious or spiritual healing groups active in the middle-class and upper-middle-class suburbs of one New Jersey county (McGuire 1988).

A considerable portion of this attention to nonmedical healing derives from older religious healing movements, many of which are now established sects, such as classical Pentecostalism or Christian Science (see Albanese 1991; Allen and Wallis 1976; Fuller 1989; Garrison 1977; Gevitz 1988; Harwood 1977; Judah 1967; Macklin 1974; Nelson 1969; Ness 1980; Nudelman 1976; Nudelman and Nudelman 1972; Pattison 1974; Schoepflin 1986; Skultans 1974; Wacker 1986; Wardwell 1973). Trying to evaluate these older movements' contemporary situation, it is sometimes difficult to distinguish their adherents from those of more recent movements. For example, in Poloma's (1991) study, 86 percent of those who reported experiencing healing as a result of prayer identified themselves as charismatic and/or pentecostal (compared with only 13 percent of the entire sample), but the study did not distinguish classical pentecostals from neo-pentecostals.

One significant difference between some older healing movements and their newer movement counterparts is whether they discourage use of medical help. Christian Science and many classical Christian pentecostal healing groups viewed medical attention as incompatible with religious healing. By contrast, most new religious healing movements combine medical and nonmedical healing approaches (cf. McGuire 1988; Poloma 1991; Trier and Shupe 1991). Nevertheless, both types of Christian healing movements differ from the biomedical system in that they hold religious conceptions of the causes of illness and power to heal. Their understanding of how healing (including medical healing) works is closely linked with their beliefs about God's actions in human lives.

The introduction of an emphasis on healing in the neo-pentecostal movements dates roughly to the latter part of the 1960s and early 1970s, and several studies document the place of healing in Episcopalian and Catholic charismatic groups (Csordas and Cross 1976; Glik 1988; McGuire 1982, 1988; Neitz 1986; Westley 1983). One interesting related development was Spiritual Frontiers Fellowship, a loosely affiliated network of spiritual healers—many kinds of healers from Methodist and Catholic clergy to psychic and metaphysical healers (Wagner 1983).

Furthermore, a growing literature reports empirical studies of healing in what has been roughly dubbed "New Age" movements (English-Lueck 1990; Foltz 1985; Glik 1988; McGuire 1988; Spickard 1990; Wallis 1985a, 1985b; Westley 1983). Most of these forms of healing are emphatically spiritual, even if they eschew a label of "religion." New Age religious movements overlap significantly with the holistic health movement, which is based on a paradigm of health and illness that opposes the paradigm of the dominant medical system. Some common features include: an emphasis on the interrelated effects for health or illness of body, mind, spirit, social and ecological environment; a notion of the fundamental interconnectedness of humans with nature, each other, and the whole cosmos (see Albanese 1990, 1991; Melton et al. 1991).

The Western esoteric and occult traditions have been a primary source of inspiration for some recent movements, such as Satanism (Bainbridge 1978; Moody 1974). Dianetics and Scientology (Wallis 1976, 1977) also claimed a focus on healing.

A related set of new religious movements has arisen in a search for an alternative women's spirituality. Some, such as certain esoteric and neo-pagan groups, are linked with New Age beliefs and practices; others are antagonistic to most New Age approaches, considering them little better than the patriarchal, dominant worldview. Some alternative women's spirituality movements emphasize their continuity with the tradition of the white witch, the wise woman who used her knowledge and craft for healing, protection, and personal efficacy. Many of these contemporary groups have made mutual healing a particular ritual focus (Jacobs 1989, 1990; Neitz 1990).

Initially, studies of the new religious movements of the second half of the twentieth century focused on mental health issues. As more movements themselves became involved with concerns for healing and emphasized their holistic conceptions of health, however, social scientists began to study and interpret all facets of healing.

## Definitions of Health, Illness, and Healing

Most early studies of new religious healing movements contented themselves with sketching those aspects of the groups' *official* teachings that deviated from the biomedical model. Their interest in movements' ideas about health, illness, and healing focused mainly on conversion and commitment to a medically deviant belief system, and on the management of cognitive dissonance when therapies failed. Early researchers generally assumed the truth of the Western biomedical model. Acknowledging that alternate healing systems sometimes "worked," researchers typically explained these successes as folk versions of medical or psychotherapeutic healing methods.

A major shift in focus and methodology began in the 1970s as anthropological approaches to healing systems were applied to Western medicine and other healing systems in industrialized societies. Accordingly, each healing system's underlying definitions of health, illness causation, and healing power must be understood as the cognitive framework within which people's actions make sense (Kleinman 1973; Young 1976). Use of ethnographic methodologies also produced a shift from emphasis on religious movements' official teachings about health and healing to trying to discover what adherents themselves believed.

This new direction is very useful, and we need much more research documenting not only the health beliefs and practices of ordinary members of new religious healing movements but also, for comparative purposes, the health beliefs and practices of persons in mainstream religious groups. Are their beliefs about religion and health all that different from those of new religious healing movements? Are they satisfied with the societal separation of religion and health? Have their life experiences (especially in the broad areas defined as illness by alternative healing groups) led them to a different stance on the need for healing? Are they, perhaps, *also* practicing alternative healing approaches, while active in their denomination? Without more data, we cannot accurately assume that members of the new religious healing movements are all that different from those of established religious groups in this society.

Medical sociologists and anthropologists have begun to examine the conceptions of health and illness held by laypersons (nonphysicians) generally. These studies are useful, because they show that relatively few laypersons hold conceptions of health, illness, and healing that closely resemble ideas promulgated by physicians' medical model (Blaxter 1983; Calnan 1987; Herzlich and Pierret 1987). Some anthropologists suggest that Western physicians lose some healing effectiveness, because they are unaware of the "explanatory models" their patients actually use to understand their illnesses (Kleinman 1988).

New religious healing movements vary widely in their definitions of health, illness, and healing. Empirical studies are only just beginning to describe some of these beliefs and the practices predicated on them. Consistent with their holistic emphasis on mind-body-spirit linkages, these healing groups hold that illness is rarely caused by physical problems alone; rather, underlying spiritual, social, and emotional difficulties work in concert with physical problems to cause an illness. Thus, in order to prevent or to heal illness, one must address all facets. For example, it is not enough to take pills to alleviate physical distress, but therapy also includes making one's social-emotional life more harmonious and attuning one's spiritual life.

These healing groups' ideas about which specific physical, social, emotional, and spiritual factors cause illness vary according to their religious outlook. Some Christian groups, for example, consider sin and the influences of Satan to be significant causal factors; by contrast, some Eastern-inspired religious healing groups refer to imbalance, disconnectedness, and disharmony as causes of illness.

Similarly, new religious healing movements hold alternative ideas about the power to heal. Modern biomedicine's focus is relatively mechanistic: The power to heal results from knowledge and skill in manipulating (e.g., through pharmaceutical or surgical intervention) the affected body system. In the medical model, while some illness is self-limiting (i.e., the disease runs its course or the body heals itself), most healing power resides primarily in professional specialists, qualified by virtue of their training, experience, and technical expertise.

By contrast, religious/spiritual alternative healing systems generally consider professionals' healing power to be very minor (although perhaps useful). Two broad alternative conceptions of healing power appear to characterize most religious healing movements: (1) healing power is concentrated in a transcendent source (described variously as God, cosmic consciousness, universal life-force, etc.), or (2) healing power resides within each individual. In the first approach, healing is accomplished by somehow channeling the transcendent healing power to the person who needs healing (e.g., by prayer, sacraments, laying-on-of-hands, psychic transmission, channeling energies through various substances, etc.). The person being healed participates by eliminating barriers to that flow of healing power (e.g., by confession of sin, reconciliation with God or others, reaffirmation of faith, etc.). In the second approach, healing is accomplished by the individual's attunement with the imminent power (e.g., by centering oneself, achieving greater harmony, balance, and clarity in spiritual, physical, social, and emotional life, etc.) and amplifying that power within by resonating with that of nature, fellow believers, or the entire cosmos (McGuire 1988). We need many more empirical studies of the diverse healing systems (including that of biomedicine) in modern Western societies; each needs to include some exploration of these basic conceptions of health and illness.

## Specific Health and Healing Practices

The health and healing practices of new religious healing groups are predicated on alternative conceptions of health, illness, and healing power. Practices that may otherwise appear weird or irrational are understandable and make sense in the context of the meaning system of their adherents. For example, the therapeutic potential of blessed oil makes sense in light of a group's beliefs about how God's healing power reaches the sick person. The importance of changing a body's alignment or physical balance as a way of producing greater emotional balance makes sense in light of a group's ideas about the holistic interconnection of body and mind and spirit.

Very few studies document healing practices in any detail. We need much more investigation and thick ethnographic description of alternative healing practices, showing their linkage with beliefs. While attention to specific rituals (group or individual) for health and healing is especially important, we also need to elicit adherents' everyday health and healing practices. Most new religious healing movements insist that health is not a separate arena, but is interwoven with all aspects of life; thus, adherents' healing practices include such seemingly ordinary behaviors as preparation of family meals, choosing healing colors for clothing or home use, or holding a sick child a special way.

Another area of health practice that needs much more study is help-seeking. Until very recently, sociological studies of help-seeking have assumed that the "proper" help to be sought was a medical professional. Recent studies show, however, that most people in modern societies do *not* usually seek medical attention in response to sickness; only a very small portion of ailments are ever brought to a physician's attention (Zola 1983, p. 111). Typically, individuals and families approach prevention of illness and response to ordinary health problems without any professional help. People rely on their own judgment, sometimes with advice from lay networks of family and friends, to respond to illness and to decide whether to seek professional help (and which help to seek). Common responses to sickness include "wait-and-see" what develops, self-dosing with prescription or nonprescription drugs, self-imposed restrictions of activities and changes in diet, and talk with family and friends (Verbrugge and Ascione 1987). Many lay responses to physical illness are nonphysical. For example, if a person believes that she is particularly vulnerable to infections when she is lonely or "blue," she might respond to the onset of the "flu" by doing things that cheer her up or by seeking the company of a close friend. Similarly if someone believes that God will intervene to heal his illness, then prayer for healing constitutes a therapeutic action.

These studies of wider lay help-seeking practices put the alternative practices of new religious healing movements in perspective. Although virtually all new religious healing movements advocate using medical help in addition to nonmedical sources, their beliefs about health and illness do modify the help-seeking process. Alternative healing systems include, for example, ideas about how to discern the "true" causes of an illness and when medical help may be ineffective (or even counter-productive). Adherents may also actively seek medical help which is consonant with their alternative beliefs and practices, such as a "Christian pediatrician" who supports their use of prayer and other Christian healing practices, or such as a family practitioner who encourages their emphasis on nutrition and meditation for health and healing.

Often, however, adherents of alternative healing systems simply do not tell their medical doctors about their nonmedical beliefs and practices. They often selectively accept their doctor's advice. For example, one woman said, "I still think they give you too much medication, which I accept gracefully and then don't take" (quoted in McGuire 1988). Medical doctors may decry this response as a "problem of patient noncompliance" with "doctors' orders." Recent studies about "noncompliance" suggest that this selectiveness is not unique to adherents of alternative healing systems, however; even persons with no particular healing alternatives often decide not to follow doctors' orders.

We have very little data on what patients actually hope to accomplish by consulting medical and nonmedical health experts, but it is entirely probable that much behavior labelled "noncompliance" is due to the fact that when people seek professional attention, they do not necessarily want to receive doctors' orders. For example, people may consult a doctor for a diagnosis, less out of physical distress from symptoms per se, than to rule out certain feared possible outcomes (cf. Zola 1983, p. 118).

Nevertheless, consultation with a professional expert is normative in our society, and there is a presumed obligation to "follow doctors' orders," despite the fact that the idea of "compliance" is a by-product of professional ideology (Trostle 1988). Such norms underpin societal responses to new religious healing movements, as discussed further below.

### The Place of Health and Healing in the Group

Findings about the place of healing generally emphasize the role of the healer and how that role is linked with the structure of authority in the group. Most early work on nonmedical healing focused on healers, perhaps because so many flamboyant healers (Christian, psychic, or esoteric) had caught the public eye. Many recent alternative healing systems, however, emphasize that all members can participate as self-healers or mutual healers. Whether a group emphasizes honored specialized healing roles or a more democratic pattern of group healing influences the exercise of authority and the distribution of informal rewards (such as prestige and recognition) in the group.

How does healing work? The foremost reason why people use a healing approach is that it makes *sense* to them. Thus, nonmedical healing systems in this culture are similar to indigenous healing systems around the world. Indigenous healing "works" partly by fitting into people's understandings of their world and how it operates. For example, if people understand their world to be one in which Satan is dangerously active, it makes sense for them to take actions to protect themselves from Satan's influence. Young (1976, p. 8) observed that therapies are considered efficacious, not only when they produce cure, but also when "they are a means by which specific, named kinds of sickness are defined and given culturally recognizable forms."

Indigenous healing forms and transforms the illness experience. It utilizes symbols and ritual action, meaningful to members, that can produce change on several levels: social, bodily, and emotional. A number of studies emphasize the importance of symbolism and ritual in effecting nonmedical healing (Csordas 1983; Dow 1986; Easthope 1985; Glik 1988; McGuire 1985, 1988; Shupe and Hadden 1989; Westley 1983). Although Western biomedicine is based on rational science, some of the effectiveness of medical doctors, too, may be based on nonscientific factors, such as symbols of power. The "placebo effect" may be a form of symbolic power (see Moerman 1983). For example, beyond whatever physical effects they may have, pills, surgery, lab tests, and diet regimens may function as ritual symbols of the power to heal (cf. Pellegrino

1976; Posner 1977). Such symbols increase trust and expectancy (thus promoting the placebo effect); the effectiveness of doctor and nonmedical healer alike are increased by such use of symbols (Frank 1973). Whether managed by a specialized healer or ordinary members of the group, ritual transformations and symbols of power may have physiological, as well as psychological, effects.

## BROADER SOCIAL SCIENCE ISSUES

Several features of modern Western societies are put into high relief by our analysis of the situation of nonmedical healing in their midst. One is the professional dominance of medicine; a related feature is the medicalization of deviance. New religious movements are one important source of alternative healing systems and, thus, implicit critiques of the dominant medical paradigm. Several observers suggest that these new religious healing movements may be part of a larger religious response to modernity, perhaps shaping a new place for religion in modern societies.

### Professional Dominance in the Courts

New religious healing movements are less likely than traditional religious healing movements to be contested in court, because they typically use medical and nonmedical healing approaches simultaneously. Nevertheless, recent legal attention to nonmedical healing raises the broader sociological issue of the professional dominance of medicine. Gradually, the society (as reflected by its courts) has come to view medical expertise as a source of authority superior to that of religious or family institutions (Fenn 1982; Willen 1983). Throughout the middle decades of this century, medical authority was ruled to supersede parental authority on matters of the well-being of children (precedent U.S. cases in 1952, 1962, and 1964 are cited in Burkholder 1974; for parallel British cases, see Wilson 1990).

For example, a number of court decisions upheld medical judgments to perform cesarian sections, over the objections of patients, their families, and religious groups. One investigation of court cases between 1979 and 1986 showed that courts generally accepted physicians' decisions to operate, despite strong patient objections (which were often religiously based) and even though subsequent medical developments showed that most of the operations were not medically necessary (Irwin and Jordan 1987).

Even in instances in which the medical ability to prevent death is doubtful, greater legitimacy is given to medical than to parental authority. In 1990, a Massachusetts court found a couple guilty of manslaughter for failing to seek a medical doctor's attention for their sick 2-1/2-year-old child, who died just five days after the onset of abdominal symptoms (see Beck and Hendon [1990b] and Richardson and DeWitt [1991] for summaries of this and related cases; a similar case involving Christian fundamentalists is being prosecuted in Louisiana—see Bridges and Chapple [1990]). These practicing Christian Scientists believed that the healing "work" they were providing the child was the best help he could get, but the court assumed that getting medical attention is the proper (i.e., nonnegligent) response to sickness. Despite the fact that the child died of a congenital bowel obstruction which probably could not have been surgically corrected, the parents were held liable for failing to try to get immediate medical help. The court ignored their assertion that if the symptoms had continued or gotten worse, they would have consulted a physician. In light of sociological data showing that wait-and-see is the *usual* response (regardless of religious persuasion) to onset of symptoms, the court's decision seems extraordinarily firm on the side of medical professional dominance.

## Medicalization of Deviance

Historically, religious, legal, and medical institutions have all contributed to the definition of deviance in society. Medicalization of deviance refers to the process whereby the dominant medical system has come to be the prime arbiter of normal or desirable behavior: Badness becomes sickness. The concept of sickness is not, however, a neutral scientific concept, but rather reflects moral judgments of normality and desirability (Freidson 1970, p. 208). The medical profession (especially its psychiatric branch) has defined a wide range of disapproved behavior as "sick": alcoholism, homosexuality, promiscuity, drug addition, arson, suicide, child abuse, and civil disobedience (Conrad and Schneider 1980).

Social control is a way the social group protects its boundaries, and labelling deviance is one obvious form of social control. A related function of medicalizing deviance is protection and expansion of prerogatives of medical professionals. There exist persuasive arguments that psychotherapy is in direct competition with religion as a shaper of worldviews and as a ritual of personal reintegration with the social group (Berger 1965; Kilbourne and Richardson 1984). If, for example, suicide is successfully labelled a "sickness," then the presumed "proper" response is to seek professional medical attention for a suicidal person. Nonmedical responses (such as prayer, counselling by nonmedical personnel, massages, hydrotherapy, meditation, etc.) represent competition to the medical monopoly over the treatment of sickness. There have been several court cases in which religious groups or leaders were found liable for "practicing medicine without a license" or for aggravating (by psychotherapeutic standards) a person's sickness, when they were using religious responses to people's emotional problems (Burkholder 1974; Beck and Hendon 1990a). The courts have thus become the locus of a struggle over professional dominance and the dominance of one therapeutic worldview over competing worldviews.

## Alternatives to the Medical Model

While new religious healing movements are interesting as religious movements per se, they are also one important contemporary assertion of a critique of the dominant medical paradigm and the medical institutions built on that paradigm. Dissatisfaction with the medical system is widespread in many Western industrialized societies, especially the United States, where basic access to adequate medical care is an important social problem. The critique implicit in adherents' attraction to alternative healing systems, such as many new religious movements, dovetails with the critiques posed by many "secular" observers.

They are dissatisfied that the medical system tends to treat the body in isolation from social, psychological, and spiritual aspects of the illness. They doubt that health is truly promoted by a paradigm that defines well-being narrowly. They criticize the extent to which modern medicine resorts too quickly or too often to treatment involving surgery or potent pharmaceuticals. They are suspicious of the possibility that medical practices address the symptoms or effects but not the real causes of illnesses, perhaps thereby merely masking or alleviating symptoms in place of promoting real healing. They criticize the tendency to depersonalize treatment, in which the sick person's expressions of distress are not heeded or are transformed into tidy medical categories rather than appreciated as human suffering.

While many critics of modern Western medicine agree about the deficiencies of the paradigm, they do not agree about the best alternative health/healing system. Many new religious movements propose alternatives that would not be widely accepted in a religiously plural society. Nevertheless, the fact that many people from diverse socioeconomic, educational, religious, and cultural backgrounds are now promulgating significant changes in society's ways of dealing with matters of health and well-being suggests that these alternative religious healing systems may be a facet of some broader social changes.

## Religion in Modern Society

Several interpretations suggest such linkages of healing movements to broader social changes. Beckford (1984) argues that new religious healing movements' beliefs and practices may represent new "world images" with important sociocultural affinities with experiences of middle classes of advanced industrial societies. These world images may, thus, create paths or directions for important social changes, especially changes regarding the relationship between the individual and society, the self and the cosmos. In this context, Beckford (1984, p. 269) asks "whether the holistic imagery common to many [New Religious Healing Movements] can be considered indicative of the place of the *sacred* in modern industrial societies." This evocation of Weber's concept of "world images" points to the possible importance of healing movements in some larger social change. Weber stated:

> very frequently the "world images" that have been created by "ideas" have, like switchmen, determined the tracks along which action has been pushed by the dynamic of interest. "From what" and "for what" one wished to be redeemed and, let us not forget, "could be" redeemed, depended upon one's image of the world (1946, p. 280).

That alternative healing movements have couched salvation in the metaphor of health and healing suggests the importance of this "world image" for shaping the direction of social change in contemporary societies. For many new religious healing groups, "health" is an idealization of a kind of self, and "healing" is part of the process by which growth toward that ideal is achieved (McGuire 1988, p. 244).

Beckford further notes that many healing movements (especially those not derived from the Christian tradition), promote an image of the self as a flexible, ever-revisable, developing entity. This image of the self is consonant with new ideas about work and identity, which may have a particular affinity with the experience of the middle classes in the modern industrial workplace (Beckford 1985). While some new religious movements emphatically reaffirm traditional norms and patterns of identity, many others promote a transformation of the self. Some alternative healing approaches, for example, encourage a reflective and reflexive attitude toward oneself, one's body, and emotional and social life. They affirm the individual's prerogative to choose the quality of one's bodily and emotional experience, to select one's own best means to achieve health and healing, indeed to assert one's chosen identity (see Dreitzel 1981). Furthermore, they promote a strong sense of connectedness with one's body and with other persons. These features of some alternative healing systems in modern society may represent socialization into new modes of identity, new patterns of individual-to-society linkage.

# REFERENCES

Albanese, C.L. 1990. *Nature Religion in America: From the Algonkian Indians to the New Age.* Chicago: University of Chicago Press.

_____. 1991. *America: Religions and Religion.* Belmont, CA: Wadsworth.

Allen, G., and R. Wallis. 1976. "Pentecostalists as a Medical Minority." Pp. 110-137 in *Marginal Medicine,* edited by R. Wallis and P. Morley. New York: Free Press.

Bainbridge, W. 1978. *Satan's Power: A Deviant Psychotherapeutic Cult.* Berkeley: University of California Press.

Beck, R., and D.W. Hendon. 1990a. "Notes on Church-State Affairs." *Journal of Church and State* 32: 180.

_____. 1990b. "Notes on Church-State Affairs." *Journal of Church and State* 32: 684-686.

Beckford, J.A. 1984. "Holistic Imagery and Ethics in New Religious and Healing Movements." *Social Compass* 31: 259-272.

_____. 1985. "The World Images of New Religious and Healing Movements." Pp. 72-93 in *Sickness and Sectarianism,* edited by R.K. Jones. London: Gower.

Berger, P.L. 1965. "Toward a Sociological Understanding of Psychoanalysis." *Social Research* 32: 26-44.

Blaxter, M. 1983. "The Causes of Disease: Women Talking." *Social Science and Medicine* 17: 59-69.

Bridges, T., and C. Chapple. 1990. "Death Puts Quiet Faith in Spotlight." *The Times Picayune* [*New Orleans*] (November 29), A1, A8.

Bromley, D.G., D.M. Johnson, and J.S. Williams. 1986. "Religion, Health and Healing: Findings from a Southern City." *Sociological Analysis* 47: 66-73.

Burkholder, J.R. 1974. "The Law Knows No Heresy: Marginal Religious Movements and the Courts." Pp. 27-52 in *Religious Movements in Contemporary America,* edited by I. Zaretsky and M. Leone. Princeton: Princeton University Press.

Calnan, M. 1987. *Health and Illness: The Lay Perspective.* New York: Tavistock.

Conrad, P., and J.W. Schneider. 1980. *Deviance and Medicalization: From Badness to Sickness.* St. Louis: C.V. Mosby.

Csordas, T.J. 1983. "The Rhetoric of Transformation in Ritual Healing." *Culture, Medicine and Psychiatry* 7: 333-375.

Csordas, T.J., and S. Cross. 1976. "Healing of Memories: Psychotherapeutic Ritual among Catholic Pentecostals." *Journal of Pastoral Care* 30: 245-257.

Dow, J. 1986. "Universal Aspects of Symbolic Healing: A Theoretical Synthesis." *American Anthropologist* 88: 56-69.

Dreitzel, H.P. 1981. "The Socialization of Nature: Western Attitudes Towards Body and Emotions." Pp. 205-223 in *Indigenous Psychologies: The Anthropology of the Self,* edited by P. Heelas and A. Lock. New York: Academic.

Dubos, R. 1959. *Mirage of Health.* Garden City, NY: Doubleday.

Easthope, G. 1985. "Marginal Healers." Pp. 52-71 in *Sickness and Sectarianism,* edited by R.K. Jones. London: Gower.

English-Lueck, J.A. 1990. *Health in the New Age: A Study in California Holistic Practices.* Albuquerque: University of New Mexico Press.

Fenn, R. 1982. *Liturgies and Trials: The Secularization of Religious Language.* Oxford: Basil Blackwell.

Foltz, T. 1985. "An Alternative Healing Group as a New Religious Form: The Use of Ritual in Becoming a Healing Practitioner." Pp. 144-157 in *Sickness and Sectarianism,* edited by R.K. Jones. London: Gower.

Frank, J. 1973. *Persuasion and Healing.* New York: Schocken.

Freidson, E. 1970. *Profession of Medicine: A Study of the Sociology of Applied Knowledge.* New York: Dodd, Mead.

Freund, P.E.S., and M.B. McGuire. 1991. *Health, Illness and the Social Body: A Critical Sociology.* Englewood Cliffs, NJ: Prentice-Hall.

Fuller, R.C. 1989. *Alternative Medicine and American Religious Life.* New York: Oxford University Press.

Garrison, V. 1977. "Doctor, Espiritista or Psychiatrist: Health-seeking Behavior in a Puerto Rican Neighborhood of New York City." *Medical Anthropology* 1: 67-183.

Gevitz, N., ed. 1988. *Other Healers: Unorthodox Medicine in America.* Baltimore: The Johns Hopkins University Press.

Glik, D.C. 1988. "Symbolic, Ritual and Social Dynamics of Spiritual Healing." *Social Science and Medicine* 27: 1197-1206.

Gordon, D. 1988. "Tenacious Assumptions in Western Medicine." Pp. 19-56 in *Biomedicine Examined,* edited by M. Lock and D.R. Gordon. Dordrecht, The Netherlands: D. Reidel.

Harwood, A. 1977. *Rx: Spiritist as Needed: A Study of A Puerto Rican Community Mental Health Resource.* New York: John Wiley.

Herzlich, C., and J. Pierret. 1987. *Illness and Self in Society.* Baltimore: The Johns Hopkins University Press.

Irwin, S., and B. Jordan. 1987. "Knowledge, Practice and Power: Court-ordered Cesarean Section." *Medical Anthropology Quarterly* 1: 319-334.

Jacobs, J.L. 1989. "The Effects of Ritual Healing on Female Victims of Abuse: A Study of Empowerment and Transformation." *Sociological Analysis* 50: 265-279.

————. 1990. "Women-centered Healing Rites: A Study of Alienation and Reintegration." Pp. 373-383 in *In Gods We Trust: New Patterns of Religious Pluralism in America,* edited by T. Robbins and D. Anthony. New Brunswick, NJ: Transaction.

Judah, J.S. 1967. *The History and Philosophy of the Metaphysical Movements in America.* Philadelphia: Westminster.

Kilbourne, B., and J.T. Richardson. 1984. "Psychotherapy and New Religions in a Pluralistic Society." *American Psychologist* 39: 237-251.

Kleinman, A.M. 1973. "Some Issues for a Comparative Study of Medical Healing." *International Journal of Social Psychiatry* 19: 159-165.

————. 1988. *The Illness Narratives: Suffering, Healing and the Human Condition*. New York: Basic.

Macklin, J. 1974. "Belief, Ritual and Healing: New England Spiritualism and Mexican-American Spiritism Compared." Pp. 383-417 in *Religious Movements in Contemporary America*, edited by I. Zaretsky and M. Leone. Princeton: Princeton University Press.

McGuire, M.B. 1982. *Pentecostal Catholics: Power, Charisma and Order in a Religious Movement*. Philadelphia: Temple University Press.

————. 1985. "Religion and Healing." Pp. 268-284 in *The Sacred in a Secular Age*, edited by P. Hammond. Berkeley: University of California Press.

————. 1988. *Ritual Healing in Suburban America*. New Brunswick, NJ: Rutgers University Press.

Melton, J.G., J. Clark, and A.A. Kelly. 1991. *New Age Almanac*. New York: Visible Ink Press.

Moerman, D. 1983. "Physiology and Symbols: The Anthropological Implications of the Placebo Effect." Pp. 156-167 in *The Anthropology of Medicine: From Culture to Method*, edited by L. Romanucci-Ross, D. Moerman, and L. Tancredi. South Hadley, MA: Bergin & Garvey.

Moody, E. 1974. "Magical Therapy: An Anthropological Investigation of Contemporary Satanism." Pp. 355-382 in *Religious Movements in Contemporary America*, edited by I. Zaretsky and M. Leone. Princeton: Princeton University Press.

Neitz, M.J. 1986. *Charisma and Community: A Study of Religious Commitment within the Charismatic Renewal*. New Brunswick, NJ: Transaction.

————. 1990. "In Goddesses We Trust." Pp. 353-372 in *In Gods We Trust: New Patterns of Religious Pluralism in America*, edited by T. Robbins and D. Anthony. New Brunswick, NJ: Transaction.

Nelson, G.K. 1969. *Spiritualism and Society*. New York: Schocken.

Ness, R. 1980. "The Impact of Indigenous Healing Activity: An Empirical Study of Two Fundamentalist Churches." *Social Science and Medicine* 14B: 167-180.

Nudelman, A.E. 1976. "The Maintenance of Christian Science in Scientific Society." Pp. 42-60 in *Marginal Medicine*, edited by R. Wallis and P. Morley. New York: Free Press.

Nudelman, A.E., and B. Nudelman. 1972. "Health and Illness Behavior of Christian Scientists." *Social Science and Medicine* 6: 253-262.

Pattison, E.M. 1974. "Ideological Support for the Marginal Middle Class: Faith Healing and Glossolalia." Pp. 418-458 in *Religious Movements in Contemporary America*, edited by I. Zaretsky and M. Leone. Princeton: Princeton University Press.

Pellegrino, E.D. 1976. "Prescribing and Drug Ingestion: Symbols and Substances." *Drug Intelligence and Clinical Pharmacy* 10: 624-630.

Poloma, M.M. 1991. "A Comparison of Christian Science and Mainline Christian Healing Ideologies and Practices." *Review of Religious Research* 32: 337-350.

Poloma, M.M., and B. Pendleton. 1991. *Exploring Neglected Dimensions of Religion in Quality of Life Research*. Lewiston, NY: Edwin Mellen Press.

Posner, T. 1977. "Magical Elements in Orthodox Medicine." Pp. 141-158 in *Health Care and Health Knowledge*, edited by R. Dingwall, C. Heath, M. Reid, and M. Stacey. London: Croom Helm.

Richardson, J.T., and J. DeWitt. 1991. "Christian Science Spiritual Healing, the Law, and Public Opinion." Paper presented at the annual meeting of the Society for the Scientific Study of Religion, Pittsburgh, PA.

Schoepflin, R.B. 1986. "The Christian Science Tradition." Pp. 421-446 in *Caring and Curing: Health and Medicine in the Western Religious Traditions*, edited by R. Numbers and D. Amundsen. New York: Macmillan.

Shupe, A., and J. Hadden. 1989. "Symbolic Healing." *Second Opinion* 12: 75-97.

Skultans, V. 1974. *Intimacy and Ritual: A Study of Spiritualism, Mediums and Groups*. London: Routledge and Kegan Paul.

Spickard, J.V. 1990. "Spiritual Healing among Followers of a Japanese New Religion: Experience as a Factor in Religious Motivation." *Research in the Social Scientific Study of Religion* 3: 135-156.

Trier, K.K., and A. Shupe. 1991. "Prayers, Religiosity, and Healing in the Heartland, U.S.A.: A Research Note." *Review of Religious Research* 32: 351-358.

Trostle, J.A. 1988. "Medical Compliance as an Ideology." *Social Science and Medicine* 27: 1299-1308.

Verbrugge, L.M., and F.J. Ascione. 1987. "Exploring the Iceberg: Common Symptoms and How People Care for Them." *Medical Care* 25: 539-569.

Wacker, G. 1986. "The Pentecostal Tradition." Pp. 514-538 in *Caring and Curing: Health and Medicine in the Western Religious Traditions,* edited by R. Numbers and A. Amundsen. New York: Macmillan.

Wagner, M.B. 1983. *Metaphysics in Midwestern America.* Columbus: Ohio State University Press.

Wallis, R. 1976. "Dianetics: A Marginal Psychotherapy." Pp. 77-109 in *Marginal Medicine,* edited by R. Wallis and P. Morley. New York: Free Press.

―――. 1977. *The Road to Total Freedom: A Sociological Analysis of Scientology.* New York: Columbia University Press.

―――. 1985a. "Betwixt Therapy and Salvation: The Changing Form of The Human Potential Movement." Pp. 23-51 in *Sickness and Sectarianism,* edited by R.K. Jones. London: Gower.

―――. 1985b. "The Dynamics of Change in the Human Potential Movement." Pp. 129-156 in *Religious Movements: Genesis. Exodus and Numbers,* edited by R. Stark. New York: Paragon.

Wardwell, W.I. 1973. "Christian Science and Spiritual Healing." Pp. 72-88 in *Religious Systems and Psychotherapy,* edited by R. Cox. Springfield, IL: Charles C. Thomas.

Weber, M. 1946. *From Max Weber: Essays in Sociology.* Translated and edited by H.H. Gerth and C.W. Mills. New York: Oxford University Press.

Westley, F. 1983. *The Complex Forms of the Religious Life.* Chico, CA: Scholars Press.

Willen, R.S. 1983. "Religion and Law: The Secularization of Testimonial Procedures." *Sociological Analysis* 44: 53-64.

Wilson, B.R. 1990. *The Social Dimensions of Sectarianism: Sects and New Religious Movements in Contemporary Society.* Oxford: Clarendon.

Young, A. 1976. "Some Implications of Medical Beliefs and Practices for Social Anthropology." *American Anthropologist* 78: 5-24.

Zola, I.K. 1983. *Socio-Medical Inquiries.* Philadelphia: Temple University Press.

# LIFE CYCLE, GENERATION, AND PARTICIPATION IN RELIGIOUS GROUPS

Wade Clark Roof and Karen Walsh

## ABSTRACT

The purpose of this paper is to pull together two differing strands of research literature: on life cycle and on generation. Much attention has been given to both life cycle and generation as they relate to religious involvement and disaffiliation, but only recently has it become apparent that it is important to study both sets of experiences in relation to one another. Drawing off the experiences of the 1960s, this paper examines three distinct processes: religious disaffiliation, or how pools of potential recruits get created; cult recruitment as it occurs in the early adult years; and recent religious and spiritual trends of the generation growing up in the 1960s. The paper concludes with some exploration of new research possibilities when life cycle and generation are studied together.

Over the past two decades a considerable body of research has emerged on the general theme of the life course. Much of this research has focused on the psychological or personal development of people as they progress through successive stages of the life cycle. Sociologists have added an important dimension to this inquiry by examining changing roles which accrue to new social expectations and obligations as people age. As a result of this growing attention to the stages of the life course, a new set of distinctions has emerged in the literature distinguishing between "life cycle" and "generational" effects: the former referring to the impact of the aging process itself and the latter to the experiences of generations or specific cohorts within a population as they age.

Religion and the Social Order, Volume 3B, pages 157-171.
ISBN: 1-55938-715-7

Now there is growing interest in the relationship of both of these—life cycle and generation—to religious belief and participation. This line of inquiry is promising for several reasons. One is that it recognizes that levels of religious commitment vary over the span of a human life and differ by cohort, one from another. The religious inclinations of an adolescent are different from those at mid-life, and the latter different still from those of old age. Because of generational differences in styles of believing and belonging, obviously a developmental approach to religion is helpful. Hence approaches to religion that look to change over time are appealing. A second is that it promises to yield greater clarity about why some time periods have greater religious and spiritual ferment than others. While many factors come into play in explaining the rise of new religious movements, life cycle and generation are among the most important to be considered, especially for any kind of analysis that extends over a long period of time. Even since Tocqueville's astute observations about American society, we have known that in this country religious life ebbs and flows over time, but we have not always fully grasped how and why this is so.

All of this has sensitized researchers to the fact that there is no simple relationship between age and religion. And for a good reason—the aging process itself is fundamentally very complex, including both the aging of individual persons and the aging of cohort-specific aggregates of individuals. Age is a human universal, yet a principal tenet of the sociology of age is that aging is not inevitably prescribed, either for the individual life course or for aggregates sharing common life experiences and cultural values. This being the case, much attention is given today in the sociology of age to describing the meaning of age trajectories across time and to sorting out individual and group variations. For religious and cultural analysis, this means that greater concern must be given to specifying age-related patterns.

Yet the sociology of religion as a field has been slow to assimilate these new approaches to age. Despite the huge proliferation of literature on cults and sects since the 1960s, virtually no attention has been given to thinking about life cycles and generational cohorts. A quick check of the many volumes on new religious movements that have appeared over the past several decades reveals that life cycle as a topic rarely appears in the index, and if generation does, it is usually as a descriptive, and not an analytic, term. This is partly because sophisticated empirical research techniques are required for truly sorting out the various influences—techniques which are impossible to apply to the historical and ethnographic accounts so common to the study of religious movements. And as we shall see, historical research on cults and sects prior to the 1960s offers almost no clues as to the importance of these factors. But also, because the sociological study of religion is somewhat isolated from developments in other fields, as for example, the sociology of age, it suffers from a lack of intellectual input from the larger discipline.

The purpose of this paper is to demonstrate how an analysis of life cycle and generation can inform the general study of religion in contemporary society, and then to speculate as to the possible advantages of applying this approach to the study of new religious movements. Our focus is largely on the so-called baby boom generation, a huge constituency that today is roughly one-third of the American population. Our concern is to sort out life cycle and generational experiences as themes in the research literature on this 1960s generation and how they interact with one another. We look at three distinct processes: (1) religious disaffiliation, or how pools of potential recruits for religious movements get created; (2) cult recruitment as it occurred in the early adult years for this generation; and (3) recent religious and spiritual trends for this generation now considerably older. We conclude the paper with some exploration of some new research possibilities.

## LIFE CYCLE

Scholars in various fields of social science are giving considerable attention to the aging process today. Much of it has focused on the discrete stages of the life course, and there is a substantial literature on childhood, adolescence, middle age, and social gerontology, cast in both psychological and sociological terms. There is also considerable emphasis in psychology on developmental stages, as in Erikson's (1950) influential paradigm of eight stages of life. Unlike his mentor Sigmund Freud, religion for Erikson is of paramount concern as a positive force in the ego. The fundamental religious aspects of Erikson's stages are evident in the very labels that he gives them (e.g., autonomy versus doubt, intimacy versus isolation, integrity versus despair). Popular interpretations of the discrete stages are found in Levinson's *Seasons of a Man's Life* (1978) and Sheehy's *Passages* (1976). Building upon Erikson's work, many have sought to link basic religious responses such as trust and faith as well as cognitive conceptions of religious reality to the sequence of stages in the life cycle. Progression through adulthood is associated with a passage from a phase of doubting/questioning/exploring to a more meaningful reconciliation of the dynamics of faith and life, often resulting in a more integrated, crystallized perspective. The best-known of these are Kohlberg's (1976) stages of moral development and Fowler's (1981) stages of faith development.

Sociologists have looked upon the life cycle from a different vantage point, though not necessarily in a mutually exclusive way. They have regarded the life cycle as having to do with maturation, but primarily as involving movement from one social role to another. With a change of role come new social expectations and obligations. Here again, religion is an important consideration. With shifts in roles from childhood to adolescence, from single status to married status and parenthood, and from young adulthood into older adulthood, there are implications for religion. Role transitions, and those especially surrounding adolescence, are thought to be crucial times of heightened vulnerability to joining religious movements. Applied to involvement in organized religion, the life-cycle pattern is often characterized as follows: children grow up attending religious services with their parents, but often wander away in late adolescence and early adulthood, get married, have children, and then return to the fold with their families (Schroeder 1975; Roozen 1980; Wuthnow and Mellinger 1978). The marginality of the young in society helps to explain the wandering away. Students, single persons, the unemployed, and the geographically mobile are on the fringes of the labor force, of religious institutions, of society itself. Family and parental responsibilities combined with a more stable community life are major themes in accounting for their return later on to religious involvement.

## GENERATION

The age structure of a society is a predisposing factor to religious change, especially when there are disproportionate numbers of the young. Because the younger cohorts typically are more affected than others by social and cultural changes, age-graded distinctions are of importance to understanding what happens religiously. Much earlier in this century, Mannheim (1952) spoke of "The Problem of Generations," alluding to the fact that those who belong to the same generation share a "common location in the historical dimension of the social process." Although Mannheim (1952) did not define a generation with great precision, he did emphasize that it was a social creation rather than a biological necessity. He assumed that each generation receives a distinctive imprint from the social and political events during its youthful years. Subsequently amplified by Ryder (1965), Mannheim's essay shows how each new cohort, beginning its life course at a unique point in time, has distinctive characteristics owing to historical context or the particular knowledge or attitudes acquired in childhood.

It is important to note an affinity between Mannheim's thinking and life-cycle theorizing. Implicit was a rudimentary concept of "life cycle" in his understanding of a generation. Although he is not entirely clear on the point at which a cohort begins to develop a generational character, he does mention "the age of 17, sometimes a little earlier and sometimes a little later," as a time when a generational consciousness should begin to develop. He appears to have assumed, as have developmental psychologists ever since, that "late adolescence and early childhood are the formative years during which a distinctive personal outlook on politics emerges" (Rintala 1968, p. 93). Schuman and Scott's (1989) analysis of American generations, indeed, offers empirical support for this hypothesis: people of all ages tend to remember events and changes from their youth, and these collective memories inform and shape their subsequent lives. In other words, as Ryder argued many years ago, the notion of a cohort is crucial to understanding the norms and values that individuals have internalized, and how all of these vary for differing sectors of the population. Historian John Modell (1989) more recently has shown that the transitions in the life course (e.g., age at marriage and entry into the work force) have varied for youth growing up in the twentieth century as a result of differing cohort, or generational, cultures.

## TOWARD A CONCEPTUAL PARADIGM

Riley argues convincingly that a paradigm is needed which integrates and reinterprets these two seemingly disparate strands of ideas: changes in people as they grow up and grow older, and changes in the society and its age-graded roles. These two notions of change are actually quite distinct and should not be confused.

> Two different dynamisms are involved, each with its own tempo. Society changes as it undergoes wars, famines, economic fluctuations; revolutions in beliefs and tastes; changes in the state of science and the arts; shifts in social norms, roles, and institutions; revisions in the age criteria for role entry and exist. Meanwhile, people change. They age over the life course from birth to death. And they are replaced by a succession of new cohorts, each composed of people who are aging (Riley 1978, p. 40).

Riley suggests that it is helpful to conceptualize the paradigm schematically as a series of horizontal bars, staggered across the axis of historical time. Each bar represents the people born during the same time period. Within each cohort, people are aging—biologically, socially, and psychologically. New cohorts succeed one another. This rather simple scheme has the advantage of reminding us that each cohort has its own unique segment of historical time, and that changes are occurring both within the bars and in the successive pattern of bars. Because society changes, the life-course patterns of people in differing cohorts vary considerably. Or to quote Riley:

> because of social change, *different cohorts age in different ways.* Cohorts born recently in this country differ from earlier cohorts because of intervening social changes of many sorts: in education, in nutrition, in the occupational and income level at which people begin their careers, in the political zeitgeist surrounding their first voting experience. If for no other reason, then, the members of each new cohort *cannot follow precisely* in the footsteps of their predecessors" (1978, p. 41, emphasis in original).

This scheme of Riley's reminds us that the life cycle is dynamic and fluid, even more so than many of the earlier theorists have described. Much of our thinking is still dominated by linear conceptions, as if life follows a sequence of events within a prescribed timetable with predictable outcomes; but in actuality life is more complex and pluralistic, something that "develops" rather than follows narrowly defined "stages." The aging process cannot be understood apart from the society, and society itself is at any given time a composite of several distinct cohorts. But to press on to the special focus of this paper, how does such a model bear upon religious change? Of what importance is it for understanding religious movements? We think it offers a fresh perspective.

## RECRUITMENT POOL FOR RELIGIOUS MOVEMENTS

For religious movements to flourish, they must of course recruit new followers. At any given time there is a supply of potential recruits, but that supply can vary greatly from one time period to another. Though historical information on this is very limited, it is known that rates of church membership and church participation were low in colonial America (see Gaustad 1962).

The churching of the nation intensified throughout the nineteenth century. Yet we can only speculate about how demographic shifts may have affected the pool of potential recruits. It appears that marginality as a group status was a factor: blacks, women, and young people did join and lead new sects in nineteenth-century America (Pritchard 1976). People affected by urbanization, geographical relocation, and changing job structures appear to have been more receptive to new religious groups (Cross 1950; Miyakawa 1964). From these accounts we can infer that demographic dislocations were important in creating the conditions for sectarian and cult movements to emerge. It is known that later in the 1920s there was great concern in the churches about young people going astray, as was evident in a popular article at the time entitled "Sodom and Tomorrow: Will the Younger Generation Really Be Good?" in the *North American Review* (1932). Youth dropping out of the religious establishment were eligible recruits to religious movements and cults at the time, as Stark and Bainbridge (1985) have shown.

The new religious movements that flourished in the 1960s and 1970s benefitted from a large youth population, many of whom had dropped out of the mainline churches and synagogues. Both the size of the youth population and defection from the religious establishment were important. The sheer size of the baby boom generation—some 76 million born from 1946 to 1964—helped to create the structural conditions for the emergence of a distinctive youth counterculture. During this same time the religious establishment in the United States was in a downward spiral, with many of the old, high-status Protestant denominations actually experiencing net losses in membership (Hoge and Roozen 1979; Roof and McKinney 1987). For the first time, the old Protestant mainline seriously lost members brought on through abandonment by the young. It was, as Martin Marty said, unquestionably a time of "seismic shifts" on the religious landscape.

Was there any connection between the dropping out and the youth counterculture? Actually the connection becomes more apparent when we look closely at *who dropped out* of the mainline churches and synagogues and *who became involved* in the cults and religious movements. Surveys show the dropouts to be disproportionately young, single, college educated, mobile, and largely middle class (Hadaway and Roof 1988). Studies of those dropping out found that the single most important factor for why these young adults dropped out was because they had "left home," or the fact that they were no longer forced to attend religious services by their parents (Roozen 1980). In this respect, the dropouts largely reflected the middle-class, church-going constituencies that had greatly expanded in the post-World War II years.

To understand this high level of religious disengagement, we turn to the combination of life-cycle and generational patterns. Widespread defection from the mainline churches and synagogues occurred at the time, primarily because a large cohort of youth was in the life-cycle phase of dropping out (ages 15-25). The post-World War II youth cohort, the so-called baby boomers, was the largest such cohort ever in American history. Just as a decade earlier they had swelled the membership rolls of Sunday schools as children, now they left the churches in record numbers. What appeared to be a "religious revival" in the 1950s for middle-class, mainline Protestant churches especially, had by the late 1960s and early 1970s turned into a "religious depression" (see Kelley 1972; Johnson 1985). What really happened was that a large sector of the population moved out of a childhood phase that was highly conducive of church involvement into a new adolescent and early adult phase of reduced involvement—and thus created a large pool of religious dropouts.

Since the 1960s the number of those with no religious affiliation in the United States—the "nones"—has increased. Survey trends indicate that the proportion of nones rose steadily from four percent in the 1960s to upwards of eight percent in the late 1970s. While the proportion doubled in those years, it appears to have levelled off in the 1980s. Using the General Social Surveys, Greeley (1989) shows that the increase in nonaffiliation was a phenomenon of the 1960s and 1970s and was not a major secularizing trend that has continued (also see Glenn 1987). The proportion of nones jumped up significantly during those years and then levelled off, reflecting Greeley says a "demographic" shift caused by the younger age of the American population.

Demographics alone, of course, does not fully capture what is meant by a generation. The term also refers to a cohort with an historical consciousness bound together by shared cultural experiences. Generation in the social and cultural sense sheds a great deal of light on the rebellion against the religious establishment in the 1960s. A Lilly-funded survey of the baby-boom generation conducted in 1989 found that two-thirds had dropped out of church or synagogue for a period of two years or more when they were growing up or during their early adult years. This figure is considerably higher in the boomer generation than for the population as a whole (Roof forthcoming). Roozen (1980) estimates the total population figure to be 46 percent. The boomers' experience of alienation from institutions, questioning of authority, and a heightened sense of individualism and life-style freedom all help to account for the turning away from institutional religion in their earlier years.

More to the point, the Lilly survey also shows that there are considerable differences in religious defection between those who were deeply influenced by the youth counterculture at the time (smoking marijuana, attending rock concerts, taking part in marches and demonstrations for social causes) and those who were less influenced. Eighty-four percent of those who were highly caught up in the counterculture dropped out of religious involvement as compared with only 56 percent of those who were less exposed to the changing values and lifestyles. Similar patterns were reported by Wuthnow for the Bay Area in 1976. What is striking is that "exposure to the sixties," as recalled by respondents today, proves more effective as a predictor of whether young adults have stayed in the church or abandoned it than any of the variables usually relied upon in studies of religious disengagement, such as gender, level of education, or socioeconomic status. Generational experience is thus a powerful factor in shaping a lasting religious ethos.

# RELIGIOUS EXPERIMENTATION

Religious disaffiliation creates a pool of potential recruits, but people may or may not, of course, actually turn to new religious movements. Who joins cults? Why do they join? In what ways do the life-cycle and generation models help in answering these questions?

As is already apparent, it is difficult to determine historically precise connections between demographics and religion. If, as Stark and Bainbridge (1985) argue, religious movements are more common in places where or in times when church religion is weak, then colonial America would seem to have been ripe for cult movements. Older histories of Puritanism discouraged such a view, but more recent historical accounts suggest that the American religious past was far more eclectic than previous interpretations have implied. Magic and the occult, belief in miracles, faith healings, and yearnings for ecstatic spirituality appear to have been quite common in the late eighteenth and early nineteenth centuries (Butler 1990). Nature religion as expressed in its many forms—mind cure, concern with health and healing, living in harmony with nature—all flourished in the nineteenth century, and often as alternatives to more conventional religion (Albanese 1991). It is reported that those joining communal groups in the nineteenth century were typically female, young to middle-age, intelligent and optimistic, very poor or very wealthy (Nordhoff 1965). Beyond these sketchy profiles, we can only infer about their personal and social characteristics.

But accounts on who joined cults, communes, and the so-called "alternative religions" during the 1960s and 1970s lend support to the view that those who dropped out of the mainline churches and synagogues often did explore new faiths. The most convincing evidence comes from the social and demographic characteristics of the recruits themselves. Recruits look very much like the church dropouts: young, college-educated, mobile, middle-class (Snow 1976; Barker 1980; Bird and Reimer 1982; Bromley and Shupe 1979; Glock and Bellah 1976; Richardson 1983). The educated, middle-class young were the most vulnerable to the cultural strains in America at the time, and hence more alienated and more likely than working-class youth to turn to cults as an alternative to organized religion.

The expansion of higher education during the 1950s and 1960s quite clearly helped to pave the way for a closer affinity between patterns of religious defection and the attractiveness of cults. The generation reaching adulthood in those decades was the largest cohort of youth ever in America and also the most educated; they were more exposed than any other to religious pluralism, to Biblical criticism, to Eastern religious beliefs and ideas. Higher levels of education often meant loss of faith in the old traditions for many youth while at the same time predisposing them to explore new cults, or at least to have a more open and accepting attitude toward them. As a generation, they had high hopes and expectations that were sustained in part by an extended educational process that enhanced norms of civility and tolerance to new levels—even to nonbelievers and seemingly strange groups of believers.

Perhaps the most thorough statistical analysis, sorting out the life-cycle and generation models as they relate to religious experimentation, is found in Wuthnow's (1976, pp. 158-164) early work titled *The Consciousness Reformation*. Wuthnow was interested in knowing whether young people in the San Francisco Bay area espoused alternative meaning systems more than older people because they were at different points in the life cycle or because of generational trends. Using Goodman odds-ratios techniques, he was able to decipher the effects of life-cycle characteristics (e.g., employment status, marital status, mobility, parental status) on meaning systems, and he concluded that life cycle was of some importance in explaining Bay Area attraction to new religious movements. But at the same time, his analysis revealed that young people and older people still differed considerably even when the life-cycle differences were taken into account. Because young people were more likely than old people to hold to modern meaning systems, even when both were the same with respect to maturation, he was able to show statistically that generational effects were of greater impact than life cycle.

## MID-LIFE SPIRITUAL YEARNINGS

Up to this point we have looked at youth trends during the 1960s and 1970s. But what about religious and spiritual developments in more recent times? What is happening now that boomers are in their thirties and forties?

The life-cycle model offers some predictions. Sociologists emphasize that as people mature into a more settled life and marry and raise children, they are likely to return to active religious involvement. Parenting even more than marriage takes people back to religious participation: "And a little child shall lead them," so the adage goes. Church dropouts of an earlier time therefore should now be returning to church. Psychologists see midlife as a time of transition and as a time when adults experience an innate capacity for growth. It is the time when, as Roschen (1991) says, a person's most important journey into "self" begins, the exploration of a deeper and richer life. This may or may not lead to religious involvement, but it does signal a stage in life of introspection and of assessing life and its possibilities, of inward turning but also often a moving outward toward others as well.

In the Lilly boomer study, we found evidence in support of both predictions. There is a return to active religious involvement on the part of many: 40 percent of those who dropped out, some as many as 20 years ago, are now exploring out religion again. Returnees tend to be older, married with children, and more conservative in lifestyle matters than those not returning. Similar evidence of a return to organized religion is found by Roozen, McKinney, and Thompson (1990) who speak of the "big chill warming to worship." Evidence of a broader spiritual quest abounds as well. Members of the boomer generation, no matter what their age or life situation, strongly endorse individualism, tolerance, and exploration in matters of belief and personal commitment. The openness characterizing moral and lifestyle freedom in their years growing up is carried over into the religious realm. The survey conducted in 1989 asked "Is it good to explore many differing religious teachings and learn from them, or should one stick to a particular faith?" and found that 60 percent of the sample favored exploring rather than committing to a single faith. Among those most influenced by the cultural climate of the 1960s in their years growing up, that figure is 80 percent.

Spiritual quests, then, might be thought of as the individual, personal equivalents currently to religious movements for many in the boomer generation. It may be that a new type of participant is emerging—the "career seeker," or the person who is always striving for a deeper spiritual understanding. Loose networks among those sharing common quests (e.g., weekend seminars or readings at particular bookstores) suggest that such seekers are more like a "cult audience" than a "cult movement," to use Stark and Bainbridge's terms. Festivals appear to have replaced congregations as places of formal ritual. "Seekers" may have replaced "followers" for a generation that has matured and which now explores spiritualities in a more individualistic manner and must make responsible spiritual choices (see Anthony, Ecker, and Wilbur 1987). Though hard data are not easily obtained on such activity, impressionistic evidence points to something like a "circulation of the seekers," with people moving from one spiritual following to another. Within the New Age movement itself, there are many differing subgroups organized around differing transformational, cosmological, environmental, and holistic themes. Though constituencies do cluster, by the very nature of New Age teachings boundaries are fluid and ever evolving. New Agers know one another through their language far more so than through rigid beliefs or communal belonging: they speak of visions and vibrations, of chakras and centering, of health and healing. Image is more central than word, journeying more important than a fixed faith or following.

There is an affinity between age and spiritual quests, just as life-cycle theory would predict. Wuthnow (1976, p. 285) observed in the Bay Area study years ago that the personal growth movements appealed to a somewhat older audience than did the countercultural movements. Though good data again are hard to come by, human potential groups especially appear to be flourishing today at a time when more Americans than ever are in their thirties and early forties. One study of the neo-Pagan movement finds that most participants fall in the 30-40-year range, underscoring the ties between this age group and themes of ecology, feminism, Goddess worship, women's power and mysteries, and cycles of birth and death (Walsh 1991; also see Neitz 1990). A growing self-help movement—books, audio and video cassettes, and 12-step groups— appeals to these same themes plus more explicit psychological concerns of guilt, anxiety, self-hatred, resentment, and shame. A generation that grew up exploring drugs and sex now finds itself deeply concerned about victimization and the many forms of addiction; self-help groups and recovery theology emerge as cutting-edge strategies helping many approaching mid-life to arrive at a meaningful belief system. The burgeoning men's movement and its ties to age is noteworthy as well, with themes of male mysteries, father-son relationships, masculinity and sexuality, and ritual bondings.

# FURTHER CONSIDERATIONS

As we have seen, life cycle and generation interact in complex dynamic ways. There is no single fit, no one way to describe how they relate, in part because the very meanings of life cycle and generation are themselves culturally defined. Riley points out in her seminal piece on aging that one of the dangers of generational, or cohort, analysis is "cohort-centrism." That is, we tend to define "*the* life course" as we have it experienced it in our own particular cohort, and then we assume that the course follows a similar pattern in every generation.

Theories and conceptional paradigms about the life course often lead us to overgeneralize. Erikson, Kohlberg, Fowler and others postulate stages of life and of religious and moral development as if there were commonalities across time and across cultures. If there is universality of stages and sequences, then the aging process should be fundamentally the same, whenever and wherever it occurs. But if the life course is not immutably fixed and is widely flexible, then does its meaning not vary with social change? Neugarten (1974) refers to the "fluid life cycle," arguing that we should interpret more loosely the view of life as expounded in developmental psychology, in which adults are supposed to grow through several well-defined stages. Even the terms "the young," "the middle-aged," or "the old" are themselves subject to widely disparate definitions, and there is some evidence to suggest that over the past two decades Americans have become less sure of what the normative expectations are between specific ages and life stages and activities (Gerber et al. 1989, p. 4). Fluidity makes for less predictable age-specific behavior and a greater range of potential options.

Because of this fluidity, scholars should be cautious in drawing inferences about patterns of religious meaning and belonging *across* generations. The fact that the majority of boomers who dropped out of religious involvement have *not* returned to organized religion is reason enough to ponder whether there has been some shift in the life course or a rewriting of the script for life's stages. To expect that this generation should follow in the same path as their parents' generation is to be "cohort-centric," by failing to recognize that the process of aging and its religious correlates are different for the two cohorts. It may be the case that proportionately many more in the boomer generation, for example, are spiritual seekers rather than religious belongers. If so, much of the strain felt between generations over religious matters may simply follow from the way cohort-specific values and behavior are held up as the normative expectations of others. The force of such expectations may in fact lead to interest in religious movements that offer novel ideas and interpretations of life.

The notion of a "career seeker" raises an important conceptual question about conversion. Conversion typically refers to a radical change in a person's life, but in fact this is often not what happens. Many members simply explore new meanings, re-orient their perspectives, and pick and choose from a variety of traditions to create an individually tailored belief system. Conversion can take many complex forms (see Snow and Machalek 1984), but probably the two most common are the "adhesional" layering of beliefs around some core as described by Nock (1933) or "combinatory conversion" which, as Manning (1991) suggests, involves a more syncretistic restructuring of beliefs. Whitehead (1987) argues that believers can hold on to the content of belief while at the same time rejecting the symbolic framework surrounding belief. For example, a defecting Scientologist might switch to Zen Buddhism in a quest to understand past-life experiences in much the same way that an evangelical might switch from watching one televangelist to another. This all suggests more a pilgrimage of the mind than anything else, a shifting of mental imageries, and the cultivation of a type of spirituality that is different from that found in many religious movements seeking to indoctrinate converts and to maintain rigid boundaries with the rest of the world.

## NEED FOR FURTHER RESEARCH

Several lines of inquiry for research are opened up by the conceptual model proposed in this paper. First, what is the relative importance of life-cycle and generational factors in accounting for the breaking away from old religions and the rise of new religious movements? What produces periods of great religious and cultural ferment—"moments of effervescence," to use Durkheim's phrase? The fact that some periods (e.g., the 1920s and the 1960s), had more new religious movements than other periods in American history has to mean that life-cycle considerations alone are insufficient for explaining the rise of such religious phenomena. Religious breakthroughs would appear to occur in times of generational discontinuities and when many members of a generation are in the adolescent and early adulthood phases.

Second, what is it about a generation that is so important—its size or its distinctive subculture? There seems to be no question that the demographic bulge of boomers in the 1960s created a large market of potential recruits to cults and religious movements. Can the same be said for the 1920s? Or for any other periods in American history? Of course, both demographics and counterculture were important in the rise of religious movements. If cultural themes are more significant than demographics, what aspects of the value shifts in the 1960s were the most telling—the greater individualism, the subjectivism and turning inward, the greater tolerance for lifestyle differences and civil liberties?

Third, how are religious groups born in the 1960s different today now that they are into the marital and parenting phase? The Unification Church is a good case in point. Having held off on marriage and family formation in earlier years, many of their members now have moved into this family-formation phase. How has marriage and child-rearing affected their energies as a religious movement? Compared with other groups in the 1960s that moved more quickly into parenting, such as the Divine Light Mission, what difference has this made for the Unification Church insofar as styles of commitment?

Fourth, to the extent that life-cycle considerations help to explain who joins new religious movements, is the same true for defection from these groups? That is, are participants within cults likely to drop out as they move out of the early adult years and into mid-life? Research has not been framed in these terms although there is enough evidence to suggest that further inquiry is warranted. Many of the nineteenth-century utopian communes fell apart as their constituencies grew older. Since the 1960s interest in communal living appears to have waned as the population most attracted to them has grown older.

Fifth, what new models might be proposed describing people's spiritual trajectories or biographies? Americans appear increasingly to move in and out of religious groups with great ease as their life situation and life-cycle needs change (Albrecht and Cornwall 1989); significant numbers report switching religions more than once (Roof 1989). We know remarkably little about patterns of religious and spiritual movement. Surveys indicate that sizable numbers of Americans, and young adult Americans especially, believe in reincarnation, practice yoga, read Starhawk and Shirley McClaine on spirituality, respect Native American teachings on the earth, while at the same time identifying as Protestant, Catholic, or Jewish. We know even less about the ways in which such beliefs and practices combine with more traditional faiths.

Sixth, what is the relation of religious deviance and generational cultures? Stark and Bainbridge (1985, p. 417) are probably right when they argue that "our society has moved into a phase in which cults are less deviant than before." The decline of traditional faiths and the appeal of new religious and quasi-religious movements among the more educated classes all suggest a changing normative environment. Balch and Taylor (1977) have shown that, among individuals socialized into the cultic milieu, conversion to a nontraditional religion is neither deviant nor a radical departure from one's existing beliefs; it is merely a logical extension of their spiritual quest. We need further research identifying aspects of cults which lead to their being labeled as deviant and examining how social perceptions of groups once judged as deviant have changed over time. The fact that the 1960s generation now occupies positions of power and influence in the country is not inconsequential: members of this generation now shape the norms, the tastes, and the climate of opinion—including religious and spiritual styles.

Obviously we raise more questions than we can answer. But we are convinced that a framework as proposed here—comparing life cycle and generation—promises to be useful. The two concepts must be looked at in conjunction with one another. Focusing on one without the other can be misleading, especially if longitudinal or comparative inferences are drawn. And increasingly, as the body of research on religious movements grows and we know more about developments over time, we are in a better position to place what we know in a broader perspective. We think the time has come to do just that—to expand our perspective along these lines.

# REFERENCES

Albanese, C.L. 1991. *Nature Religion in America*. Chicago: University of Chicago Press.
Albrecht, S.L., and M. Cornwall. 1989. "Life Events and Religious Change." *Review of Religious Research* 31: 23-37.

Anthony, D., B. Ecker, and K. Wilbur. 1987. *Spiritual Choices.* New York: Paragon House.

Balch, R.W., and D. Taylor. 1977. "Seekers and Saucers: The Role of the Cultic Milieu in Joining a UFO Cult." *American Behavioral Scientist* 20: 839-860.

Barker, E. 1980. "Free to Choose? Some Thoughts on the Unification Church and Other Religious Movements." *Clergy Review* 65: 365-368.

Bird, F., and B. Riemer. 1982. "Participation Rates in New Religious and Para-Religious Movements." *Journal for the Scientific Study of Religion* 21: 1-14.

Bromley, D., and A. Shupe. 1979. "Just a Few Years Seems like a Lifetime: A Role Theory Approach to Participation in Religious Movements." Pp. 159-185 in *Research in Social Movements, Conflicts and Change,* edited by L. Kriesberg. Greenwich, CT: JAI Press.

Butler, J. 1990. *Awash in a Sea of Faith.* Cambridge, MA: Harvard University Press.

Cross, W. 1950. *The Burned Over District.* New York: Harper Torchbooks.

Erikson, E.H. 1950. *Childhood and Society.* New York: W.W. Norton.

Fowler, J.W. 1981. *Stages of Faith: The Psychology of Human Development and the Quest for Meaning.* San Francisco: Harper Collins.

Gaustad, E.S. 1962. *Historical Atlas of Religion in America.* New York: Harper and Row.

Gerber, J., J. Wolff, W. Klores, and G. Brown. 1989. *Lifetrends: The Future of Baby Boomers and Other Aging Americans.* New York: Stonesong Press.

Glenn, N. 1987. "No Religion Respondents." *Public Opinion Quarterly* 51: 293-315.

Glock, C.Y., and R.N. Bellah. 1976. *The New Religious Consciousness.* Berkeley: University of California Press.

Greeley, A.M. 1989. *Religious Change in America.* Cambridge, MA: Harvard University Press.

Hadaway, K., and W.C. Roof. 1988. "Apostasy in American Churches: Evidence from National Surveys." Pp. 29-46 in *Falling from the Faith,* edited by D. Bromley. Newbury Park, CA: Sage.

Hoge, D.R., and D.A. Roozen. 1979. *Understanding Church Growth and Decline: 1950-1978.* New York: Pilgrim Press.

Johnson, B. 1985. "Liberal Protestantism: End of the Road?" *The Annals of the American Academy of Political and Social Science* 480: 39-52.

Kelley, D.M. 1972. *Why Conservative Churches are Growing.* New York: Harper and Row.

Kohlberg, L. 1976. "Moral Stages and Moralization." Pp. 31-53 in *Moral Development and Behavior,* edited by T. Lickona. New York: Holt, Rinehart, and Winston.

Levinson, D. 1978. *The Seasons of a Man's Life.* New York: Knopf.

Mannheim, K. 1952. *Essays on the Sociology of Knowledge.* New York: Oxford University Press.

Manning, C. 1991. "The Psychology of Conversion to Modern Paganism." M.A. thesis, University of California at Santa Barbara.

Miyakawa, T.S. 1964. *Protestants and Pioneers.* Chicago: University of Chicago Press.

Modell, J. 1989. *Into One's Own: From Youth to Adulthood in the United States 1920-1975.* Berkeley: University of California Press.

Neitz, M.J. 1990. "In Goddess We Trust." Pp. 353-372 in *In Gods We Trust: New Patterns of Religious Pluralism in America,* edited by T. Robbins and D. Anthony. 2nd ed. New Brunswick, NJ: Transaction.

Neugarten, B. 1974. "Age Groups in American Society and the Rise of the Young-Old." *The Annals of the American Academy of Political Science* 415: 187-198.

Nock, A.D. 1933. *Conversion.* New York: Oxford University Press.

Nordhoff, C. 1965. *The Communistic Societies of the United States.* New York: Schocken Books.

Pritchard, L.K. 1976. "Religious Change in Nineteenth-Century America." Pp. 297-330 in *The New Religious Consciousness,* edited by C.Y. Glock and R.N. Bellah. Berkeley: University of California Press.

Richardson, J.T. 1983. "New Religious Movements in the United States: A Review." *Social Compass* 30: 85-110.

Riley, M.W. 1978. "Aging, Social Change, and the Power of Ideas." *Daedalus* 107: 39-52.

Roof, W.C. 1989. "Multiple Religious Switching." *Journal for the Scientific Study of Religion* 28: 530-535.

————. Forthcoming. *To Dwell in Possibility: America's Baby Boomers and Their Quest for a Spiritual Style*. San Francisco: Harper Collins.

Roof, W.C., and W. McKinney. 1987. *American Mainline Religion*. New Brunswick, NJ: Rutgers University Press.

Roozen, D.A. 1980. "Church Dropouts: Changing Patterns of Disengagement and Re-Entry." *Review of Religious Research* 21(Supplement): 427-450.

Roozen, D.A., W. McKinney, and W. Thompson. 1990. "The 'Big Chill' Generation Warms to Worship." *Review of Religious Research* 31: 314-322.

Roschen, J.F. 1991. "Baby Boomers Face Midlife: Implications for Faith Communities in the '90s and Beyond." Publication of Adult Faith Resources.

Ryder, N.B. 1965. "The Cohort as a Concept in the Study of Social Change." *American Sociological Review* 30: 843-861.

Schroeder, W. 1975. "Age Cohorts, the Family Life Cycle, and Participation in the Voluntary Church in America: Implications for Membership Patterns, 1950-2000." *Chicago Theological Seminary Register* 65: 13-28.

Schuman, H., and J. Scott. 1989. "Generations and Collective Memories." *American Sociological Review* 54: 359-381.

Sheehy, G. 1976. *Passages: Predictable Crises of Adult Life*. New York: Dutton.

Snow, D.A. 1976. "The Nichiren Shoshu Buddhist Movement in America: A Sociological Examination of Its Value Orientation, Recruitment Efforts and Spread." Ph.D. dissertation, University of California at Los Angeles.

Snow, D.A., and R. Machalek. 1984. "The Sociology of Conversion." *Annual Review of Sociology* 10: 67-190.

Stark, R., and W. Bainbridge. 1985. *The Future of Religion*. Berkeley: University of California Press.

Walsh, K. 1991. "We All Come from the Goddess: Perspectives on Neo-Paganism in Modern America." Unpublished paper, Department of Religious Studies, University of California at Santa Barbara.

Whitehead, H. 1987. *Renunciation and Reformulation*. Ithaca, NY: Cornell University Press.

Wuthnow, R. 1976. *The Consciousness Reformation*. Berkeley: University of California Press.

Wuthnow, R., and G. Mellinger. 1978. "Religious Loyalty, Defection, and Experimentation: A Longitudinal Analysis of University Men." *Review of Religious Research* 19: 234-245.

# FEMINIST PERSPECTIVES ON NEW RELIGIOUS MOVEMENTS

Lynn Davidman and Janet Jacobs

## ABSTRACT

In the past twenty years the study of new religious movements has brought new vitality to the sociology of religion. This field has flourished during precisely the same time period as the growth of feminist scholarship documenting women's invisibility in social research as producers and subjects of knowledge and illustrating the need for new concepts and theories that place women at the center of analysis and begins with women's experiences. This paper assesses the state of knowledge about women and gender within the literature on new religious movements in order to determine whether and in what ways feminist knowledge has transformed empirical and theoretical work in the sociology of religion. After concluding that gender has not become a category of analysis that informs most studies of "new religions," we present some of the emerging feminist research that illustrates how an approach that places gender at the center of analysis challenges and transforms our knowledge of religion in contemporary society.

In the past twenty years the sociology of religion has flourished as its practitioners took advantage of the burgeoning of "new religious movements" to expand its empirical and theoretical bases. The emergence of several kinds of religious activity attracted attention and contributed to a widespread impression that, far from being moribund, as predicted by secularization theory, religion was alive and well in the late twentieth-century United States. Most prominent among these emerging trends were movements inspired by Asian

Religion and the Social Order, Volume 3B, pages 173-190.
ISBN: 1-55938-715-7

religious traditions, the various groups, techniques, and spiritual disciplines that were part of the human potential movement; and the widespread attraction of what was in some ways "old time religion," albeit in newly packaged, neotraditionalist forms—the fundamentalist and charismatic revivals. Several students of contemporary religion have asserted that the study of "cults" might be contributing to the transformation of the sociology of religion by broadening its horizons and developing empirical and conceptual links with other subareas of sociology such as the study of social movements, medical sociology, and the sociology of organizations and deviance (Robbins 1988a; Robertson 1985).

During this same 20-year period, the feminist movement has produced a generation of scholars who recognized the importance of the category of gender for an understanding of all social experience. Feminist scholarship began with a critique of the invisibility of women in all fields of inquiry, both as producers of knowledge and as subjects of scholarly analyses. The next stage—and these stages are not simply sequential but continuous and perhaps spiraling—was the attempt to fill in the gaps in our knowledge of women by studying their lives according to the priorities and categories of male scholarship. However, these concepts and models often missed a great deal of women's distinctive experiences; women's lives reveal different patterns and concerns than those that shape men's lives. This realization has sparked the third stage of feminist inquiry: the development of a scholarship that places women at the center and begins with women's experiences. This focus on gender challenges and expands conventional categories of thought and analysis.

The sociology of religion has been flourishing during precisely the same time period as the growth of this feminist scholarship. What impact has this growing body of feminist knowledge and conceptual development had on the development of research and theory within the sociology of religion? This paper assesses the state of knowledge about women and gender within the sociological study of new religious movements to determine whether and in what ways this knowledge has challenged and transformed the scholarship and theory in the field. Our analysis focuses on three of the most central areas of research in the field—studies of the origins of new religious movements, issues of family and community, and conversion and commitment—all topics in which, we reasoned, the importance of gender should be evident.

Our review of the literature indicates that overall, gender has not become a basic category of analysis that informs all research on "new religions." Instead, the use of gender as an analytic category is generally confined to questions of marriage, sexuality, and family as they are reflected in contemporary religious phenomena.[1] An awareness of the centrality of gender does not inform most other topics in the field, including the analyses of the origins of new religions or theories of conversion and commitment. This paper examines this literature from a feminist perspective and presents the emerging feminist research in the field to show how an approach that places gender, as well as race and social class, at the center of analysis, can transform research and theory in the field.

# ORIGINS OF NEW RELIGIOUS MOVEMENTS

A vast amount of the sociological literature on new religious movements has been devoted to analyzing how and why these movements developed and what factors in the American social scene during the late 1960s through the 1970s could account for the growth of such unusual and diverse religious movements. Theories of the origins of new religious movements are explained primarily in relation to structural and cultural transformations or the intersection of the two. While *structural transformation* refers to shifts in broad social patterns such as economic and geographic mobility and changing family patterns, *cultural transformations* refer to changes in values, beliefs, attitudes, and sexual and gender ideologies. Many theorists often combine these two in a way that shows how particular structural dislocations are concomitant with shifts in basic cultural meaning systems.

## Cultural Transformations

Although scholars who adopt a cultural perspective recognize the importance of structural factors such as increased urbanization and economic and geographic mobility, they generally assume that changes in culture are independent variables that can produce structural transformations.[2] Many of these theories describe a "culture crisis" produced by the decline of coherent, cohesive systems of meaning that had previously integrated society and offered plausible ways for individuals to understand their lives and how they fit into the larger social order (Bellah 1975, 1976; Eister 1974; Robbins and Anthony 1978, 1979; Wuthnow 1976).

Most theorists within this tradition speak of a "crisis of meaning;" a climate of "deepening moral ambiguity" due to the decline of shared moral agreements in a highly differentiated and pluralistic society (Bellah 1976; Glock 1976; Robbins and Anthony 1978, 1979; Wuthnow 1976). Tipton's (1982) work exemplifies such an approach as he seeks to explain the emergence of new religious movements in connection with the failures of the counterculture of the 1960s. As the counterculture challenged the utilitarian individualism of mainstream Protestant ethics, an expressive ideal replaced self-interest as the basis for human action. The emphasis on self-awareness and self-expression, however, were enmeshed with the politics of the Vietnam war and the failures of liberal society. In the disillusionment that followed the social chaos of the 1960s, some young Americans sought refuge in religious movements that appeared to combine expressive ideals with the rules, authority, and normative structure of utilitarian culture—a merger of tradition with innovative religious organizations.

Tipton's analysis relies on the major themes in another of the most widely known cultural explanations—that of Bellah in *The Broken Covenant* (1975). In this book Bellah argues that the cultural dislocation of the 1970s is due to the decline of those shared values of Biblical religion and utilitarian individualism that had previously served to integrate U.S. society (Bellah 1976) and the subsequent erosion of the legitimacy of American institutions. The significance of Biblical religion for providing a "sacred canopy" (Berger 1969) to integrate society is that it led to a "notion of Americans as elect people with exemplary significance for the world," "God's New Israel" (Bellah 1976, p. 334).

What is missing from Bellah's sweeping cultural generalization is a sense of who actually held and benefited from this particular view. Certainly not the Native Americans, whose way of life was destroyed by prophets of America's place in the moral order, nor other disadvantaged and marginalized groups within American society, including women. A feminist analysis reveals that the biblical religion that defended the privilege of the white, Anglo-Saxon Protestant male was patriarchal and included a limited role for women.

Similarly, the value of "utilitarian individualism," in which the guiding theme is "interest" and which is defined by Bellah as a belief in a "neutral state in which individuals would be allowed to pursue the maximization of their self-interest" (1976, p. 335) is not a value that could be espoused by all individuals living in the United States. Many individuals continue to occupy roles that are defined by the utilitarian interests of the members of the dominant groups: in general, persons of color work at low paying and low status jobs that benefit white society while women's roles are often limited to being helpmates for men under conditions of economic disadvantage. As nurturers and caretakers, women are often less able to act in pursuit of their own maximum "interest," an understanding of which is itself defined by gender socialization. Feminist theoretical analyses highlight the ways in which women act to secure and affirm connections with others, a value system that differs from the individualism which is assumed to be a cultural universal by theorists such as Bellah (Chodorow 1978; Gilligan 1982; Miller 1976).

A feminist analysis reveals that a theory of shared values that unite "Americans" must be deconstructed; we cannot speak of patterns in the United States as if it is monolithic. Similarly, a woman-centered perspective suggests that the apparent "crumbling" of these "shared systems of meaning" in the late 1960s and 1970s is a positive indicator of the growing empowerment and visibility of those who had not benefitted from dominant cultural patterns, such as women, blacks, and other disadvantaged groups.

Other theorists who see cultural changes as central claim that the rise in science, technology, and higher education have contributed to the unique crisis of consciousness in the late 1960s and early 1970s. Some suggest that the growth of scientific world views has led to a decline in theism (Wuthnow 1976). Others propose that the spread of social scientific explanations has resulted in a decline of individual sense of responsibility (Wuthnow 1976; Glock 1976) and that the growth of relativist positions, such as the "social construction of knowledge" approach, makes the belief in any inherent, fundamental order increasingly implausible. Thus individuals may come to feel that there is no way of controlling their destiny, and they therefore face a crisis of moral legitimation and seek out alternate structures of meaning.

A feminist perspective suggests that gender would be relevant for a more accurate understanding of all the above trends. Most studies of Christian belief show that women score higher on measures of belief than do men (Argyle and Beit-Hallahmi 1975; Nelson, Cheek, and Au 1985). In order to have a more refined and nuanced understanding of the decline in theism, then, these shifts in belief need to be understood in terms of gender, as well as race, social class, and age. Similarly, if the rise in numbers of students in college is partly responsible for the search for new systems of meaning, given that in the late 1960s and early 1970s men were the majority of students in colleges, there might have been differences in the degree of searching among young women and men. Men outnumber women in the fields of natural science. This makes it difficult to accept general statements about the societal impact of the rise of science and education because there are great variations in the exposure of different groups to these perspectives. More fundamentally, individuals with low status and little privilege in society rarely feel in control of their destiny, suggesting that the crisis experienced by young white males in the early 1960s and 1970s is the ongoing social reality of marginalized groups. Thus, it is not surprising that white middle-class males comprised the largest number of converts to new religious movements, as the search for meaning was contextualized by the privileged assumptions of the dominant class.

## Structural Explanations

In explaining the rise of new religious movements sociologists often point to the need for community and coherence that results from the major structural changes and transformations that constitute modernization. Factors such as urbanization, increased population growth, structural differentiation, rationalization, and bureaucratization are all said to produce conditions of alienation, anomie, and dislocation. Individuals thus turn to "new" communities and meaning structures in an attempt to create frameworks for their lives.

Some theorists highlight the contemporary changes in the American political and economic scene—such as the Vietnam war and the failure of the liberal society—as factors in the rise of social ferment and the proliferation of new religious movements. Although these analyses are insightful, this discussion of political change and social movements has paid little attention to the women's movement and women's consciousness raising. In fact, many of the explanations of the origins of new religious movements build an analysis of their sources as if these were distinct from the sources of other contemporary social changes. The impact of feminism therefore has not been integrated into the theoretical work on the contemporary sociology of religion. This point will be further elaborated in the discussion of the women's spirituality movement and its relationship to other new religions.

Within the structural perspective, differentiation is frequently cited in discussions of the origins of new religious movements (Hunter 1981; Westley 1978, 1983). By fragmenting individual life-space into functionally specific roles, differentiation leads to difficulty in forming a coherent sense of personal identity. Proliferating new religious and therapeutic movements offer participants a holistic sense of "who am I" that transcends their otherwise diverse roles and limited instrumental commitments.

This theory of the origins of new religious movements is not fully satisfying because it is not subtle or nuanced: if we all live in the same differentiated society, then why do we all not join religious movements? We need theories that will give us more information on the particular ways differentiation affects individuals and their likelihood of joining religious movements.

For example, a gendered analysis of differentiation would ask whether women who work at home are less subject to differentiation in their lives than are men. We know that greater numbers of men than women join new religious movements, particularly those that require a higher degree of breaking away from one's past life. Might men be more likely to join because they experience greater differentiation in their lives than do women? This is one way we can begin to unravel the particulars of how the structural feature of differentiation affects the members of a population in distinct ways.

The breakdown of community is an additional structural factor that is widely believed to contribute to contemporary religious resurgence. Robbins and Anthony (1978, 1979) have written of the contemporary crisis of community that has led individuals to seek and create new communal forms. Marx and Ellison (1975) assert that because social change is eroding the traditional mediating structures—such as extended families and homogeneous communities—between the individual and large-scale formal structures, new "social inventions" such as communes and encounter and spiritual movements are arising to take their place. The formation of these alternative communities "represents contemporary attempts to create new intermediate relations between individual and primary groups on the one hand, and traditional (communitarian, associational, and occupational) secondary groups on the other, through extended primary relations" (Marx and Ellison 1975, p. 455). These groups wean individuals away from the nuclear family and create contexts for "extended communal relations transcending kinship ties."

In this early analysis gender is not considered to be an important factor in analyzing the differential attractiveness of these groups to young people. It is likely that there are gender differences in the desire and need to be weaned away from one's nuclear family and to form alternative family forms. A gendered analysis might examine the part that the feminist movement and its disruption of conventional kinship relations plays in the formation of these groups, as well as the differential family relations of women and men and how they shape the attractiveness of the new spiritual and communal forms.

The "crisis in the American family" is also posited by many as a significant factor in the formation of alternative social forms, including new religious movements. Some theorists write that the family's loss of its expressive and instrumental functions and their transferral to other social institutions is a major structural transformation that contributed to the rise of alternative religious groups (Robbins and Anthony 1982; Kilbourne and Richardson 1982). Kilbourne and Richardson write that other macrolevel shifts in gender and the family, such as women's increased participation in the paid labor market, the sophistication of birth control technology, and changes in divorce and marital styles, are connected with contemporary religious conversion.

Because many of the family's former functions are now performed by other institutions and gender roles are in a state of flux, individuals experience a widening gap between themselves and the society. They are confused by the growing differences between the highly institutionalized public realm and the de-institutionalized private realm (Hunter 1981). Like that of Kilbourne and Richardson, Hunter's analysis highlights such gender-related themes such as the current flux and uncertainty in key areas of private life including the norms governing courtship, marriage, sexuality, and child-rearing.

## NEW RELIGIOUS MOVEMENTS AND THE FAMILY

A major factor in the attractiveness of new religious movements to young people is that they offer solutions, difficult to find elsewhere, to the contemporary dilemmas of private life. For example, if a young adult is experiencing tension with her or his own family, joining one of these groups offers the possibility of entering a new, extended, surrogate family (Bromley et al. 1982). That new religious movements attempt to operate as surrogate families is clearly evident in the way members refer to each other as brother and sister, and even refer to the leader as "father." Fichter (1985) writes that family is very important in the Unification Church theology both in terms of the large surrogate family it is trying to create and also in terms of its positing of the husband-wife dyad as the basic unit of society.

Parsons (1986) further elaborates on the significance of family and surrogate ties in the Moonies' ideology and institutional structure. Because the Unification Church stresses emotional intimacy among followers, a church member assumes both the role of the child to his or her superiors and the role of the father (and less frequently, the mother) to the devotee's subordinates. The emphasis on patriarchal authority is made clear as Reverend Moon is the embodiment of the spiritual parent who presides over all other Church members. By bringing a feminist perspective to this field, Jacobs (1989) has pointed out that the appeal of father figures such as Reverend Moon is a cultural manifestation of patriarchal societies in which fathers are both idealized and absent from the caretaking of children in the traditional nuclear family.

Another solution sought by young adults joining new religious movements is a sense of clarity about the norms governing the most intimate areas of their lives: gender, sexuality, marriage, and the family. Aidala's (1985) study comparing young adults who join religious and nonreligious communes found that although all of these groups were ideologically concerned about gender and sexuality, the nonreligious communal groups were much less likely to offer specific models and guidelines. Instead, members continually negotiated and renegotiated these norms, often aspiring to some ideal of gender equality. Despite these egalitarian intentions, however, women in these movements frequently found that freedom from gender restrictions existed in the spiritual realm only, as women in these communities remained responsible for reproduction, child care, and household chores (Culpepper 1978; Jacobs 1984, 1986; Aidala 1985).

The religious communal groups, in contrast, all did offer a "definition and implementation of a particular vision of male/female" (Aidala 1985, p. 289) that was a major attraction to potential converts. Frequently they proposed conventional models in which gender differences and roles were clearly articulated through behavioral controls, regulations, and ideological principles that supported the notion of biological determinism. Many other studies of contemporary religious groups similarly found that the delineation of distinct roles for men and women and the provision of clear norms for family life were primary elements in their attractiveness to potential converts. In studies of such diverse communities as the Hare Krishnas, Evangelical and Fundamentalist Christian groups, Pentecostal Catholics and Orthodox Jews, sociologists have found that the conventional guidelines for nuclear family life were central in the religious construction of reality and its appeal to new members (Aidala 1985; Ammerman 1987; Aviad 1983; Danzger 1989; Davidman 1990a, 1990b, 1991; Kaufman 1991; McGuire 1982; Neitz 1987; Rochford 1985; Rose 1987; Warner, 1988).

A feminist analysis that begins with the experiences of the women in these groups reveals the double-edged nature of the women's embracing conventional religious models of gender and family life. One the one hand, many of these groups are patriarchal: power resides in the men, Christian wives are encouraged to be "submissive" to their husbands, and Jewish women are subject to a system of laws regulating their sexuality that were made entirely by men for the protection of their own ritual purity (Davidman 1991; Kaufman 1991; Rose 1987; Stacey 1990). Nevertheless, joining these groups actually yields many latent advantages for the women within the home. For example, because the religious groups place such a high value on nuclear family life, the men are encouraged to dedicate themselves to caring for their children. The religion offers men a source of identity beyond work and offers women the possibility of finding mates who will be supportive and responsible within the home (Davidman 1991, p. 117; Rochford 1985). Rose's (1987) and Stacey's (1990) studies of Evangelical Christians reveal that although the religious teachings of these groups are manifestly patriarchal, they also incorporate many contemporary feminist goals, such as the value of mutual open communication, support, and nurturance within a marriage. The women within these groups negotiated and willingly made compromises in order to "build up" their men into responsible, and responsive partners who would cooperate in the maintenance of a stable family unit.

Feminist researchers differ in their interpretations and assessments of these women's choices. Some see them primarily as victims of a patriarchal culture in which their socialization to traditional female roles makes them willing to forego gender equality and other forms of personal achievement in order to satisfy their desire for the primary goal of a woman's life—marriage and childbearing. Other feminist scholars see these women as agents in shaping their own fates, who, in the context of the disadvantaged position held by women in the larger society, actively make choices and develop strategies to "reshape family life in postmodern and postfeminist directions" (Stacey 1990, p. 261).

## GENDER AND THEORIES OF CONVERSION

In addition to scholarly emphases on the origins of new religious movements and gender and family within them, a great deal of research energy has been directed to understanding the processes of recruitment, conversion, and commitment into new religious movements; "it is the phenomenon that students of new religious movements examine most frequently" (Robbins 1988b, p. 63; Snow and Machalek 1984, pp. 167-168).

Among the various models proposed by sociologists, the most widespread acceptance has been enjoyed by those theories which highlight the importance of affective bonds and intensive interactions in the conversion process. These studies indicate that there are varieties of conversion experiences, that they do not all involve a mystical experience, and that many are effected through interpersonal relationships (Balch and Taylor 1978; Beckford 1978; Bromley and Shupe 1986; Lofland and Skonovd 1981; Lofland and Stark 1965; Rochford 1982; Snow et al. 1980; Snow and Phillips 1980; Stark and Bainbridge 1980a, 1980b; Travisano 1970). In reviewing ten models of the dynamics of conversion and commitment, Greil and Rudy (1984, p. 305) conclude that "only 'formation of affective bonds with group members' and 'intensive interactions' seem to be indispensable prerequisites for conversion." In effect, one is likely to be recruited to a movement to the degree that one is already linked to members through extra-movement social networks and to the degree that one is not inhibited by countervailing influences including alternative social networks and commitments "such as spouse, children, debts and occupational reputation" (Snow et al. 1980, p. 794).

Given recent theoretical developments on the ways in which women and men have distinct approaches to relationships, it is striking that the literature in the sociology of religion on the importance of affective bonds does not differentiate between women's and men's experiences. Are there differences in the kinds of bonds sought by women and men and in the nature of the relationships that attract them into the religious communities? The self-in-relation school in feminist theory (Chodorow 1978; Gilligan 1982; Miller 1976, 1984; Rubin 1976; Surrey 1984) suggests that women experience themselves as more interconnected with others than do men. Chodorow traces this to early childhood development and to the fact that boys, unlike girls, must separate themselves from their primary love object, their mother, in order to form their proper gender role identity. Consequently, thereafter males experience themselves as less interconnected with others than do females. Gilligan (1982, p. 171) writes that "in view of the evidence that women perceive and construe social reality differently from men and that these differences center around experiences of attachment and separation, life transitions that invariably engage these

experiences can be expected to involve women in a distinctive way." Thus this
feminist literature suggests that women would be more motivated to act in their
lives by factors having to do with relationships with others than would men.
How does this gender distinction apply within the field of conversion?

A feminist analysis might highlight the relationship between the higher
predilection for relationality among women and their recruitment and
conversion to new religious movements. It is evident that the large majority of
members of groups that require a radical departure from ordinary social life
are males. As Greil and Rudy (1984, p. 317) have written, depending on how
"deviant" the group is, the more it will require breaking bonds with the people
in one's life. In six out of their ten cases conversion appeared to be associated
with the neutralization or absence of extra-group affective ties. Joining a group
that involves a radical discontinuity of social roles almost by definition entails
breaking off contacts with individuals with whom one associated in previous
roles. Might this factor account for men's greater percentages in new religious
movements and women's higher numbers in occult groups, in contrast, which
require less breaking off of former ties (Tiryakian 1973)?

In recent years several studies of recruitment and conversion have appeared
which do show the influence of gender. Three studies in which gender and
conversion are discussed are Rochford's (1985) book on the Hare Krishna,
Jacobs' (1984, 1986, 1989) study of individuals who "deconvert" from new
religious movements, and Davidman's (1990a, 1990b, 1991) research on secular
Jewish women who become Orthodox.

In a chapter of his fine study of the Hare Krishna in America, Rochford
(1985) examines the way gender is a salient feature differentiating the
recruitment and socialization of men and women in the Hare Krishna
movement. He found that women were more likely to be recruited through
networks of friends and relatives while men are more likely to be recruited
through contact in public places. This research lends support to the feminist
self-in-relation theory, which highlights women's affiliative tendencies.

In her study of why women *leave* nontraditional religious movements,
Jacobs found that intimate relationships are central in women's conversion into
these groups. The women she spoke with all emphasized a relationship with
a guru or religious leader that played a critical role in their socialization into
membership. The women "deconverted," or left these religious groups, when
this special intimacy with the male religious figure deteriorated. She found that
"female religious commitment involves a love-centered economy in which
conversion is experienced as an emotional exchange" involving feelings of
affection, approval, and intimacy. She concludes that "gender is a defining
characteristic in religious commitment to alternative movements and that the
demands and obligations of spiritual commitment are specified according to
criteria which are sex-linked" (Jacobs 1984, p. 170).

In her study of *ba'alot teshuvah,* newly Orthodox Jewish women, Davidman
(1990a, 1990b, 1991) found that the search for nuclear family is a the most
important type of interpersonal bond sought by these "converts." Although

most studies of conversion report that the formation of interpersonal bonds between members and recruits is a central factor in the recruitment of members, the type of bonds they describe are those of friendship between peers, or even of surrogate family. But they do not highlight the desire to form a nuclear family as the kind of relationship that would be critical in bringing recruits into a religious community. By beginning with women's experiences, Davidman revealed a concern that may be important in many experiences of conversion in contemporary religious communities.

## INSIGHTS EMERGING FROM FEMINIST STUDIES OF RELIGION

In the above sections we have shown how feminist scholarship, with its emphasis on women's experiences and the centrality of the category of gender, can transform some of our basic understandings of critical phenomena in the study of new religious movements—their origins, family and gender patterns, and dynamics of recruitment and commitment. We have suggested ways in which attention to gender would further refine our empirical knowledge and theoretical understandings in these fields. In this section, we move beyond a critique and reformulation of those areas of research that arose out of the concerns of (mostly) male scholars to an examination of some new research foci and insights that emerge when the scholarship begins with women's distinctive experiences. Here we show how feminist scholarship in two new areas—studies of sexual exploitation and of women-centered religious groups—reveals and brings into focus aspects of social life that are invisible in mainstream research.

### Feminist Perspectives on Sexuality and Sexual Exploitation

One new area of interest arising from feminist concerns is the regulation and control over sexuality, and the deliberate sexual exploitation of women, within new religious movements (Jacobs 1984, 1989; Jones 1989, 1990; Goldman 1990). A review of the literature indicates the limited roles accorded women who were defined as either seductresses or concubines, depending on the ideology of the movement and the prerogatives of the men in power. In one of the earliest studies of a Christian community, Harder, Richardson, and Simmonds (1976) reported on the controls that were placed on women as a result of their potential harm: "Women are simultaneously viewed as sensuous beings and as temptresses. Because their bodies may cause men to desire pleasures of the flesh, women must dress and conduct themselves so as not to sexually arouse (cause to stumble) men and must take responsibility for avoiding potentially sexually charged situations" (1976, p. 157). Similar attitudes and regulations have been found in orthodox Hindu and Buddhist sects as well.

At the other end of the spectrum are those groups in which sexual service is defined as part of the female devotee's role within the movement. Within these religious communities, the women are expected to attract new recruits with their sexuality and to provide sexual partners to the men in the group (Wallis 1978; Jacobs 1984, 1989; Jones 1989, 1990). Spiritual growth is tied to sexual service as a place of privilege is accorded those women who are chosen to serve high-status men. Female recruits who reject such demands may be shunned or abused, while those who comply express a consciousness of submission that, as in the case of the fundamentalist appeal, may be seen as a reflection of the extent to which traditional female socialization informs religious experience and sexual identity.

The kind of sexual exploitation that has been found within these movements seems to be tied to the prevalence of charismatic leaders who value female recruits for the sexual pleasure they provide. Three significant examples, among others, discussed in the research are Father David Moses of the Children of God (Wallis 1978), Jim Jones of the People's Temple (Jones 1989, 1990), and Love Israel of the Love Family (Balch and Cohig 1985). In the Love Family, for example, Balch and J. Cohig report that Love Israel, the founder and "king" of the religious community, had two wives as well as sexual liaisons with other female devotees from whom he selected favorite partners to live in his household and accompany him on trips. This form of sexualization can become particularly destructive when one considers the paternal role of the charismatic leader. The affective bonds that inform such relationships confound the demands for sexual service with the promise of emotional caretaking from a godly parent, an attachment that is contextualized by gender inequality, a spiritual hierarchy, and competing relationships with other female followers.

## Women-Centered Religious Communities

Feminist analyses highlight the patriarchal nature of authority and leadership in many new religious movements. Their finding that male dominance and prescribed gender roles characterize the structure and ideologies of many "new" religious movements has led to new areas of inquiry on the meaning of gender differences in contemporary religious phenomena. One question that naturally arises is what differences might exist if the leaders of a movement were female rather than male? Would religious authority be expressed and practiced differently than what has been described thus far?

To answer this question, Wessinger (1990) pursued a study of Siddha Yoga, one of the few spiritual communities in which a female guru currently resides. Her findings offer a view of an alternative religious movement which is faced with the challenge of redefining gender within a larger religious tradition that equates the female with suffering and entrapment.

Although the female leadership in Siddha Yoga has attracted many professional women in the United States, the majority of teachers are men, while the philosophy stresses the significance of the divine masculine and feminine. Siddha Yoga thus represents a movement in which female leadership has begun to transform the foundations of patriarchal structure and theology. As such transformations are often painfully slow, however, a second area of inquiry has been focused on those new religious movements in which patriarchal hierarchies have been eliminated altogether and a feminine notion of the divine has replaced the masculine god image.

These goddess-centered groups, having emerged at the same time as the more authoritarian movements, were greatly influenced by the feminist movement and the desire for social change evident in the early 1970s. As an alternative to both the ethics of utilitarianism and self-expression described by Tipton, the women's spirituality movement has emphasized the significance of relational values and interconnectedness within a spiritual cosmology that seeks to restore a balance to humanity through the inclusion of a feminine spiritual presence and the practice of women-centered rituals (Culpepper 1978; Starhawk 1979, 1982; Ruether 1985).

Compared with the other forms of new religions, the women's groups have been studied much less extensively by contemporary sociologists. One notable exception is the work of Neitz (1990a) on feminist witchcraft as a mystery religion. In her research, she discusses the meaning of goddess symbology and the relationship between the witchcraft revival and the feminist movement. Neitz explores what it means to be a witch and the process of empowerment that is achieved through spiritual images and practices that validate the female self and affirm a feminine identity. As a result of her ethnographic research among feminist witches and neopagans, Neitz suggests a new understanding of the concept of power. Within conventional sociology, power is usually conceived in Weberian terms as the power of A to get B to do what A wants (i.e., "power over"). Within these discussions of power, "women and religion both get left behind, likely to be mentioned only to note their relative lack of power" (Neitz 1990b, p. 1). However, her fieldwork suggests that "part of what is going on for women in current religious movements is the attempt to gain legitimacy for power defined as A's ability for A to do what A wants" (1990b, p. 2). For women, who are often socialized to be responsive to others' needs, the idea that they can be free to explore and do what they themselves want is actually quite empowering.

By focusing on women's distinctive experiences, feminist researchers reveal significant dimensions of contemporary religion—such as the sexual exploitation of women in "new" religious movements, the nature of groups with women leaders, and the construction of a woman-centered religious form and symbology—that are generally not highlighted in the mainstream literature. Their scholarship suggests new meanings of conventional concepts such as power, religious authority, and magic. This newly emerging scholarship suggests that by beginning with women's experiences and including gender as a central analytic category in studies of religion, we will be able to expand our empirical and conceptual understanding of contemporary religious phenomena.

## GENDER, SOCIAL CHANGE, AND THE FUTURE OF NEW RELIGIOUS MOVEMENTS

In placing the research on new religions within the larger context of the sociology of religion, it is apparent from our analysis here that several gaps in the field still need to be addressed. From both an empirical and theoretical point of view, a more pluralistic perspective on religious experience would enhance our understanding of the complexity and diversity of cult and sect growth. The study of gender, race, and ethnicity provides a perspective in which movements such as the women's spirituality movement, the Black Muslims, and Santeria might be more fully investigated for differences and similarities to the other more well-researched groups that have dominated the scholarship in the field.

In particular, a more inclusive approach would expand the theoretical foundations on which the sociology of religion is built. Cultural and historical explanations, which until now have ignored the significance of marginalization in the emergence of alternative religious communities, might consider the social conditions and political realities affecting women and people of color as they seek to find spiritual expression in movements which are empowering and transformative.

One area that could be further elaborated is the relationship between religious conversion and social change. Here the women's spirituality movement offers a range of scholarly possibilities as we try to understand the ways in which religious innovation is a response to political and social oppression. Wiccan communities as well as other female-centered groups such as Women Church (Ruether 1985) present an opportunity to study nontraditional leadership styles and the success or failure of nonauthoritarian social structures. Further, these groups also provide a window into the study of social change because the ethics of any spiritual community have an impact on the world around it. A truly comprehensive understanding of new religions can thus benefit greatly from the study of women's experience and the identification of feminist innovations in the area of spiritual growth and development.

Scholars of new religious movements have been excited by the prospect of their research expanding the links between the sociology of religion and other subareas of sociology. The inclusion of the experiences of women and other marginalized groups in the development of research and theory in the sociology of religion will not only enrich this particular subfield, but will also expand its connections with the concerns of the larger discipline of sociology. Many articles, panel presentations, and efforts at curriculum development currently focus on the development of a more inclusive scholarship, one which will help us to understand social life from the perspectives of groups who have hitherto been marginalized. The discipline is beginning to move toward a broader conception of knowledge and theory, one which recognizes that all of social experience is fundamentally structured by gender, age, race, and social class. We hope that sociologists of religion will move further in this direction as well.

## ACKNOWLEDGMENT

The authors gratefully acknowledge the able research assistantship of Janet Stocks and Larry Greil's careful reading of two successive drafts of this paper.

# NOTES

1. This point—about the confinement of gender analyses to the domestic sphere and the lack of their incorporation in other areas—is made about the entire discipline of sociology in Stacey and Thorne's oft-cited article, "The Missing Feminist Revolution in Sociology" (1985).

2. This argument is highlighted in the discussion between Wuthnow and Stark in the *Journal for the Scientific Study of Religion* (1981).

# REFERENCES

Aidala, A. 1985. "Social Change, Gender Roles, and New Religious Movements." *Sociological Analysis* 46: 287-314.

Ammerman, N.T. 1987. *Bible Believers: Fundamentalists in the Modern World.* New Brunswick, NJ: Rutgers University Press.

Argyle, M., and B. Beit-Hallahmi. 1975. *The Social Psychology of Religions.* London: Routledge & Kegan Paul.

Aviad, J. 1983. *Return to Judaism: Religious Renewal in Israel.* Chicago: University of Chicago Press.

Balch, R.W., and J. Cohig. 1985. "The Magic Kingdom: A Story of Armageddon in Utopia." Paper presented at the annual meeting of the Society for the Scientific Study of Religion, Savannah, GA.

Balch, R.W., and D. Taylor. 1978. "Seekers and Saucers: The Role of the Cultic Milieu in Joining a UFO Cult." Pp. 43-64 in *Conversion Careers: In and Out of the New New Religions,* edited by J. Richardson. Beverly Hills, CA: Sage.

Beckford, J.A. 1978. "Accounting for Conversion." *British Journal of Sociology* 29: 249-262.

Bellah, R. 1975. *The Broken Covenant.* New York: Seabury.

————. 1976. "The New Religious Consciousness and the Crisis of Modernity." Pp. 335-352 in *The New Religious Consciousness,* edited by C. Glock and R. Bellah. Berkeley: University of California.

Berger, P. 1969. *The Sacred Canopy: Elements of a Sociological Theory of Religion.* Garden City, NY: Anchor Books.

Bromley D.G., and A.D. Shupe. 1986. "Affiliation and Disaffiliation: A Role-Theory Interpretation of Joining and Leaving New Religious Movements." *Thought* 61: 192-211.

Bromley, D.G., A.D. Shupe, and D.L. Oliver. 1982. "Perfect Families: Visions of the Future in a New Religious Movement." Pp. 119-130 in *Cults and the Family,* edited by F. Kaslow and M. Sussman. New York: Haworth.

Chodorow, N. 1978. *The Reproduction of Mothering: Psychoanalysis and the Sociology of Gender.* Berkeley: University of California Press.

Culpepper, E. 1978. "The Spiritual Movement of Radical Feminist Consciousness." Pp. 220-234 in *Understanding New Religions,* edited by G. Baker and J. Needleman. New York: Seabury Press:.

Danzger, H. 1989. *Returning to Tradition: The Contemporary Revival of Orthodox Judaism.* New Haven: Yale University Press.

Davidman, L. 1990a. "Accommodation and Resistance: A Comparison of Two Contemporary Orthodox Jewish Groups." *Sociological Analysis* 51: 35-51.

————. 1990b. "Women's Search for Family and Roots: A Jewish Religious Solution to a Modern Dilemma." Pp. 385-407 in *In Gods We Trust,* edited by T. Robbins and D. Anthony. 2nd ed. New Brunswick, NJ: Transaction Books.

————. 1991. *Tradition in a Rootless World: Women Turn to Orthodox Judaism.* Berkeley: University of California Press.

Eister, A.W. 1974. "Culture Crises and New Religious Movements." Pp. 612-627 in *Religious Movements in Contemporary America,* edited by I. Zaretskky and M. Leone. Princeton: Princeton University Press.

Fichter, J.H. 1985. *The Holy Family of Father Moon*. Kansas City, MO: Leaven.

Gilligan, C. 1982. *In a Different Voice: Psychological Theory and Women's Development*. Cambridge, MA: Harvard University Press.

Glock, C. 1976. "Consciousness Among Contemporary Youth: An Interpretation." Pp. 353-366 in *The New Religious Consciousness*, edited by C. Glock and R. Bellah. Berkeley: University of California Press.

Goldman, M. 1990. "From Promiscuity to Celibacy: Sexual Regulation at Rajneeshpuram." Paper presented at the annual meeting of the Society for the Scientific Study of Religion, Virginia Beach, VA.

Greil, A.L., and D.R. Rudy. 1984. "What Have We Learned From Process Models of Conversion? An Examination of Ten Studies." *Sociological Focus* 17: 305-323.

Harder, M.W., J.T. Richardson, and R. Simmonds. 1976. "Lifestyle: Courtship, Marriage, and Family in a Changing Jesus Movement Organization." *International Review of Modern Sociology* 6: 155-172.

Hunter, J. 1981. "The New Religions: Demodernization and the Protest Against Modernity." Pp. 1-20 in *The Social Impact of New Religious Movements*, edited by B. Wilson. Lewiston, NY: Edwin Mellen Press.

Jacobs, J.L. 1984. "The Economy of Love in Religious Commitment." *Journal for the Scientific Study of Religion* 23: 155-171.

_____. 1986. "Deconversion from Religious Movements: An Analysis of Charismatic Bonding and Spiritual Commitment." *Journal for the Scientific Study of Religion* 26: 294-308.

_____. 1989. *Divine Disenchantment*. Bloomington: University of Indiana Press.

Jones, A.C. 1989. "Exemplary Dualism and Authoritarianism at Jonestown." Pp. 209-227 in *New Religious Movements, Mass Suicide, and Peoples Temple*, edited by R. Moore and F. McGehee III. Lewiston, NY: Edwin Mellen Press.

_____. 1990. "Revolutionary Sex in Jonestown." Paper presented at the annual meeting of the Society for the Scientific Study of Religion, Virginia Beach, VA.

Kaufman, D.R. 1991. *Rachel's Daughters: Newly Orthodox Jewish Women*. New Brunswick, NJ: Rutgers University Press.

Kilbourne, B.K., and J.T. Richardson. 1982. "Cults vs. Families: A Case of a Misattribution of Cause." Pp. 81-100 in *Cults and the Family*, edited by F. Kaslow and M. Sussman. New York: Haworth Press.

Lofland, J., and L.N. Skonovd. 1981. "Conversion Motifs." *Journal for the Scientific Study of Religion* 20: 373-385.

Lofland, J., and R. Stark. 1965. "Becoming a World-Saver: A Theory of Conversion to a Deviant Perspective." *American Sociological Review* 30: 862-875.

Marx, J.D., and D.L. Ellison. 1975. "Sensitivity Training and Communes: Contemporary Quests for Community." *Pacific Sociological Review* 18: 441-460.

McGuire, M.B. 1982. *Pentecostal Catholics: Power, Charisma and Order in a Religious Movement*. Philadelphia: Temple University Press.

Miller, J.B. 1976. *Toward a New Psychology of Women*. Boston: Beacon Press.

_____. 1984. *The Development of Women's Sense of Self*. Work-in-Progress Series. Wellesley, MA: Wellesley Center for Research on Women.

Neitz, M.J. 1987. *Charisma and Community: A Study of Religion and Commitment Among the Catholic Charismatic Renewal*. New Brunswick, NJ: Transaction.

_____. 1990a. "In Goddess We Trust." Pp. 353-371 in *In Gods We Trust*, edited by T. Robbins and D. Anthony. 2nd ed. New Brunswick, NJ: Transaction.

_____. 1990b. "Contemporary Witches and the Feminist Reconceptualization of Power." Paper presented at the annual meeting of the Association for the Sociology of Religion, Washington, DC.

Nelson, H.M., N.H. Cheek, Jr., and P. Au. 1985. "Gender Differences in Images of God." *Journal for the Scientific Study of Religion* 24: 396-402.

Parsons, A.S. 1986. "Messianic Personalism in the Unification Church." *Journal for the Scientific Study of Religion* 25: 141-159.

Robbins, T. 1988a. "The Transformative Impact of the Study of New Religious Movements on the Sociology of Religion." *Journal for the Scientific Study of Religion* 27: 12-31.

————. 1988b. *Cults, Converts, and Charisma.* London: Sage.

Robbins, T., and D. Anthony. 1978. "New Religious Movements and the Social System: Integration, Disintegration or Transformation." *Annual Review of the Social Sciences of Religion* 21: 1-28.

————. 1979. "The Sociology of Contemporary Religious Movements." *Annual Review of Sociology* 4: 75-89.

————. 1982. "Cults, Culture and Community." Pp. 57-59 in *Cults and the Family,* edited by F. Kaslow and M. Sussman. New York: Haworth Press.

Robertson, R. 1985. "Beyond the Sociology of Religion." *Sociological Analysis* 46: 219-242.

Rochford, E.B. 1982. "Recruitment Strategies: Ideology and Organization in the Hare Krishna Movement." *Social Problems* 29: 339-410.

————. 1985. *Hare Krishna in America.* New Brunswick, NJ: Rutgers University Press.

Rose, S. 1987. "Women Warriors: The Negotiation of Gender in a Charismatic Community." *Sociological Analysis* 48: 245-258.

Ruether, R.R. 1985. *Woman-Church.* New York: Harper and Row.

Rubin, L. 1976. *Worlds of Pain: Life in the Working Class Family.* New York: Basic Books.

Snow, D., and R. Machalek. 1984. "The Sociology of Conversion." *Annual Review of Sociology* 10: 167-190.

Snow, D., and C. Phillips. 1980. "The Lofland-Stark Conversion Model: A Critical Reassessment." *Social Problems* 27: 430-447.

Snow, D.A., L.A. Zurcher, and S. Ekland-Olson. 1980. "Social Networks and Social Movements: A Microstructural Approach to Differential Recruitment." *American Sociological Review* 45: 787-801.

Stacey, J. 1990. *Brave New Families, Stories of Domestic Upheaval in Late Twentieth Century America.* New York: Basic.

Stacey, J., and B. Thorne. 1985. "The Missing Feminist Revolution in Sociology." *Social Problems* 32: 301-316.

Starhawk. 1979. *The Spiral Dance: A Rebirth of the Ancient Religion of the Great Goddess.* New York: Harper and Row.

————. 1982. *Dreaming the Dark.* Boston: Beacon Press.

Stark, R., and W.S. Bainbridge. 1980a. "Networks of Faith: Interpersonal Bonds and Recruitment to Cults and Sects." *American Journal of Sociology* 85: 1376-1395.

————. 1980b. "Towards a Theory of Religion: Religious Commitment." *Journal for the Scientific Study of Religion* 19: 114-128.

Surrey, J. 1984. *Self-in-Relation: A Theory of Women's Development.* Work-in-Progress Series. Wellesley, MA: Wellesley Center for Research on Women.

Tipton, S.M. 1982. *Getting Saved from the Sixties: Moral Meaning in Conversion and Cultural Change.* Berkeley: University of California Press.

Tiryakian, E. 1973. "Toward a Sociology of Esoteric Culture."*American Journal of Sociology* 78: 491-512.

Travisano, R.V. 1970. "Alternation and Conversion as Qualitatively Different Transformations." Pp. 594-606 in *Social Psychology through Symbolic Interaction,* edited by G. Stone and H. Farberman. Waltham, MA: Ginn-Blaisdell.

Wallis, R. 1978. "Recruiting Christian Manpower." *Society* 14: 72-74.

Warner, R. S. 1988. *New Wine in Old Wineskins: Evangelicals and Liberals in a Small-Town Church.* Berkeley: University of California Press.

Wessinger, C. 1990. "The Legitimation of Feminine Religious Authority: The Siddha Yoga Case." Paper presented at the annual meeting of the Society for the Scientific Study of Religion, Virginia Beach, VA.

Westley, F. 1978. "The Cult of Man: Durkheim's Predictions and the New Religious Movements."
    *Sociological Analysis* 39: 135-145.
————. 1983. *The Complex Forms of the New Religious Life: A Durkheimian View of New
    Religious Movements.* Chico, CA: Scholars Press.
Wuthnow, R. 1976. *The Consciousness Reformation.* Berkeley: University of California Press.
————. 1981. "Two Traditions in the Study of Religion." *Journal for the Scientific Study of
    Religion* 20: 16-32.

# PART IV

## THE ROAD TO MATURITY. FROM EPISTEMOLOGY TO A COMPREHENSIVE RESEARCH AGENDA

# WILL THE REAL CULT PLEASE STAND UP?
## A COMPARATIVE ANALYSIS OF SOCIAL
## CONSTRUCTIONS OF NEW RELIGIOUS MOVEMENTS

Eileen Barker

## ABSTRACT

Sociologists of religion are but one group of people who offer society a secondary construction of the social reality of new religious movements (NRMs). This paper examines the logic behind rival constructions in order to gauge how adequately they (compared with those constructed by sociologists) might be expected to reflect the NRMs' primary construction. Two fundamental differences emerge: one is concerned with the evaluations that are included in the construction, and the other with selection of the available data. It is argued that, although the NRMs may, in some ways, be the best able to reproduce the reality that they have created, there are ways in which this is not the case, and their representation of reality is less acceptable to society than other constructions. The anti-cult movement, being primarily concerned to convince others of the wrongfulness of the movements, will select only data that confirm a negative image of "destructive cults." The media, being concerned with producing "a good story" under constraints of limited time and space, are unlikely to reproduce the complexity of reality. Although no claim is made that all sociological versions of reality are superior to those produced by members of the NRMs, the ACM, or the media, the main thrust of the paper is that the logic of the sociological enterprise is more likely than that of the others to result in a version that can adequately reflect the primary construction of reality.

Religion and the Social Order, Volume 3B, pages 193-211.
ISBN: 1-55938-715-7

Members of a new religious movement (NRM) create and sustain a social reality in the most fundamental sense—through their actions, they *are* the reality. This primary construction of reality can be distinguished from secondary constructions which describe it. The distinction is, however, a fragile one which could be as confusing to make as to ignore, for there is an oft-permeated boundary between the two types of construction. Insofar as the members of NRMs are aware of and take account of secondary constructions of their reality, these enter into the realm of the ongoing primary construction. This paper is an exercise in tertiary construction in that it examines secondary constructions of NRMs by the NRMs themselves, by the anti-cult movement (ACM), by the media, and by sociologists of religion.

## A SOCIOLOGICAL PERSPECTIVE

Many of the challenges of social science stem from the fact that social reality is *both* an objective reality in the sense that individuals cannot wish it away, *and* idealistic in the sense that it exists only insofar as it is recognized by the actors who take it into account and whose actions are "thereby oriented in [their] course" (Weber 1964, p. 88; Berger and Luckmann 1967). The functioning of any society, and, indeed, of any human being, would be impossible without some shared understanding of the nature of social reality, but the fact that social reality exists only insofar as it is mediated through the minds of individuals means that different people will see and will respond to the same situation in different ways. Even identical twins in the most homogeneous or totalitarian of societies will see the world from a slightly different perspective.

It is, however, a basic assumption of the sociology of knowledge that differences in individuals' perceptions are not completely random, but that many of the disparities are systematically related to such variables as values, ideological or economic interests, subcultural assumptions, previous experiences, position in society, and so on. The sociologist would expect the youthful convert, the leader, the parent of the convert, and the sociologist of religion to construct images of an NRM in what are, to at least some extent, *systematically different* ways.

Furthermore, just as one cannot assume that there is a single verity to be known, so one cannot assume that "anything goes." Concepts of truth and falsity are not irrelevant to secondary constructions of reality. Insofar as social reality is "out there" and has to be taken into account by others, it is, to some extent at least, empirically testable by any human being who is capable of recognizing its existence. This is true whether the knowledge needed to attain that information is gleaned directly from members through participation, observation, interview, or questionnaire, or through a variety of more indirect means. It is quite obvious that some secondary constructions of reality are simply not true—that is, they bear no relation to the empirically observable primary reality. Anyone claiming that the Unification Church was part of the 1990s drug scene or that the Brahma Kumaris indulged in sexual orgies would have an extremely difficult task to convince anyone who was seriously concerned with the investigation of what these movements actually believe and practice. On the other hand, it would be comparatively easy to demonstrate that Rastafarians have made use of an illegal drug and followers of Bhagwan Rajneesh have been encouraged to explore all manner of sexual practices.

This is not to say that myths do not abound which bear very little resemblance to the reality revealed by empirical scrutiny. Thus, the number of members in a movement may be grossly exaggerated both by the movement, which wishes to give an impression of its success, and by deprogrammers, who wish to deny the high rate of voluntary turnover in the movement as this would challenge their version of reality which insists that the members are incapable of leaving the movement without outside intervention. The membership might also be grossly exaggerated in the minds of people who are continually hearing about the movements in the media and come to confuse high visibility with high numbers.

## Producers and Consumers of Secondary Constructions

While this paper concentrates on the production of images of NRMs, it should not be forgotten that production is usually intended for consumption. As in any market, the consumers may create a demand for the production of particular kinds of goods and the producers will respond to this demand. In other words, consumer demand for a particular kind of knowledge can have an effect not only on the secondary constructs but also, in some circumstances, on the primary reality of the NRM.

In the comparisons that follow, the aim is not to expose deception or stupidity (although one can certainly find examples of both in all the categories), but to explore the *logic* of the differing positions and interests. The complexity of the subject matter and the shortage of space means that the differences within the different categories cannot be explored in the detail they deserve, but it is possible to suggest by way of ideal-type characterizations (or, perhaps, caricature-like sketches) the differences to be found between the various categories.

# NEW RELIGIOUS MOVEMENTS' CONSTRUCTIONS

## The Constantly Changing Nature of Primary Construction

No attempt is being made here to describe the variety between primary constructs of NRMs, but a brief comment ought to be made about the ways in which any movement is likely to change over a relatively short time, for rarely do the secondary constructions take these into account in any detail. The primary reality of an NRM is usually constructed in its original format from the perspective of the individual who is the movement's founder. If, however, movements are to become *social* realities, their founders must have followers, which means that the founders must communicate knowledge (in the widest sense) that is taken sufficiently seriously by enough people to construct an NRM.

With the passage of time, the reality becomes more complex and more differentiated; knowledge of its various aspects will be more or less shared by different people from a number of different perspectives. Various factors will promote the growing complexity: an increasing number of followers may play a role in negotiating the construction, emphasizing those parts that are more easily assimilated, and, later, the followers may "elect" those features that fit their particular interests or with which they have a particular "affinity" (Weber 1948, p. 63). Structural changes occurring through a growth in membership will be accompanied both by the increase of secondary rather than face-to-face relations and by the development of more or less institutionalized communication networks and power structures. There will also be demographic changes with the aging of first-generation converts and the birth of second-generation children and, eventually, the death of the founder (Barker 1991a).

Further changes can be expected due to interaction with the "outside." Not only political, economic, legal, and social pressures, but, as already mentioned, the competing definitions of the NRM may have to be taken into account. Results may include antagonisms, accommodation, withdrawal, or a variety of other responses that will alter the processes involved in the continuing construction of the primary reality—and the processes involved in the continuing construction of secondary realities.

### NRMs' Secondary Constructions in Relation to Those of Sociologists

It might appear, and many members of NRMs might assert, that it was a simple, logical step to move from the level of a primary construction of reality to a secondary one, but only a few seconds' reflection would show that this is by no means the case. Of course, one would expect that an NRM (and, indeed, an old religious movement) would want to create as good an impression of itself as possible. NRMs will want to proclaim (or, in the case of more esoteric movements, try to keep secret) the "truth" which the members will want to *live* and use to change themselves and, perhaps, to change the world (Barker 1988). Important validatory sources of knowledge for the NRM are likely to be divine revelation or personal experiences of an untestable nature. Some NRMs explicitly reject rational thought or intellectual endeavors on the grounds that these can interfere with "'true understanding."

Sociologists have no expertise with which to judge the truth or falsity of the theological or ideological claims that the NRM makes. They may not invoke God as an independent variable; they can merely observe that, under certain circumstances, members have reported that they have been guided or influenced by God, the Holy Spirit or, possibly, satanic forces. While sociologists may try to persuade the NRM that the restriction imposed by their methodological agnosticism on what they can include in their secondary descriptions of reality is neutral so far as the truth of the movement's supernatural beliefs is concerned, the NRM may quite reasonably view the sociologists' theological reductionism as a denial of the movement's most central and significant message. In such circumstances, the sociological construction may be seen as at best irrelevant. But sociologists may also be seen as a nuisance or even as a threat. They might expose knowledge that the NRM would rather keep undisclosed because it is naturally anxious to present a face that, even if it is not acceptable to the world, would at least be acceptable to its actual and potential members.

### Physical Access for Purposes of Secondary Constructions

All this can, of course, give rise to technical problems of physical access, raising ethical and methodological issues about the use of covert research to acquire otherwise unobtainable data. While originally several NRMs were not averse to being studied in the perhaps somewhat naive belief that sociologists would further their aims by publicizing their new truths, they were later to become more cagey. This scenario was clearly illustrated in the early 1960s when John Lofland persuaded the early members of the Unification Church in California to let him study how the movement went about gaining members and building itself up (Lofland [1966] 1977, p. 269). In this, it seemed at first that his interests largely coincided with those of the members, who were eager to improve their skills of proselytization. Within less than a year, however, the local leader told Lofland that, because he was displaying no interest in converting to the movement, his presence was no longer welcome; so far as she was concerned, "to present only the 'sociological part' would be to grossly distort the movement" (p. 274). To complete his study, Lofland relied on information that was gained by a young sociology undergraduate who feigned conversion and was accepted by the movement as a convert (p. 275).

Thirty years later, several developments have been observed, one of which is that a few of those NRMs which had become most suspicious and difficult to access have started approaching sociologists asking to be studied by them. Of course, this apparent faith in the sociological approach is not without its problems for sociologists, several of whom have been accused of being "apologists for the cults." It should also be pointed out that there are still several NRMs who are extremely resistant to any attempts to find out anything about their beliefs, practices, or organization.

But why, it might be asked, would any NRM be turning to sociologists rather than promoting its own secondary constructions of its own reality for outside consumption? There are several reasons, one being that the general image now held by most consumers (with good reason in several instances) is that NRMs are not to be trusted, however glossy the packaging or sincere their members may seem to be. A related reason is that the expertise of sociologists is at least relatively well respected in society, so their construction is more likely to be listened to. Moreover, on the whole, sociologists' accounts of NRMs have been less negative than the images created by the anti-cultists and much of the media, so it is supposed that, even if the sociologist does not construct exactly the kind of image the NRM would choose, at least there is a fair chance that the movement will not be falsely accused of beliefs which it does not hold or actions in which it insists it does not (at least now) indulge. A further reason why the NRMs might be wise to offer the market sociologists' constructs rather than their own is probably a reason unrecognized by most NRMs: the reason is not so much that the reputation or status of social science means that sociologists will be *listened to,* but that the logic of its approach means that they are more likely to be *heard.*

## Subjective Access for Purposes of Secondary Construction

To elaborate this point is to explore a bit further a wider issue of subjective access—that is, whether believers (primary constructors) are the only people who can really know what the reality of the movement is (Barker 1989a). There is a sense in which it might seem obvious, at least to the members, that no one could know the truth about their movement better than they themselves. In one sense, of course, this is correct. But there is another sense in which a movement may not be as able as outsiders to give as complete, balanced or contextualized a picture of themselves as others might. As Wilson (1970, p. ix) has pointed out:

> there is a sense in which it could be said that no one but a medieval man could possibly understand medieval society. But there is also a sense, and the statement is no less comprehensible to us, in which we may say that medieval man had little or no chance of ever understanding medieval society.

## The Communication of Social Reality

There is also a sense in which it is often easier for nonmembers to *communicate* the social reality of an NRM than it is for the insiders themselves. This is because all secondary constructions of reality are likely to be both more and less than the reality itself: "less" in that clearly every single action of every single member cannot be faithfully be reproduced—some selection is necessary; "more" in that, because the consumer of the information has not been in the same situation and does not share the same assumptions as the member, some kind of contextualization and *translation* has to be carried out. This is where one might suggest that sociologists have to add art to their science if they are to be successful in their endeavor *to reproduce–by not reproducing precisely.* Perhaps an analogy taken from the theater could make this clearer: the actor depicting a bore on stage is successful only in so far as he is *not* boring, *yet* is reproducing boringness in such a way that it is recognizable as part of a shared understanding of what a boring person is like.

This is not to suggest that believers and practitioners cannot produce excellent studies of their own religion. Some clearly have done that very thing: Jules-Rossette (1975), Hornsby-Smith (1991), Mickler (1980), Pearson (1990), and Smith (1987) are but a few examples. But the very success of these authors lies in the fact that, having embraced the interests and methods of the social scientist, they have not written as though they were members of their religion. Their writing has been impeccably scholarly and objective—even to the extent that it can be argued that, although one receives a considerable amount of accurate and valuable knowledge from these studies, they reveal remarkably little in the way of insight as to what it is like actually to be a member (Barker 1987, pp. 138-139). Such insight for the nonmember consumer can sometimes appear to come more readily from nonmembers.

In other words, it is possible that the sociological believer, aware of the potential accusation of producing a biased account of his or her own reality, is extra cautious not to paint a picture which would depict the more sensual aspects of membership. By "sensual," I am not referring to sexual connotations of the concept, but to a general subjective "feel." Indeed, to try to impart this sense of what it is like to be a member can be to open oneself to accusations of being a covert believer. Drawing on my own personal experience, which several conversations with colleagues suggest is far from unique, I have been accused at various times of being a Unificationist, a Krishna devotee, a New Ager, a pawn of the Church of Scientology, and a fundamentalist Christian who rejects the theory of evolution (as the result of my writing an article on "scientific creationism"). Needless to say, I deny all charges, but confess that I have not yet found a way of getting round the problem that actors in the theater or television have of portraying a character and having some of their audience assume that they are really portraying themselves.

Part of the problem is that, like the dramatic actor, but unlike the natural scientist, sociologists, especially when engaged in participant observation, *do* draw on their own emotions and experiences in order to empathize (but not necessarily sympathize) with the character in order to try to understand how it feels to be in a particular situation—and then to communicate this understanding to the consumer-audience. At the same time, however, sociologists in the field (like actors on the stage) must be continually aware of what is going on—recognizing that they are both feeling from within and, as it were, watching from outside themselves. While the actor is waiting for a laugh to die down, or checking that the properties are correctly set, the sociologist is observing the communication structure, noting undercurrents in the group interaction, noticing which actors are allowed to interrupt others, which are sitting as though alert and interested, which are bored, apathetic or angry, and so on (Barker 1987, pp. 142-143).

In other words, the suggestion in this section has been that primary constructors of reality are not necessarily the most effective persons to construct for others an accurate image of their own reality. It is not so much that sociologists are likely to paint a "better" picture of reality, but that for a social reality to be understood by nonparticipants, more than a straightforward description to which they may have access is necessary. The sociologist will certainly want to have access to the members—they are a necessary part of his or her data, but they are not sufficient.

## THE ANTI-CULT MOVEMENT'S (ACM'S) CONSTRUCTIONS

Just as few members of NRMs like to be called cultists or, indeed, for their movement to be called an NRM and thus "lumped together with all those bizarre cults," so do few people like to be called anti-cultists. Sometimes the term "cult watchers" is employed. The term anti-cultist is, however, being used in this paper in order to make a distinction between those whose primary interest or concern is with what are perceived as the negative aspects of NRMs, rather than with merely watching them. Included in this very broad category are groups of concerned relatives of members, certain sections of mainstream religions (especially, but by no means exclusively, some evangelical Protestant groups) and, in the United States, some concerned members of the Jewish community. "Professional deprogrammers" (those who charge fees of tens of thousands of dollars for kidnapping and holding members of NRMs against their stated will in order to dissuade them from membership of their movement) are certainly to be included among the anti-cultists, but the majority of anti-cultists would not, at least publicly, applaud this illegal and extreme type of action. While there have always been a few loners in the ACM, most anti-cultists belong to, or are in close communication with, one or other of the organizations that have grown up during the past two decades or so. There now exists an international network, exchanging information and speakers between such groups as the American Family Foundation (AFF) and the Cult Awareness Network (CAN) in the United States, Family Action Rescue and Information (FAIR) in the United Kingdom, Schweizerische Arbeitsgruppe gegen Destruktive Kulte (SADK) in Switzerland, Aktion für geistige und psychische Freiheit (AGPF) in Germany, L'Union Nationale des Associations de Défense des Familles et de L'Individu (UNADFI) in France, and the Concerned Christians Growth Ministries (CCG Ministries) in Australia. A sizeable literature has been published both by and about the ACM (Beckford 1985; Saliba 1990, pp. 618-652; Shupe and Bromley 1980; Shupe et al. 1984).

All members of the ACM are committed to a negative evaluation of NRMs or, as they commonly call them, "destructive cults" (Robbins 1988, p. 143). However, the extent to which they are motivated to do something about this interest ranges from wanting to expose the movements and warn others of actual or potential dangers associated with the movements, to wanting to ban them or at least some of their practices, and/or to destroy them altogether, possibly through crippling litigation. The methods that the ACM employs at the societal level in pursuit of its goals include lobbying, legal actions, feeding the media with "atrocity tales," "outrageous incidents" (Shupe and Bromley 1980, pp. 170-173), or "negative summary events" (Beckford 1985, pp. 224-230). At the individual level, methods include "strategic intervention therapy," "exit counselling" (Hassan 1988) and, in extremis, deprogramming (Patrick 1976). Clearly, in order to persuade people that "something ought to be done" about NRMs, it is only logical that the ACM would be disposed to construct pictures of the movements in which mainly or exclusively negatively evaluated aspects are included; any of the more positive or even ambiguous factors are likely to be rejected or ignored.

It might be noted, however, that some evangelically oriented groups (e.g., the Dialog Center in Denmark and the Christian Research Institute in California) have some of the best data available on NRMs, and *because* of rather than in spite of their commitment to both evangelistic and educational purposes, they construct a less distorted picture of NRMs than do many of the more secular anti-cultists. Their primary interest being in sound doctrine, and their point of reference being Biblically based, they are less tempted to select and concentrate on only the negative aspects of empirically observable behavior. For the religiously motivated members of the ACM, the main criterion for judging an NRM is their own source of revelation. Books by evangelical Protestants in particular meticulously survey the beliefs and practices of NRMs, citing Holy Scripture to expose the wrongness of the movement (e.g., Allan 1980; Martin 1980). This, of course, is not a debate into which the sociologist can enter, except perhaps to point out where the ACM has misunderstood the NRM's beliefs, possibly because concepts are being used with a different meaning by the two parties.

The source of information on which the more secular sections of the ACM rely for construction purposes tends predominantly to be bitter ex-members and antagonistic relatives and friends of members. Such people can be a valuable source of knowledge, but, by themselves, they are liable to produce as biased a picture of the movement as using divorcees to construct a picture of marriage would produce. The ACM does have one other important source of information: the media. It should, however, be noted that there is a close symbiotic relationship between the ACM category and a subgroup of the media, with each feeding the other a continually recycled stock of atrocity tales about the NRMs. It is not uncommon for members of the ACM to produce as evidence of a particular phenomenon a newspaper description of an NRM that has, itself, originated from the ACM. This will be discussed further in the next section.

One source of data that members of the ACM are unlikely to turn to directly is the raw data of the NRMs themselves. They may offer several reasons for this: the cults would not allow the ACM to study them, the cults would only lie, and the cults are dangerous and might exert some kind of mind control over ACM researchers. Of course, the ex-members on whom the ACM relies have had firsthand experience with their movement, and many of them have now written informative accounts of their experiences. It should, however, be borne in mind that several studies have shown that the descriptions of NRMs that have been constructed by ex-members who have been associated with the ACM have a more negative evaluation than those produced by ex-members who have not been so affected. Indeed, part of the exit counselling (and deprogramming) that is carried out by members of the ACM is explicitly intended *to teach* ex-members what happened to them during their sojourn in the movement—especially that they had been under the influence of mind control and that few if any of the decisions that they thought they were making were in fact the outcome of their own volition (Barker 1984, p. 129; Lewis 1986; Solomon 1981; Wright 1987).

Another source that the ACM does not turn to very frequently is sociology. It is true that there are a few sociologists of religion who are quoted with some frequency; Ronald Enroth and Richard Ofshe are examples of respected professional sociologists who have produced publications acceptable to the ACM; Ofshe is a Director of the American Family Foundation; Enroth is associated with the Christian Research Institute. But, generally speaking, there has developed a sharp rift between sociologists, especially those who have studied the movements at first hand, and members of the ACM. Those within each category tend to cite colleagues in the same category; if they do cite members of the other category, this tends to be in a fashion that cursorily dismisses the evidence or construction of reality that the other has offered. It is probably true that the sociologists tend to read the ACM literature more frequently than the anti-cultists read that of the sociologists. However, sociologists are likely to be doing so, not so much because they believe that there is intrinsically anything reliable in the ACM construction of reality, but because they are viewing the ACM and its literature as part of their data.

So far as the ACM attitude toward the sociological studies of the NRMs is concerned, it sometimes appears that these are seen to pose a greater threat to the ACM's construction of reality than do those of the NRMs. It is not just that consumers might pay more attention to sociologists' constructs than they do to those of the NRMs (something that has been true only so far as limited, though significant, groups of consumers are concerned), but that the sociologists' constructs have challenged those of the ACM in a way that the constructs of the NRMs have not. Sociological constructions tend to be more complicated, perhaps more tentative and certainly less obviously evaluative than those of either the NRMs or the ACM.

On a number of occasions, when trying to demonstrate to anti-cultists that they are factually wrong about a relatively straightforward piece of information (such as the Moonies' rate of voluntary defection), the evidence and/or argument has not been refuted or debated so much as dismissed. In a similar vein, pointing out that changes have occurred within an NRM with the passage of time is likely to be greeted with the rejoinder that such information "only muddies the waters"—unless, of course, the change is for the worse and some new sins can be exposed.

The message is clear enough: I and other sociologists have been given it enough times by members of both NRMs and the ACM: "you are either with us or against us;" "fudging the issue doesn't help matters; it just makes them worse"; and so on. I have been present on at least two separate occasions when ex-members have spoken at meetings about their experiences with a certain amount of ambivalence, stating that although they now realize that they made a mistake or that it was time to move on, they had gained much of value from the time spent with their erstwhile movement. On each occasion, anti-cultists who were present refused to accept that these were "really" ex-members; it was, they declared, clear that they were still in the clutches of their NRMs (although most of the ex-members had left their movements several years earlier). "Real" ex-members, according to the ACM's construction of reality, must be totally opposed to the NRM if they have really left. On the first of the two occasions, one anti-cultist actually got up when an ex-member was trying to answer a question and started shouting hysterically, "We don't want to hear this! It's just deceit and lies. It's not helpful at all. We don't want to hear any more!" (Barker 1990, p. 4).

In other words, the ACM, like some of the NRMs to which it is opposed, prefers to keep matters simple and have clear boundaries separating the members from the nonmembers, and, even more specifically, from ex-members; the "in"/"out" distinction must not allow for either ambiguity or ambivalence. In fact, the ACM and the NRMs often agree over boundaries—the disagreement is on the evaluation and characterization of the content of what is on either side of the boundary. Some of the NRMs, particularly the Church of Scientology, are actively constructing pictures of the ACM which focus exclusively on the worst excesses of the movement, ignoring the very real attempts that have been made to help people who have suffered because of some of the NRMs' worst excesses. Each side can, in fact, through its construction of the other's reality, reinforce the boundary between them and even provide the other side with a justification for behaving in a more extreme (and negative) manner through "deviance amplification" (Wallis 1976, pp. 214ff).

The logic is undeniable. If the primary concern is to expose the harmfulness of the NRMs, it is counterproductive to distinguish too carefully between the "destructive cults" on the one hand, or not to distinguish carefully enough between cultists and ex-cultists on the other hand. Furthermore, general pronouncements that offer an all-encompassing negative evaluation are less likely to be successfully challenged than those which give precise details about a particular movement. In this way, without giving rise to direct allegations, the sins of one can be visited on all, or the consumer at least does not have to face the complexity of discovering that not all "destructive cults" are equally guilty of the same anti-social patterns of behavior. While Ross and Langone (1988, p. 3) carefully make the point that every case is unique, they say that they "intentionally avoid listing 'bad groups' in order to emphasize the parents' responsibility to find out about the cult to which *their* child belongs." One might be excused for wondering whether other reasons for not mentioning the NRMs by name include a reasonable desire to keep clear of libel suits—and a desire not to find themselves in the position of "muddying the waters." The book contains a great deal of useful advice as to how parents might react to their offspring's joining an NRM, but most sociologists who have studied the movements would find it difficult to endorse without qualification the one-sided picture it draws of the movements. In reading the section that outlines the characteristics of destructive cults, for example, it would certainly be difficult for a parent with no other knowledge not to receive the impression that "destructive cults" are shrouded in secrecy and use unethical means to manipulate and recruit members (which frequently lead to drastic and destructive personality changes and the break-up of families), quite apart from the fact that they "have been known to engage in deceptive and unlawful practices that violate the very fabric of our democratic society" (Ross and Langone 1988, p. 20).

It is, of course, true that some NRMs have engaged in deceptive and unlawful practices, but this applies to relatively few of the movements that have been the subject of investigation by the American Family Foundation. It is also true that quite a few people *not* in NRMs have engaged in deceptive and unlawful practices—including, one might add, several members of the ACM. And, like most members of the ACM, Ross and Langone make full play of the People's Temple tragedy in Guyana (almost the only movement to be mentioned by name), without raising the point that the membership, beliefs, and practices which were to be found in Jonestown were patently dissimilar to those found in the majority of the so-called "destructive cults" (Richardson 1980).

The main argument in this section has been that if the main purposes of a secondary constructor of reality are to demonstrate that the primary reality is a bad thing, and to lobby against this bad thing, then directly opposing perspectives (those of the NRMs) may be used with a mirror evaluation placed on them—good turning to bad, truth to deception, right to wrong, or godly to satanic. At the same time, secondary constructions of reality that are full of qualifications (illustrating the different ways in which a primary reality may be experienced) and that also refuse to become clearly embroiled in evaluative judgments, can be seen as more threatening than the unambiguously "wrong" construction. The ambiguous and/or complex pictures are at best (and here the ACM and the NRM might at times find themselves in agreement) irrelevant or distracting and a watering down of the truth; at worst they are a competitor that threatens to discredit both the movement (NRM or ACM) and its constructions and so prevent it from fulfilling its mission. The logic of such a situation is to deny or, if possible, dismiss or ignore the sociological construction.

## THE MEDIA'S CONSTRUCTIONS

The media have produced some excellent and accurate information about NRMs; they have also produced some of the most irresponsible and fantastic constructions. People working in the media need to sell "newsworthy" stories, and are nearly always under considerable constraints of both time and space. Journalists usually have to work to a deadline, and will be allotted only a few hundred or a few thousand words; if the medium is radio or television, the time for transmitting a construction of reality is usually limited to minutes. There are occasions when members of the media have written books. Among the most impressive of these are Fitzgerald's (1987) account of Rajneeshpuram, originally published in *The New Yorker,* and the investigation into the School of Economic Science by Hounam and Hogg (1984). Two *Standard* reporters, Kilduff and Javers (1978) of the *San Francisco Chronicle* and Krause et al. (1978) with his team of staff from the *Washington Post* managed to produce books on "the Suicide Cult" within days of the "Guyana Massacre." Given the speed with which these two books were produced, they were remarkably informative, but for fullness and balance of a construction of reality, they can bear no comparison to Hall's (1987) sociological description and analysis of the history, ideology, and final tragedy of the People's Temple.

Numerous studies have been made of ways in which the media create realities and some of the factors that influence their creations (e.g., the Glasgow University Media Group 1976, 1980; Gumpert and Cathart 1982; Gurevitch et al. 1982). Sociologists of deviance (e.g., Cohen and Young 1973) have illustrated ways in which the media not only distort but actually manufacture news, creating a mythical movement which can then become a reality. Van Driel and Richardson (1988, p. 37) summarize their analysis of print media coverage of NRMs as showing that:

> News about "cults" in the United States is "clearly information by outsiders for outsiders" and, although not uniformly negative, can best be described as "a stream of controversies" with little attention to the history or human side of the new religions.

While van Driel and Richardson concluded that the majority of stories could not be categorized as mouthpieces for the ACM (with the notable exception of those appearing during the months following the Jonestown suicides), they did find that the overall tone of coverage was negatively slanted because it was almost always the controversies that made the news. Thus the "continual reporting of controversies and accusations may have fostered a climate in which NRMs became synonymous with 'problematic', 'controversial,' and 'deviant'" (van Driel and Richardson 1988, p. 57). Beckford and Cole (1988, p. 218) found that the print media in Britain was considerably more negative in its reporting of NRM stories than it was in stories about other religious minorities, 12.5 percent of stories about NRMs (compared to 1 percent about other religious minorities) being "extremely negative," 35.8 percent (13.75 percent) being "negative," 46.3 percent (55 percent) "neutral," and 5.4 percent (30 percent) being "positive" or "extremely positive." Beckford and Cole (1988, p. 217) note, furthermore, that the neutral and positive stories tended to be brief news reports, while the longer stories tended to be the more negative ones.

The extent to which NRMs have literally "had a bad press" has been illustrated on a number of occasions when people, most of whose knowledge of NRMs has been built up by the media alone, have been asked their opinion about the movements. In one public opinion survey, over one-quarter of the respondents expressed an unfavorable attitude toward a nonexistent "spoof" cult (Lindt and Gollin 1979, p. 18). In the early 1980s, I asked the control group for my study of the Unification Church what they knew about the "Moonies." Nearly all the respondents who admitted to knowing anything offered a negative evaluation, using words such as "scary," "fake," "bizarre," and "dangerous," with only a few remembering any factual information that might have given rise to such evaluations. Overwhelmingly, their source of information had been the media, although some had talked to a Unificationist in the street and one or two knew of someone who had joined the movement (Barker 1984, pp. 2-3). Similarly, Beckford (1985, p. 231) reports that his research into family responses to the Unification Church in Britain has shown that "the mass media are frequently the single most important influence on people's attitudes towards the movement."

The very success of the media in reaching more consumers than any other group in society means that this accumulation of controversies, at the expense of noncontroversial stories, builds up a conventional wisdom that is almost bound to be biased against the movements. Perfectly true stories relating a genuine tragedy can come to constitute part of a taken-for-granted public assumption that the tragedies are peculiarly related to NRMs rather than to other sections of society which are not singled out as being so newsworthy. If, for example, a member of a NRM commits suicide, this may be accurately reported under the heading "Cultist Kills Herself." It is, however, unlikely that one would read a headline declaring "Methodist Kills Herself"—in the second case the woman's religious affiliation is not normally considered newsworthy. Thus, with the passage of time, the impression might be given that members of NRMs are especially prone to committing suicide. Members of the media rarely have the time or inclination to pursue the comparative approach which is central to the scientific enterprise and which would, in this instance, require that the rate of suicides in NRMs was compared to that of nonmembers of a similar age and social background. If such an exercise were to reveal that members of NRMs were less likely to kill themselves than were the nonmembers, the question might be raised as to whether NRMs played a role in preventing suicide (Barker 1989b, pp. 40-41). The point is, of course, that newsworthiness leads to selective visibility, and that selective visibility does not necessarily reflect the primary reality.

The sources of information used by the media vary enormously, but to the extent that the pressures of time are great and the slot is short, the more likely it is that easily accessible information will be used—other things being equal. This propensity, together with the need for "newsworthiness," tends to make "the grieving mother," "the abandoned wife," or the ex-member who wishes to air a grudge against his erstwhile movement likely to be among the more tempting sources. It takes far more time and effort to seek out ex-members who have no particular axe to grind and now want to resume a "normal" life in peace, or parents who are not overly concerned by their sons' or daughters' unconventional beliefs and life-style; and even if (perhaps because) such people are more "ordinary," they are less likely to produce an interesting story. While media stories frequently focus on a particular individual (grieving mother, abandoned wife, rescued victim) with the NRM forming a "sinister," "secret," or "bizarre" backcloth, there are occasions when the NRM is given the opportunity to present its side of the story. However, as Beckford and Cole (1988, p. 220) point out, even if it appears "as if 'equal time' has been allowed to the two sides... this kind of objectivity conceals the fact that these typically, if not uniformly, adversarial structures only reinforce the image of NRMs as primarily controversial."

Sociologists are quite frequently approached, but their carefully considered writings are rarely read by the media constructors, who may be looking for a quick introduction to the movement, an "angle," or perhaps the name of someone who can provide a "personal story." Occasionally "the dispassionate expert" will be invited to comment with a few pithy remarks, but only very occasionally will there be the opportunity to develop a more sophisticated discussion. And, even when the media producers do present a more sophisticated picture, it is unlikely that the consumer public would be able to absorb it in the limited space and time. Despite their enormous impact on the public, the media are selectively ephemeral. It is the more disturbing cuttings that are preserved or programs videoed for recycling by the ACM; mostly the stories are thrown away within hours of being read, and the television program has faded into the ether. There is rarely the opportunity to question or to check for references or, indeed, to examine what was actually presented. Memories are not always reliable; evaluations may stick, but often it is only the odd phrase or visual image, perhaps memorable for its unusualness, that will be recalled.

Although there have been libel cases brought by some NRMs, these have been few, and not notably successful. In England, the Unification Church lost a 6-month libel case that it brought against the *Daily Mail* for a story alleging the movement brainwashed its members and broke up families (Barker 1984, pp. 2, 120-121; 1989c, pp. 197-198). In 1988, an article in *La Suisse* suggested that the leaders of the Unification Church push the members into prostitution and suicide. Three years later, a court in Geneva ruled that the story was libellous and had not been substantiated by the evidence; but, the court also ruled, the journalists had written what they did in good faith as the image of the movement was such that it was understandable that they should write such things (*Jugement du Tribunal de Police*, Cause No. 1-P/4465/89, Geneve 1991). In other words, the assumption was that journalists might be expected to take seriously the versions of the reality of the Unification Church that had been constructed by others and that they could be at least partially absolved from responsibility for not making the kinds of enquiries that the court had made after the church had brought the case.

Finally, mention might be made of some of the ways in which language may be employed by the media to promote loaded images. The metaphor of "brainwashing" is a favorite concept, and adjectives such as crazy or sinister are used with remarkable frequency. Indeed, one may recognize whole phrases such as "parents fight brainwashing by bizarre sect" being repeated over and over again, presumably as the result of a pressurized journalist going through the clippings files for a quick reference point. Bundles of ideas can be communicated through the use of a single concept, and although there may be no conscious intention of communicating more than a straightforward description of a particular phenomenon, in practice certain concepts are almost bound to suggest a moral evaluation. The label "cult" has been recognized for some time as doing this. Indeed, many of the movements have now come to dislike being referred to as new religions because they see it as associating them with other groups with whom they, perhaps quite correctly, believe that they have little in common but which are known to be "bad."

Polemical use is made not only of evocative concepts but also of other semantic techniques, such as the use of the passive rather than the active voice for the verb, and the infiltration of unexamined assumptions about what is "natural" or "normal." Thus what might otherwise be viewed as "choice" can be translated into coercion, and, conversely, what might otherwise be viewed as "coercion" translated into liberation. To caricature somewhat: "John was an innocent victim who was brainwashed into an exploitative cult which promoted ideas that no one in their right mind could believe. He was forced to lead an unnatural life, renouncing his childhood sweetheart. His anguished parents had to pay an undisclosed sum, said to involve the mortgage of their family home, for John to be rescued and given the opportunity to see for himself how he had been deceived and manipulated."

Let me repeat, it is not being denied that the media do not produce some excellent and accurate information about NRMs. The discussion in this section has been to highlight the fact that the media have a primary interest in selling a story to their audience. They have to ensure that they hold the interest of their readers, listeners, and viewers—and keep their longer-term loyalty to the paper, magazine, program, or channel. Media constructors of reality usually work under considerable constraints due to the limited time and space available to them; there is always another story waiting to be written or program to be produced. Few media professionals will be specialists in any field as specific as that of NRMs; most will rely on secondary, tertiary or even more distant sources for the information from which they construct their images.

## CONCLUDING REMARKS

According to its own rules of methodological procedure, the sociological approach is limited. It cannot pronounce on the truth or falsity of a theological or ideological position, although it can observe who accepts which beliefs and under what conditions they are more likely to adopt a particular position. It cannot decide between opposing moral claims, although it can point to the potential conse-quences of following one moral position rather than another. It cannot make Platonic statements about what is the true content of a definition, although it can report what people believe is, say, a "real" religion; and, *given* a particular defini-tion, it can say whether a particular movement is or is not a religion (Barker 1991b).

All secondary constructions must select some aspects and leave out other aspects of the social reality that they claim to be describing. The NRMs can be expected to select those aspects that they believe (rightly or wrongly) will put them in the best light; the ACM will select those that put the NRM in a bad light; the media will select what they believe, according to a range of criteria, will make a good story.

It has already been claimed that one of the meta-values of social science is that the selection it has to make will be based not on evaluation, but on how, in the most balanced way, the sociologist's secondary construction can reflect the primary construction of the reality concerned. Of course, there are plenty of inefficient, even bad sociologists, and values do enter into the sociological enterprise in ways that they should not, according to the discipline's own standards. But the logic of the sociological method is one that, at least in principle, invites criticism and empirical refutation (Popper 1963). A sociological criterion for judging a sociological account is the degree to which it furthers our understanding of a social phenomenon, not the degree to which it furthers the advancement or the curtailment of the phenomenon or how good a story it makes.

Jealous of the reputation of the sociology and psychology of religion, professional bodies in the United States, including the Society for the Scientific Study of Religion and the Association for the Sociology of Religion, have recently taken steps to preserve the standards that they felt the ACM and the NRMs were threatening to erode in the name of their professional expertise. Statements have been made available to the courts by both the SSSR and the ASR about the limitations of the sociological method in declaring that members of an NRM (or any other organization not using physical coercion) are incapable of being responsible for their own actions. As a result of some members of NRMs offering papers that relied on supernatural revelation (in the face of contrary empirical evidence) to make their argument, the Council of the SSSR has recently passed a resolution explicitly requiring what it had previously taken for granted—that certain standards of scholarship have to be observed in papers presented to its annual meetings.

This does not mean that members of NRMs cannot form as important a part of the sociological discipline as Catholics, Jews, or agnostics do; nor does it mean that anti-cultists should not give evidence in courts. What it might suggest, however, is that sociologists may continually need to clarify the basis of their approach to secondary constructions of social reality, reaffirming that some of its limitations could, in fact, be its strengths.

# REFERENCES

Allan, J. 1980. *The Rising of the Moon.* Leicester: Inter-Varsity Press.
Barker, E. 1984. *The Making of a Moonie: Brainwashing or Choice?* Oxford: Blackwell.
———. 1987. "Brahmins Don't Eat Mushrooms: Participant Observation and the New Religions." *LSE Quarterly* (June): 127-152.
———. 1988. "Kingdoms of Heaven on Earth: New Religious Movements and Political Orders." Pp. 17-39 in *The Politics of Religion and Social Change: Religion and the Political Order,* edited by A. Shupe and J.K. Hadden. Vol. 2. New York: Paragon House.
———. 1989a. "And What Do You Believe?" Pp. 32-50 in *Investigating Society,* edited by R. Burgess. London: Longman.
———. 1989b. *New Religious Movements: A Practical Introduction.* London: HMSO.
———. 1989c. "Tolerant Discrimination: Church, State and the New Religions." Pp. 185-208 in *Religion, State, and Society in Modern Britain,* edited by P. Badham. Lewiston, NY: Edwin Mellen Press.

————. 1990. "Reborn or Misused?" *LSE Magazine* (Spring), pp. 4-7.

————. 1991a. "Changes in New Religious Movements." Pp. 759-781 in *New Religious Movements,* edited by M. Fuss. Vol. 2. Rome: International Federation of Catholic Universities, Center for Coordination of Research.

————. 1991b. "But is it a Genuine Religion?" *Report from the Capital.* (April): 10-14.

Beckford, J.A. 1985. *Cult Controversies: The Societal Response to New Religious Movements.* London: Tavistock.

Beckford, J.A., and M.A. Cole. 1988. "British and American Responses to New Religious Movements." Pp. 210-224 in *Sects and New Religious Movements,* edited by A. Dyson and E. Barker. Manchester, England: The Bulletin of the John Rylands University Library of Manchester.

Berger, P., and T. Luckmann. 1967. *The Social Construction of Reality.* London: Allen Lane.

Cohen, S., and J. Young, eds. 1973. *The Manufacture of News: Deviance, Social Problems and the Mass Media.* Beverly Hills, CA: Sage.

Fitzgerald, F. 1987. *Cities on a Hill.* New York: Simon and Schuster.

Glasgow University Media Group. 1976. *Bad News,.* London: Routledge and Kegan Paul.

————. 1980. *More Bad News.* London: Routledge and Kegan Paul.

Gumpert, G., and R. Cathart, eds. 1982. *Inter/Media: Interpersonal Communication in the Media World.* New York: Oxford University Press.

Gurevitch, M., T. Bennett, J. Curran, and J. Woollacott, eds. 1982. *Culture and Society and the Media.* London: Methuen.

Hall, J. 1987. *Gone from the Promised Land: Jonestown in American Cultural History.* New Brunswick, NJ: Transaction.

Hassan, S. 1988. *Combatting Cult Mind Control: Protection, Rescue and Recovery from Destructive Cults.* Wellingborough: Aquarian Press.

Hornsby-Smith, M. 1991. *Roman Catholic Beliefs in England.* Oxford: Oxford University Press.

Hounam, P., and A. Hogg. 1984. *Secret Cult.* Tring, Herts: Lion Publishing.

Jules-Rossette, B. 1975. *African Apostles: Ritual and Conversion in the Church of John Maranke.* New Haven, CT: Yale University Press.

Kilduff, M., and R. Javers. 1978. *The Suicide Cult: The Inside Story of the Peoples Temple Sect and the Massacre in Guyana.* New York: Bantam.

Krause, C.A., L.M. Stern, R. Harwood, and the Staff of the *Washington Post.* 1978. *Guyana Massacre: The Eyewitness Account.* Berkeley: Berkeley Publishing.

Lewis, J.R. 1986. "Reconstructing the 'Cult' Experience: Post Involvement Attitudes as a Function of Mode of Exit and Post-Involvement Socialization." *Sociological Analysis* 47: 151-159.

Lindt, G., and A. Gollin. 1979. "Religious Cults in America: Public Opinion and the Media." Unpublished paper, American Association of Public Opinion Research.

Lofland, J. [1966]. 1977. *Doomsday Cult: A Study of Conversion, Proselytization, and Maintenance of Faith.* New York: Irvington.

Martin, W. 1980. *The New Cults.* Santa Anna, CA: Vision House.

Mickler, M. 1980. *A History of the Unification Church in the Bay Area: 1960-74.* M.A. thesis, Graduate Theological Union, Berkeley, CA.

Patrick, T., with T. Dulack. 1976. *Let Our Children Go!* New York: Ballantine.

Pearson, M. 1990. *Millennial Dreams and Moral Dilemmas: Seventh-day Adventism and Contemporary Ethics.* New York: Cambridge University Press.

Popper, K. 1963. *Conjectures and Refutations: The Growth of Scientific Knowledge.* London: Routledge and Kegan Paul.

Richardson, J.T. 1980. "People's Temple and Jonestown: A Corrective Comparison and Critique." *Journal for the Scientific Study of Religion* 19: 239-255.

Robbins, T. 1988. *Cults, Converts and Charisma: The Sociology of New Religious Movements.* Beverly Hills, CA: Sage.

Ross, J.C., and M.D. Langone. 1988. *Cults: What Parents should Know, A Practical Guide to Help Parents with Children in Destructive Groups.* Weston, MA: The American Family Foundation.

Saliba, J. 1990. *Social Science and the Cults: An Annotated Bibliography.* New York: Garland Publishers.

Shupe, A.D., and D.G. Bromley. 1980. *The New Vigilantes: Deprogrammers, Anti-cultists and the New Religions.* Beverly Hills, CA: Sage.

Shupe, A.D., D.G. Bromley, and D.L. Oliver. 1984. *The Anti-Cult Movement in America: A Bibliography and Historical Survey.* New York: Garland.

Smith, P. 1987. *The Babi and Baha'i Religions: From Messianic Shi'ism to a World Religion.* New York: Cambridge University Press.

Solomon, T. 1981. "Integrating the 'Moonie' Experience: A Survey of Ex-Members of the Unification Church." Pp. 275-294 in *In Gods We Trust: New Patterns in Religious Pluralism in America,* edited by T. Robbins and D. Anthony. New Brunswick, NJ: Transaction.

van Driel, B., and J.T. Richardson. 1988. "Print Media Coverage of New Religious Movements: A Longitudinal Study." *Journal of Communication* 36: 37-61.

Wallis, R. 1976. *The Road to Total Freedom: A Sociological Analysis of Scientology.* London: Heinemann.

Weber, M. 1948. *From Max Weber: Essays in Sociology.* London: Kegan Paul.

————. 1964. *The Theory of Social and Economic Organization.* Toronto: Free Press.

Wilson, B.R., ed. 1970. *Rationality.* Oxford: Blackwell.

Wright, S. 1987. *Leaving Cults: The Dynamics of Defection.* Washington, DC: The Society for the Scientific Study of Religion.

# PROBLEMS OF RESEARCH AND DATA IN THE STUDY OF NEW RELIGIONS

James T. Richardson, Robert Balch, and J. Gordon Melton

## ABSTRACT

This paper reviews problems with research on new religious movements, indicating reasons for the difficulties, and ways to alleviate them. More comparative studies and more historical research from a global perspective are recommended. Major problems with current research include (1) too many one-shot study designs; (2) problems with "compounded accounts" deriving from the interaction of subject accounts with researcher perspectives; (3) need for more longitudinal research with "triangulation" of methods and sources, and better approximations of control group studies; (4) more replication and use of standardized instrumentation in research; (5) difficulties using therapy settings as data gathering situations; and (6) limitations of "happy member" research. Areas where more research is needed include (1) organizational level studies; (2) economic considerations; (3) healing within new religions; (4) contacts between new religions and traditional religions and other institutions; (5) roles of mass media in mediating views about new religions; (6) relations between and among new religious groups; (8) popular fears about groups referred to as "cults;" (9) "corruption of power" in new religions; (10) sex roles in the groups; (11) recruitment processes; (12) what happens to children in the groups; (13) defectors from the groups; (14) ties between ethnic communities and new religious groups; (15) and the alleged "succession problem" brought on when leaders of groups die or leave.

Religion and the Social Order, Volume 3B, pages 213-229.
Copyright © 1993 by JAI Press Inc.
All rights of reproduction in any form reserved.
ISBN: 1-55938-715-7

There has been a tremendous amount of research conducted on new religions in America and other Western societies (Choquette 1985; Robbins 1988; Saliba 1990). Although scholars have been studying these phenomena for over two decades, there are a number of issues that have been inadequately researched. Some favored areas of investigation need more systematic, sophisticated research to support conclusions that have been drawn, sometimes on the basis of limited evidence. This paper briefly discusses a number of methodological problems that have plagued the study of new religions and comments on areas of study needing more research.

One major reason for the dearth of information in some areas of interest is that there are relatively few scholars studying new religious phenomena. A few dozen researchers have undertaken the bulk of the research that has been published on the new religions. Understandably, this cadre of researchers has focused on certain groups and specific problems, to the exclusion of others. It now appears that more social scientists and graduate students are directing their efforts toward religious phenomena (Robbins 1988, pp. 190-207). Hopefully, this resurgence of interest in religion among social scientists will facilitate knowledge-building on the role of religion in the modern world, and specifically about the plethora of new religious phenomena.

Another reason for both the high level of interest and the relatively checkered pattern of research is the controversial nature of the new religions (Barker 1984; Beckford 1985a; Bromley and Richardson 1983). Attention focused on new religions by social control agents and the mass media has diverted attention from a number of important questions. At the same time, however, focus on the new religions by the media and social control agents has engendered interest among scholars, some of whom have then made efforts to gather data on certain aspects of new groups and movements, especially controversial ones. This tendency for scholarship to follow the lead of the media, however, has detracted from a thorough and balanced research agenda. Major areas of study remain largely unexplored, including further explication of some issues crucial to settling controversies about new religious groups and movements.

This paper presents a discussion of several general research issues that should be addressed if we are to understand more fully the meaning of new religions in modern society. The proposed research agenda cannot be exhaustive, but hopefully will offer some direction to those interested in this area of study.

## COMPARATIVE STUDIES

There has been little effort to undertake comparisons between different groups and movements. Considerable data have been amassed, but often the data have been gathered in ways not allowing easy comparisons. Many studies therefore are idiosyncratic and difficult to relate to other research. Different concepts and theoretical perspectives are used, and limited ad hoc methodologies discourage comparisons. In a rare example of efforts at comparison, Greil and Rudy (1984) note the difficulties of making comparisons because different approaches are used to test ostensibly the same theory in the most intensively researched area of study concerning new religions—recruitment and conversion. They acknowledge that comparative research is problematic because the groups differ on so many dimensions that complete comparisons are impossible. However, they also identify other problems such as the lack of agreement about the unit of analysis (e.g., group or individual) and conceptual confusion about terms such as conversion and recruitment.

Economic practices of new religions is another controversial area where there has been some comparative research (Richardson 1982). These studies typically suffer from lack of comparable information, as demonstrated in the one collection of research on this topic (Richardson 1988). We know some details about a few groups, but little about most. What we do know allows few generalizations to be made about this important area of group life.

Balch (1985, pp. 36-37) and Richardson (1977) have independently constructed "data frames" that propose the kinds of information that researchers should systematically gather about the new religious groups. If ethnographic researchers did attempt to gather such comparable data, then the study of new religions might eventually be organized similarly to the Human Relations Area Files in anthropology, a data base that contains systematic information on hundreds of pre-literate tribes. Compiling standardized data on groups studied would be analogous to replication research, which would allow more confidence in research results. Suggestions for systematic data-gathering, however, have rarely been followed.

## HISTORICAL RESEARCH AND WORLDWIDE PERSPECTIVE

Most research on new religions suffers from a pervasive ahistoricity (Melton 1991). Sociologists and psychologists in particular are often surprisingly uninformed about ties a given group has to various long-standing religious traditions. This lack of historical appreciation both blinds researchers to important research questions and leads them to assumptions that might not hold up if examined. As Bainbridge (1985, p. 159) has noted, "In modern society, cults are born out of older cults, and most of them are known to cluster in family lineages."

Failure to recognize relationships between specific groups and established traditions has led researchers to misunderstand what may be happening with the rise of new religions in the West. For instance, groups that are labeled "new religions" in the West sometimes are simply manifestations of missionary activities directed toward the West by non-Western religious traditions. A variant on this pattern is the explication of ties with ancient religious traditions by new groups within Western countries, once the new groups have a foothold in the new society. Whatever the exact relationship with a religious tradition, these new groups may function similarly to the way Christian mission groups behave in non-Western countries. Indeed, one might predict this to be the case. However, these kinds of research questions may not even be addressed if the researcher knows little about religious history and about other religious traditions. Instead, the researcher may treat the group as just another exotic group which developed *ex nihilo*. Ahistoricity, thus, shifts the focus of attention to why some people join culturally strange groups rather than, for example, to an examination of similarities and differences between missionizing experiences in different cultures, or why such mission activity is taking place at all, or whether it is successful.

American scholars appear to take for granted the notion of pluralism within the United States, but failure to understand the history of various individual religious traditions is compounded by a lack of understanding of the diversity of world religion. There are obvious signs of a worldwide pluralism within the United States, as representative groups from other non-Western traditions are finding a niche within American society. Fruitful areas of inquiry currently are being missed as a result of scholarly ethnocentricity. American scholars need to adopt a *global* perspective on pluralism analogous to their perspective on pluralism *within* American culture.

## IMPROVED RESEARCH DESIGNS

### One-Shot Studies

Most scholarly studies are "one-shot" research designs capturing but a single moment in the developmental history of a group. Such snapshots may be insightful but they are inherently suspect when assertions about long-term effects or causation are offered. These single-shot studies can be maximally valuable if replicated repeatedly using similar methodologies that allow comparisons.

Balch and Taylor's (1978) study of a flying saucer group exemplifies the problem of depending on one-shot studies. In that study the researchers concluded that the group had succeeded in obtaining and retaining committed members without application of strong social influence processes often used by other new and exotic groups. Follow-up research, however, revealed that the group had come close to disintegrating before leaders instituted significant changes, including ceasing recruitment activities in favor of developing commitment in current participants. The organizational structure created, thus, was consistent with what researchers of other new religious groups had found: increased isolation and development of more direct methods of social influence designed to promote deindividuation and to enhance involvement and commitment of members (Balch 1990).

### The Problem of "Compounded Accounts"

The one-shot design is particularly prone to problems deriving from the fact that (1) most data from subjects/participants are retrospective, and (2) most researchers have some biases or preconceived conceptions about events and practices within the group being studied. Accounts of interview data are sometimes treated as an "objective reality" by scholars who are, in fact, creating and interpreting the meaning of interviewee accounts. Scholarly interpretations are themselves another variety of account and should be recognized as such. This "compounding of accounts" raises serious epistemological questions, and claims based on such information should be accepted with caution. Much corroboration of data and replication are necessary before information can be used by scholars and policymakers.

The phenomenon of compounded accounts also presents an intriguing research topic in its own right that should attract scholarly investigation. Attempting to demonstrate the efficacy of the notion of compounded accounts and to explain how such accounts are constructed is a fruitful line of research. Interactions between "conversion accounts" and "scholarly accounts" might yield especially useful insights for understanding the meaning of research results in this controversial area of study.

### Longitudinal Research, Triangulation, and Control Groups

There has been little longitudinal research in the area of new religions. Groups and individuals must be studied through time to determine how they change and if earlier predictions and conclusions stand the test of time. Taslimi, Hood, and Watson (1990) is one exception of longitudinal work on the individual level, and Bromley (1985, 1988a) presents follow-up research on finances of one of the more controversial groups. Balch's (1990) follow-up work on the flying saucer group, combined with the earlier report, is a rare example of longitudinal research.

One important problem that could be addressed through longitudinal research involves the most prominent theory of development of new religions. Most scholars attribute the rise of new religions in the 1960s and 1970s to the social unrest of that period. However, Melton (1991) has presented some provocative data suggesting that the number of new groups has been increasing constantly over the past few decades. If Melton is correct, then another explanation is required to account for the rise of new religions within the West.

Triangulation involves utilizing a number of data sources simultaneously but from different perspectives (Beckford 1985a, p. 143). In the case of research on new religious groups, triangulation would mean that data should be gathered from members *and* ex-members, from apologists *and* detractors, from leaders *and* followers within the group, from parents *and* from sons and daughters who are members, and so on. There should be an attempt to approximate stratified sampling of all relevant categories related to a group being studied, with representative samples of all relevant groups being included.

All of these various data sources should be treated as accounts (Scott and Lyman 1968; Beckford 1978; Richardson et al. 1984), of course, but together the multiple accounts allow better understanding of the reality construction process. Multiple data sources make the researcher more aware of perspectives of those external to the groups, a needed corrective to much research which ignores or minimizes the societal context and meaning of groups being studied.

Use of control groups is difficult to attain in the usual field or ethnographic research being conducted on new religions. The term control group refers to a group matched with the experimental group in all characteristics except the experimental variable. Matching can be accomplished through random assignment or through deliberate pairing on characteristics thought to be important. Use of control groups is normal in laboratory experiments but should be approximated whenever possible in field research, especially if generalizations about a larger population are formulated.

Individual characteristics associated with participation in new religions can be identified only by showing that those who do not join possess different characteristics. Heirich (1977) accomplished this in his excellent study of factors contributing to conversion to Pentecostalism. Barker (1984) approximated a control group in her research on joining the Unification Church, selecting a sample of similarly aged and situated people to compare with members. This approach added much support to her claims about reasons for joining. Wright (1987) employed a matched sample that contained equal number of "leavers" and "stayers" in his well-respected study of defection from new religions.

There are a variety of alternatives to full-fledged control groups. Some researchers have used data from national surveys of youth to make comparisons of joiners and nonjoiners (Richardson et al. 1979). Use of standardized personality assessment instruments also is roughly analogous to the use of control groups (see Richardson 1985b, 1990 for summaries of such research). Other researchers have used comparison groups from other new religions to allow some conclusions to be drawn about types of people attracted and the impact of variations in the recruitment process, as well as of differences in theology or ideology (Pilarzyk 1978; Gerlach and Hine 1970; Gordon 1984a, 1984b). Thus, while it is difficult to construct a pure control group, there have been productive efforts toward creating viable alternatives.

In summary, more longitudinal studies and "triangulation" of data sources are necessary in order to evaluate the validity and reliability of research findings and conclusions. Further, to the extent possible the ideal of a control group for comparison purposes should be approximated.

## Replication and Standardization

Only a few research reports facilitate comparable studies through provision of complete methodological information, but the paucity of such information usually makes replication impossible. By strict canons of research methodology, there are virtually no real replications in the study of new religions, which detracts greatly from their explanatory power.

More complete reporting of research methods is needed to allow replication efforts by other researchers. In the "hard sciences," research reports usually allow complete replication because of the reported methodological detail. However, the social sciences do not have a tradition of publishing much detail about research, and finding such information is often difficult. Standardized personality assessment instruments are available and have been used in some studies (Simmonds et al. 1976; Nordquist 1978; Taslimi, Hood, and Watson 1990), but they have not been widely used even by psychologists of religion.

One way to encourage replications would be to retain copies of research instruments in a central repository with ready access. Such a repository of instruments and data would not only encourage replication, but would invite scholars to check work, follow up on research ideas and gather comparable information. A further advantage of such a repository would be the encouragement of pre-testing and validation of research instruments.

## Therapy As Research

A special research design problem concerns the selection of research subjects who have left new religions. A few researchers have focused their research almost exclusively on a small subset of participants who have departed from new religious groups under extremely unfavorable conditions, often by forcible extrication (see, e.g., Singer 1979). Because this is not the typical condition for leaving a new religious group, such research suffers from serious selection bias. Generalization either about individual experience in new religious groups or about the groups themselves is, at best, quite problematic.

This kind of research exemplifies the worst type of the "compounded account" problem identified above. New accounts are worked out within a setting that not only involves therapy but also vigorous resocialization, sometimes euphemistically labelled "deprogramming." To the extent that therapy and deprogramming are involved, accounts presented by subjects are *jointly constructed* by therapist and subject and cannot be treated as independent measurements of individuals or groups.

Research within a therapy setting could be useful for examining the *current* psychological state of individuals, including their reaction to deprogramming. However, social science knowledge of how biographies are constructed and reconstructed (Berger 1967) should cause researchers to treat information gained through such "research" methods about life in the groups with considerable skepticism. Research by Solomon (1981), Lewis (1986), and Lewis and Bromley (1987) indicates that deprogrammed individuals often have considerably different views than voluntary leave-takers of their experiences in the groups. These researchers all conclude that different perspectives are attributable to the experience of deprogramming.

## "Happy Member" Research

It also should be recognized that research on active participants in groups is not without problems. Such research depends on accounts by members that may be self-serving and group-serving. Insider accounts may well involve an element of "impression management" by members seeking to put on a good face for researchers or other visitors. New religions frequently experience high attrition; thus, members who are left are those most likely to be happy with the situation in the group, or who at least may be interested in leaving that impression with observers. Further, focusing on active participants ignores people who have withdrawn from the group.

Member-based research also frequently suffers from a bias that assumes a permanence of membership. That assumption yields the conclusion that the results of a single-sample study can be generalized to all members over time, even those who have left! These assumptions are untenable especially with groups that have high attrition rates (Bird and Reimer 1982; Barker 1984).

There is more than a little irony associated with reports based on interviews with members of a group who claim that everyone is very happy with their life in the group when the group dissolves shortly thereafter because so many members defect. One case in point is the Love Family. Group members seemed quite happy with their circumstances in the group, and there were few indications that the group might disintegrate. Later it took considerable effort to secure information that allowed an understanding of the group's rapid demise (Balch 1988). Another example is the Shiloh group, which began a major process of disintegration shortly after publication of a monograph predicting the group's persistence (Richardson, Stewart, and Simmonds 1979). These occurrences may be quite understandable in hindsight, but they are disquieting nonetheless. Such problems might be averted with more sophisticated longitudinal studies, triangulation methods, comparison groups, and more thorough participant observer research. Improved methodology could rectify validity problems for both those researching current members of groups and those undertaking studies using only data from defectors and deprogrammees.

## ORGANIZATIONAL-LEVEL STUDIES

Organizational analysis is another area where more long-term studies of new religious groups are needed. Much research on new religions is conducted on the individual level and then treated as if it were organizational analysis. For example, new religions change, sometimes very rapidly. These are typically organizational transformations and when they occur they should be analyzed structurally and organizationally and not be treated simply as extensions of individual attitudes and behavior. Questions about how the groups mobilize material resources seem especially important, but a number of studies simply ignore such issues.

There are notable exceptions to the general criticism of inadequate attention to organizational questions. For instance, Rochford (1985) presents considerable organizational information about the Hare Krishna, and Lofland's (1977) enlarged edition of his pioneering study *Doomsday Cult* presents organizational change data on the Unification Church. Lofland and Richardson (1984) develop a typology of elementary forms of religious organizations not dependent upon church-sect theory and then apply that typology to changes in some newer groups. Wallis (1975) presents a provocative analysis of organizational changes in

Scientology from a "therapeutic cult" to a "religious sect," based on a shift from "epistemological individualism" through the "arrogation of authority" by group leaders. These ideas have been extended by others to different groups (e.g., Richardson 1979). Beckford (1975, 1985a) has also addressed the organizational level of analysis in two reviews of work that are particularly valuable for their lack of dependence on the traditional church-sect theory.

These and other organizationally oriented studies notwithstanding (see Robbins 1988, pp. 100-133), little is known about the vast majority of new religious groups that have developed and evolved over the past two decades. Even the number of groups is not precisely known (but see Melton 1991). Why some groups succeed while others fail has been little addressed (see Bromley and Hammond 1987 for an exception). Nor is the process of organizational development well understood (but see Bainbridge and Stark 1979; Richardson 1985a).

## NEGLECTED SUBSTANTIVE RESEARCH AREAS

In addition to the general methodological issues already discussed, there remain a number of important substantive areas and problems that have been relatively neglected to date. Space limitations will not permit detailed discussion. In this final section we seek to briefly identify the issues and point toward the kinds of questions which, if addressed, will contribute to a more mature understanding of new religious movements.

*Economic Considerations.* Some new religions are relatively prosperous, while others operate so close to the margin that their viability is constantly threatened. In spite of this relatively obvious observation, little attention has been devoted to understanding how economic affairs relate to other aspects of group life. How do the groups raise and spend money? How much money do they raise, and are there other ways the groups obtain needed resources? How are finances handled in the groups, and how are resources distributed? Still another potentially fascinating issue is how do economic concerns relate to group ideology and theology? The role played by social and material concerns as independent variables impacting theological development should be carefully studied from something akin to a sociology of knowledge approach.

*Theology.* The issue of what new religions believe is also of special importance. Many research reports assume the primacy of theology, treating it *implicitly* as a major independent variable (see Richardson 1988). There is also often an implicit assumption that the group's theology does not change over time. These assumptions may be accurate, but they have seldom been corroborated in ways that satisfy usual criteria for causation. Theologies evolve and change, sometimes dramatically. Why this is so, and how it occurs should be primary issues for researchers. The development of systems of belief can be better understood if the perspective which views theology as a primary independent variable is questioned.

*The Healing Function.* Many individuals participate in new religious groups because of considerations of mental and physical health, but little is known about *how* this concern is manifested or *how* healing claims are articulated by the groups. Indeed, this area is quite controversial, with some arguing that new religious groups cause both mental and physical health problems. Others contend that these groups ameliorate problems, especially psychological problems (see Kilbourne and Richardson 1984 for a discussion of this controversy).

McGuire (1985) discusses the prominence of healing in new religious movements, as well in traditional churches, and her own research (McGuire 1988) demonstrates the importance of a focus on healing. Robbins and Anthony (1982) summarize specific therapeutic effects of participation of membership in what they call deviant religious groups. New Age groups clearly claim to promote physical and mental happiness. Given these and other such studies (Richardson 1985a, 1990), more attention should be paid to specifying how concern for healing is utilized to attract members and how these beliefs and practices are implemented by the groups.

*Contacts with Traditional Institutions.* All too often the societal context of new religions is overlooked, when such influences may be all-important to an understanding of events in these groups. Particular attention should be paid to the influence of churches, governmental agencies, and courts on new religions. Information about any contacts with other groups is important too, especially those engaged in social control of deviant groups (see Robbins 1985; Robbins, Shepherd, and McBride 1985), for example, local police, the IRS, and Immigration and Naturalization Service. Legal actions are important not only because of the implications for the free exercise of religion, but because defending legal actions can require a significant dedication of a group's financial and leadership resources.

Researchers should attend to relationships between new religions and more traditional religious groups. Are churches supportive, or do they join in opposition of the new religions? Do some religious groups lend morale and/ or financial support to the newer groups? Which traditional religious groups are more supportive, and why? Much research assumes that somehow the groups have managed to exist in a vacuum without assistance, which is seldom the case (Richardson 1991). All sorts of ties may exist between newer and older groups, and researchers need to investigate them. Shupe and Bromley (1980) discuss some religious groups which have been involved in the anti-cult movement, but this kind of information is just a beginning.

*The Role of Mass Media.* The general public knows of new religions substantially through the coverage they receive by the mass media, but little is known about the relationship between mass media and new religious movements. What image do the media construct and present of the new groups? Where do the media turn for information and background on new religions? Do the media utilize social science scholarship and are they informed about historical and comparative perspectives? Does what media representatives say about new religions influence their recruitment efforts?

In addition to questions pertaining to how new religions are treated by the press, attention also needs to be devoted to how new religions deal with the press. Some groups discourage contact with the media while others utilize public relations experts to try to present themselves in a favorable light. At present there are few studies that have addressed issues of relations between the media and new religions (but see Van Driel and Richardson 1988). This should be a higher priority for social science researchers.

*Relations Among New Religious Movements.* Most reported research would lead to the conclusion that new religions are isolated groups uninterested in contact with other such groups. In fact, some groups cooperate with each other and share resources, particularly in the face of strong social control efforts and attacks from outsiders. The coalition formation and cooperation that sometimes takes place (Richardson and Reidy 1980) is little understood and demands more attention. Similarly, little is known about the conflicts and tensions between new religions, although it is clear that they sometimes coalesce to attack yet other groups with which they disagree theologically, as evidenced by the efforts of the Christian World Liberation Front and its spin-off, Spiritual Counterfeits Project, which publishes critical tracts on other new groups (Heinz 1976).

*Ties Among Anti-cult Groups.* Contacts among anti-cult groups and movements are equally significant. There has been considerable merging and coalition formation in the anti-cult movement (Shupe and Bromley 1980). The study of such oppositional groups can yield valuable information about the societal context in which new religions function and also about how oppositional groups themselves develop, change, and function in our society.

*Popular Fear of "Cults."* Negative feelings about the new religious groups are strong, and there is some evidence that they may be increasing (Bromley and Breschel 1992). Hostility is significant because new religious groups must live within the same society in which many members abhor them. Why such feelings and beliefs develop is important to understand. Which groups or types of people seem most prone to anti-cult feelings and what are the sources of these emotions? Is it possible to predict which groups will be targeted in anti-cult campaigns? The role played by media manipulation efforts of the anti-cult movement needs to be researched in conjunction with counter efforts by the groups themselves. For example, an anti-cult organization claimed significant responsibility for a highly negative portrayal of Scientology in a 1991 *Time Magazine* cover story. These fascinating issues deserve more attention.

*New Religious Groups "Going Bad."* "Corruption of power" in a new religion requires explanation. By corruption of power is meant the use of structurally-based power for personal benefit in a way defined as illegitimate by members (Balch 1991). There have been a number of reported examples that seem to fit such an internally based definition. Scholars need to study these situations to determine how and why they occur, and with what frequency. Care should be taken to avoid relying simply on the accounts of those who may have lost an internal power struggle and, of course, such research should use triangulation methods to verify allegations.

There are situations extreme enough to warrant agreement from all observers, external and internal, that something violating virtually any conceivable set of norms has happened. Jonestown was an isolated and extreme incident that seems to go "beyond" notions of the corruption of power. Other tragic events also have occurred including child abuse, sexual exploitation, and other unacceptable behaviors. Whether such episodes occur more or less frequently in new religions as compared with other groups is an important empirical question, but the conditions which seem to foster such tragic episodes in new religions should be understood (Wentzel 1990).

These "corruption of power" events are often focused on by media, which serve a mediating function for most citizens in terms of their understanding of the new groups. Social scientists should not leave to journalists the researching of the "dark side" of the rise of new religions. Several valuable treatments recently have examined religious deviance without adopting an anti-cult ideological stance. Hall (1987) presents a thorough analysis of the demise of the Peoples Temple, and Levy (1982) explores issues raised by the Jonestown tragedy. Balch (1988) examines the disintegration of the Love Family. More serious studies by trained social scientists of problems and extreme deviance in new religious groups would ensure that knowledge on these issues is social scientific rather than ideologically biased journalism.

*Sex Roles.* Tremendous variation in sex role definitions exists in the new religions and, further, these definitions also change over time within a group. It cannot be assumed that traditional sex roles obtain in any group being studied. The way that sex roles function in recruitment also should be examined. There has been some excellent work concerning gender roles in new religions (Aidala 1985; Harder 1974), but more is needed, if only because so few new religious groups have been studied at all to date. Jacobs (1984) raises some profound issues in her study of exploitation of women in some new religions, and these issues require further investigation.

*Recruitment Processes and Participation Decisions.* The controversial "brainwashing" issue has been discussed extensively (Bromley and Richardson 1983), but very little is known about details of recruitment strategies of most new religious groups. Which methods are more effective and in what contexts? Which recruitment efforts lead to lower attrition? Which bring about life-long changes in the people, and which have only temporary effects? How do recruitment efforts relate to group ideology?

Great attention has been paid to application of the Lofland and Stark (1965) "world-saver" model of conversion, to the dismay of Lofland (1978, p. 18). He states that he anticipated that by now there would be "at least a half dozen qualitative process models of conversion, each valid for the range and kind of event it addressed, and each offering insights." There also has been a fixation among many who oppose new religions on so-called brainwashing, which is thought to equate physical and psychological coercion and assumes that virtually all the new religions use some form of psychological coercion to win recruits. Both of these assertions are empirical questions that have been questioned by scholars (Anthony 1990; Bromley and Richardson 1983).

*Children in New Religious Groups.* Many new religious groups now are more than two decades old. They typically recruited younger single people who, over time, married and started families. This "domestication" of the groups has forced some significant changes and has even contributed to the demise of some groups. However, many groups continued, and children currently are being raised in some of the groups. So far there has been very little attention paid to these children, but it is obvious that research is needed.

There have been accusations of child abuse in some groups, and governmental authorities have sometimes intervened (Wentzel 1990; Malcarne and Burchard 1992). Researchers should know how groups differ in their child-raising philosophies, what impact the group philosophies have on the children, any long-term effects of being reared in communal settings, and how children are being educated, particularly if the groups operate their own schools. These issues recently have become quite controversial and demand more attention from scholars.

*Defectors from New Religions.* The high attrition rates of nearly all these groups present an obvious question: What happens to people after leaving the groups? Do they have adjustment problems, or do they fit back into society easily? Were they taught any useful skills in the groups which assist them in their post-group life? Do former members reject all religion, or do they affiliate with other religious groups? Under what conditions do defectors eventually return to the group from which they defected? Why do they come back, and how are they received? What types of people return? There is some research on defection and disaffiliation (e.g., Wright 1987; Bromley 1988b), but much more information is needed.

*Ties with Ethnic Communities.* Some of the new religions have established significant ties with ethnic communities. The best known example is Hare Krishna temples becoming "neighborhood churches" for ethic Indians living in Western societies (Rochford 1985). However, there may be other such instances that are just as important to the maintenance and evolution of some newer religions. This issue relates, of course, to the earlier point about understanding the historical relationship between newer religions in the West and the religious traditions from whence they have come.

*The "Succession Problem."* Sociologists have generally accepted the assumption that groups have difficulty maintaining themselves when the original charismatic leader dies. Melton (1991) has recently claimed that the succession problem is a myth and does not bear up well when examined systematically. This conclusion, if substantiated, should cause sociologists to shift their focus somewhat from leaders to groups. Melton (1991) makes the additional important related point that little is known about the operation of the boards of directors and officers of the newer religions. Tax laws in the United States have required the establishment of such groups as a part of gaining tax-exempt status. Melton suggests this development has had important consequences in the area of succession, assisting some groups in overcoming the "succession problem." These findings and theoretical speculations need to be examined more carefully; to date few scholars have pursued them at all.

# CONCLUSIONS

In this brief treatment it has not been possible to cover all aspects of research problems with studies of new religions. We have attempted to point out several general methodological issues that should be addressed prior to implementing a research design, so that the findings based on research can be better validated. We have also attempted to list several areas where more research is needed, particularly to gather information which might inform scholars and policymakers alike. We hope that more scholars become interested in this area of study and that they will bring methodological skills to the research that will allow more confidence in the results. More skilled researchers studying new religions should eventually assist in settling some of the more controversial issues surrounding new religions in our society.

# REFERENCES

Aidala, A. 1985. "Social Change, Gender Roles, and New Religious Movements." *Sociological Analysis* 46: 287-314.
Anthony, D. 1990. "Religious Movements and 'Brainwashing' Litigation." Pp. 295-344 in *In Gods We Trust*, edited by T. Robbins and D. Anthony. 2nd ed. New Brunswick, NJ: Transaction Books.
Bainbridge, W.S. 1985. "Cultural Genetics." Pp. 157-194 in *Religious Movements*, edited by R. Stark. New York: Paragon House.
Bainbridge, W.S., and R. Stark. 1979. "Cult Formation: Three Compatible Models." *Sociological Analysis* 40: 285-293.
Balch, R. 1985. "What's Wrong with the Study of New Religions and What Can We Do About It?" Pp. 24-39 in *Scientific Research on New Religions: Divergent Perspectives*, edited by B. Kilbourne. San Francisco: American Association for the Advancement of Science.
———. 1988. "Money and Power in Utopia: An Economic History of the Love Family." Pp. 185-222 in *Money and Power in the New Religions*, edited by J. Richardson. Lewiston, NY: Edwin Mellen.
———. 1990. "Getting Off the Planet: Recruitment and Commitment in Bo and Peep's UFO Cult." Unpublished paper, Department of Sociology, University of Montana, Missoula.
———. 1991. "Religious Totalism and the Corrupting of Religious Power." Paper presented at annual meeting of the Society for the Scientific Study of Religion, Pittsburgh, PA.
Balch, R., and D. Taylor. 1978. "Seekers and Saucers: The Role of the Cultic Milieu in Joining a UFO Cult." Pp. 43-64 in *Conversion Careers: In and Out of the New Religions*, edited by J. Richardson. Beverly Hills, CA: Sage.
Barker, E. 1984. *The Making of a Moonie: Brainwashing or Choice?* Oxford: Blackwell.
Beckford, J. 1975. "Religious Organizations: A Trend Report and Bibliography." *Current Sociology* 21: 1-170.
———. 1978. "Accounting for Conversion." *British Journal of Sociology* 29: 249-262.
———. 1985a. *Cult Controversies: The Societal Response to the New Religious Movements.* London: Tavistock.
———. 1985b. "Religious Organization." Pp. 125-138 in *The Sacred in a Secular Age*, edited by P. Hammond. Berkeley: University of California Press.
Berger, P. 1967. *The Sacred Canopy.* New York: Doubleday.
Bird, F., and W. Reimer. 1982. "A Sociological Analysis of New Religious and Para-religious Movements." *Journal for the Scientific Study of Religion* 21: 1-14.

Bromley, D. 1985. "Financing the Millennium: The Economic Structure of the Unificationist Movement." *Journal for the Scientific Study of Religion* 24: 253-275.

―――――. 1988a. "Economic Structure and Charismatic Leadership in the Unification Church." Pp. 335-364 in *Money and Power in the New Religions,* edited by J. Richardson. Lewiston, NY: Edwin Mellen.

―――――, ed. 1988b. *Falling from the Faith: Causes and Consequences of Religious Apostasy.* Newbury Park, CA: Sage.

Bromley, D., and E. Breschel. 1992. "General Population and Institutional Elite Support for Social Control of New Religious Movements: Evidence from National Survey Data." *Behavioral Science and the Law* 10: 39-52.

Bromley, D., and P. Hammond, eds. 1987. *The Future of New Religious Movements.* Macon, GA: Mercer University Press.

Bromley, D., and J. Richardson, eds. 1983. *The Brainwashing/Deprogramming Controversy: Sociological, Psychology, Legal, and Historical Perspectives.* Lewiston, NY: Edwin Mellen.

Choquette, D. 1985. *New Religious Movements in America: An Annotated Bibliography.* Westport, CT: Greenwood.

Gerlach, L., and V. Hine. 1970. *People, Power and Change.* Indianapolis: Bobbs-Merrill.

Gordon, D. 1984a. "Dying to Self: Self-Control Through Self-Abandonment." *Sociological Analysis* 45: 41-55.

―――――. 1984b. "The Role of Local Social Context in Social Movement Accommodation." *Journal for the Scientific Study of Religion* 23: 381-395.

Greil, A., and D. Rudy. 1984. "What Have We Learned About Process Models of Conversion? An Examination of Ten Studies." *Sociological Analysis* 54: 115-125.

Hall, J. 1987. *Gone from the Promised Land: Jonestown in American Cultural History.* New Brunswick, NJ: Transaction.

Harder, M. 1974. "Sex Roles in the Jesus Movement." *Social Compass* 21: 345-353.

Heinz, D. 1976. "The Christian World Liberation Front." Pp. 143-161 in *The New Religious Consciousness,* edited by C. Glock and R. Bellah. Berkeley: University of California Press.

Heirich, M. 1977. "Change of Heart: A Test of Some Widely Held Theories About Religious Conversion." *American Journal of Sociology* 85: 653-680.

Jacobs, J. 1984. "The Economy of Love in Religious Commitment: The Deconversion of Women from Non-traditional Religious Movements." *Journal for the Scientific Study of Religion* 23: 155-171.

Kilbourne, B., and J. Richardson. 1984. "Psychotherapy and New Religions in a Pluralistic Society." *American Psychologist* 39: 237-251.

Levy, K. 1982. *Violence and Religious Commitment.* University Park, PA: Pennsylvania State University Press.

Lewis, J. 1986. "Reconstructing the Cult Experience: Post-Involvement Attitudes as a Function of Mode of Exit and Post-Involvement Socialization." *Sociological Analysis* 46: 151-159.

Lewis, J., and D. Bromley. 1987. "The Cult Withdrawal Syndrome: A Case of Misattribution of Cause?" *Journal for the Scientific Study of Religion* 26: 508-522.

Lofland, J. 1977. *Doomsday Cult: A Study of Conversion, Proselytization, and Maintenance of Faith.* Enlarged ed. New York: Irvington.

―――――. 1978. "'Becoming a World-Saver' Revisited." Pp. 805-818 in *Conversion Careers,* edited by J. Richardson. Beverly Hills, CA: Sage.

Lofland, J., and J. Richardson. 1984. "Religious Movement Organizations: Elemental Forms and Dynamics." Pp. 29-51 in *Research in Social Movements, Conflict and Change,* edited by L. Kriesberg. Greenwich, CT: JAI Press.

Lofland, J., and R. Stark. 1965. "Becoming a World-Saver: A Theory of Conversion to a Deviant Perspective." *American Sociological Review* 30: 862-875.

Malcarne, V., and J. Burchard. 1992. "Investigations of Child Abuse/Neglect Allegations in Religious Cults: A Case Study in Vermont." *Behavioral Science and Law* 10: 75-88.

McGuire, M. 1985. "Religion and Healing." Pp. 268-284 in *The Sacred in a Secular Age*, edited by P. Hammond. Berkeley: University of California Press.
_____. 1988. *Ritual Healing in Suburban America*. New Brunswick, NJ: Rutgers University Press.
Melton, J.G. 1991. "When Prophets Die: The Succession Crisis in New Religions." Pp. 1-13 in *When Prophets Die: The Postcharismatic Fate of New Religions*, edited by T. Miller. Albany: SUNY Press.
Nordquist, T. 1978. *Ananda Cooperative Village*. Uppsala: Religionhistoriska Institute, Uppsala University.
Pilarzyk, T. 1978. "Conversion and Alienation Processes in the Youth Culture." *Pacific Sociological Review* 21: 379-405.
Richardson, J. 1977. "A Data Frame for Communal Research." *Communal Studies Newsletter* 4: 1-13.
_____. 1979. "From Cult to Sect: Creative Eclecticism in New Religious Movements." *Pacific Sociological Review* 22: 139-166.
_____. 1982. "Financing the New Religions: Theoretical and Comparative Perspectives." *Journal for the Scientific Study of Religion* 21: 255-268.
_____. 1985a. "The 'Deformation' of New Religions: Impacts of Societal and Organizational Factors." Pp. 163-176 in *Cults, Culture and the Law*, edited by T. Robbins, W.C. Shepherd, and J. McBride. Chico, CA: Scholars Press.
_____. 1985b. "Psychological and Psychiatric Studies of New Religions." Pp. 209-223 in *Advances in the Psychology of Religion*, edited by L. Brown. New York: Pergamon Press.
_____, ed. 1988. *Money and Power in the New Religions*. Lewiston, NY: Edwin Mellen.
_____. 1990. "Religion, Psychology and the Law." Paper presented at the conference on "Religion and Psychopathology," Jagallonian University, Cracow, Poland.
_____. 1991. "Calvary Chapel: A New Denomination?" Paper presented at the conference on "Evangelicals, Voluntary Associations, & American Public Life," Wheaton College.
Richardson, J., J. van der Lans, and F. Derks. 1984. "Leaving and Labeling: Voluntary and Coerced Disaffiliation from Religious Social Movements." Pp. 97-126 in *Research in Social Movements, Conflict and Change*, edited by K. Lang and G. Lang. Vol. 9. Greenwich, CT: JAI Press.
Richardson, J., and M. Reidy. 1980. "Form and Fluidity in Two Contemporary Glossolalic Movements." *Annual Review of the Social Sciences of Religion* 4: 183-220.
Richardson, J.T., M. Stewart, and R. Simmonds. 1979. *Organized Miracles: A Study of the Contemporary Youth, Communal, Fundamentalist Organization*. New Brunswick, NJ: Transaction.
Robbins, T. 1985. "Government Regulatory Powers Over Religious Movements: Deviant Groups as Test Cases." *Journal for the Scientific Study of Religion* 24: 237-251.
_____. 1988. *Cults, Converts and Charisma: The Sociology of New Religious Movements*. Newbury Park, CA: Sage.
Robbins, T., and D. Anthony. 1982. "Deprogramming, Brainwashing, and the Medicalization of Deviant Religious Groups." *Social Problems* 29: 283-297.
Robbins, T., W. Shepherd, and J. McBride, eds. 1985. *Cults, Culture, and the Law*. Chico, CA: Scholars Press.
Rochford, B. 1985. *Hare Krishna in America*. New Brunswick, NJ: Rutgers University Press.
Saliba, J. 1990. *Social Science and the Cults: An Annotated Bibliography*. New York: Garland.
Scott, M., and S. Lyman. 1968. "Accounts." *American Sociological Review* 33: 46-61.
Shupe, A., and D. Bromley. 1980. *The New Vigilantes*. Beverly Hills, CA: Sage.
Simmonds, R., J. Richardson, and M. Stewart. 1976. "The Jesus People: An Adjective Check List Assessment." *Journal for the Scientific Study of Religion* 15: 323-337.
Singer, M. 1979. "Coming Out of the Cults." *Psychology Today* 12: 72-82.

Solomon, T. 1981. "Integrating the 'Moonie' Experience: A Survey of Ex-members of the Unification Church." Pp. 275-295 in *In God's We Trust,* edited by T. Robbins and D. Anthony. New Brunswick, NJ: Transaction.

Taslimi, C., R. Hood, and P. Watson. 1990. "An Assessment of Former Members of Shiloh: An Adjective Check List 17 Years Later." *Journal for the Scientific Study of Religion* 30: 306-311.

Van Driel, B., and J. Richardson. 1988. "Print Media Coverage of New Religious Movements: A Longitudinal Study." *Journal of Communication* 36: 37-61.

Wallis, R. 1975. "Scientology: Therapeutic Cult to Religious Sect." *Sociology* 9: 89-99.

Wentzel, S. 1990. "Charging Religious Movements with Child Abuse as Social Control Strategy." Paper presented at the annual meeting of the Pacific Sociological Association, Spokane, WA.

Wright, S. 1987. *Leaving the Cults: The Dynamics of Defection.* Washington, DC: Society for the Scientific Study of Religion.

# Research in the
# Social Scientific Study of Religion

Edited by **Monty L. Lynn,** *Department of Management Sciences, Abilene Christian University* and **David O. Moberg,** *Department of Social and Cultural Sciences, Marquette University*

**Volume 5,** 1993, 258 pp.                                            $73.25
ISBN 1-55938-301-1

*Also Available:*
**Volumes 1-4** (1989-1992)                                            $73.25 each

## JAI PRESS INC.
55 Old Post Road - No. 2    P.O. Box 1678
Greenwich, Connecticut 06836-1678
Tel: (203) 661-7602      Fax: (203)661-0792